WHAT MATTERS MOST

Four Absolute Necessities
In Following Christ

WHAT MATTERS MOST

TONY EVANS

MOODY PRESS
CHICAGO

ISBN: 0–8024–3934-9

1 3 5 7 9 10 8 6 4 2

Printed in the United States of America

*This book is dedicated to
the elders, deacons, staff, and members
of Oak Cliff Bible Fellowship,
for the strategic role they play
in the discipleship ministry of our church.*

ABOUT THE AUTHOR

DR. ANTHONY T. EVANS, SR. (B.A., Carver Bible College; Th.M., Th.D., Dallas Theological Seminary; D.H.L., Eastern College) is senior pastor of Oak Cliff Bible Fellowship Church in Dallas and president of The Urban Alternative, a ministry devoted to promoting clear understanding and application of Scripture to bring about changes in urban communities through the church. He is the author of many books, including *The Promise, America's Only Hope, Returning to Your First Love,* and *Our God Is Awesome.* He and his wife, Lois, live in Dallas, Texas, and have four children.

CONTENTS

NECESSITY FOUR
EVANGELISM

WITH GRATITUDE

Once more, I want to thank the people who helped bring this book into being. They include Greg Thornton, Bill Thrasher, Cheryl Dunlop, and the other members of the team at Moody Press, and my editor and friend, Philip Rawley.

INTRODUCTION

This is a book about discipleship. It was born out of more than thirty years of preaching and twenty-one years of pastoral experience. It appears to me that too many Christians are still far too vague about what it really means to follow Christ. Or if they are clear on what it means, they are somewhat foggy on how one gets from here to there.

This reality is further complicated by those who reduce our commitment to and development in Christ to little more than an evangelical "Ouija board" type of guessing game, or who make it seem so complicated that some want to give up trying.

It is my contention that we do not have to accept either extreme. The apostle Paul believed it was very achievable to "present every man complete in Christ" (Colossians 1:28) in the church at Colossae.

He believed that in the corporate context of this local church, each individual member could grow to maturity in Christlikeness. Nothing is said about endless programs, meetings, strategies, and activities that needed to be devised in order to bring about the spiritual development of these disciples. Instead, Scripture gives us a picture of believers coming together to learn about

Christ through the four main topics explored in this book: worship, fellowship, Scripture, and evangelism.

This is true, I believe, not because there is no place in the church for an emphasis on function, but rather because the essence of discipleship is our experience with Christ. Discipleship, then, is more than the sum total of our religious activities. It is coming to know Christ and having the completeness of His life worked out in us (Colossians 2:9–10).

The thesis of this book is that God has provided four clearly defined experiences that make possible our growth and development as Christ's disciples. These experiences are worship, fellowship, Scripture, and evangelism. When believers are dynamically experiencing these things in the context of a local church, spiritual maturity through the process of discipleship is inevitable.

To be sure, such maturity, while guaranteed, is not automatic. The individual believer bears a responsibility. It is possible to function as a Christian without having fully entered into these experiences, which means discipleship is not taking place, no matter how spiritually busy the person is.

Or, it is possible to so focus on one of these experiences that the others are lacking. This makes us unbalanced Christians, which can also stymie the discipleship process.

Some Christians are "into the Word," while others focus on worship. Some tout the need for fellowship, whereas still others emphasize evangelism. But it is not any one of these by itself that makes us authentic followers of Christ. All four together accomplish the goal of our maturity into Christlikeness.

Another great misconception about discipleship is that it can be done apart from the local church. Many Christians seek to become disciples of Christ through individual or small group relationships apart from the dynamic context of a local body of believers.

As we will demonstrate throughout this book, this is an impossibility. If there is no local church, then there is no discipleship. This is so because no one person or small group has all the necessary gifts and strengths to give any one believer all the resources needed for that person's development.

This must come from the broader body of believers, which uniquely completes Christ's body (Ephesians 1:22–23), functions as His temple (Ephesians 2:19–22), and is empowered by the Holy Spirit's presence (1 Corinthians 3:16).

This does not mean that small groups aren't important. It simply means that they are important under the local church, not apart from it. All other discipleship relationships must be viewed as supplemental to the church.

When Jesus walked this earth with the Twelve, He could pass on only strengths to them, since He had no weaknesses. He was a sinless "small group leader." This is not the case today. It is dangerous to put all of your spiritual marbles into an individual or small group "bag" that is disconnected from the local church, because unlike Jesus we don't pass on just our strengths. We pass on our weaknesses too.

This is why Jesus left the discipleship process in the hands of His body (expressed in local assemblies). This explains why the Scripture puts so much emphasis on the local church and not just the universal church. This is why the apostle Paul, the master church builder, wrote not to Christians everywhere, but to Christians somewhere. So let me state my thesis again. When believers encounter, through the Holy Spirit, the four vital experiences described in this book and make them a dynamic part of their lives, discipleship takes root and spiritual maturity, Christlikeness, is achieved.

It is my prayer that by the time you complete this book you will have a functional handle on what it takes to be an authentic follower of Jesus Christ. I also pray that you will order your life around these four necessities that will take you where you want to go.

When you and I do this, our lives will take on a dimension of joy, power, peace, and victory we may have never known before, one that will be ours regardless of circumstances. This is so because we will have discovered *what matters most.*

CHAPTER ONE

WHAT MATTERS
TO JESUS

I f you want to find out what mattered most to someone, read his last words. Usually, whatever a person
considers to be most important is on his mind when he
comes to his last days on earth. That's why we pay so
much attention to last words, especially those of people
important to us.

As those who seek to be obedient followers of Jesus
Christ, we need to know what matters most to Him so it
can matter most to us. Thankfully, we don't have to wonder about it. After His resurrection from the dead, and
just before His ascension back into heaven, Jesus told
His disciples—and us—what was uppermost on His
mind. His last words on earth are recorded for us in
Matthew 28:18–20.

Notice verse 19: "Go therefore and make disciples of
all the nations." There it is, the mission of the church,
stated in clear and concise terms: to disciple the people
of God so that they affect the world for Christ. If Christ's
mandate for the church is to *make* disciples, then His
will for us as individual believers is that we would
become disciples.

The way we achieve Christ's will for us is what we're
going to talk about in the four sections that follow these

introductory chapters, what I'm calling four absolute necessities in following Christ: worship, fellowship, Scripture, and evangelism. These are the essential elements in becoming a mature, fully functioning disciple of Jesus Christ.

To be a disciple of Christ means that we become like Him. That's why Jesus said in Matthew 10:25, "It is enough for the disciple that he become as his teacher." So becoming a disciple is where we ought to be heading in our Christian lives. This is the goal toward which we are to aim. In this chapter I want you to see what discipleship is, because before we can begin the process we have to see and understand the goal we're aiming for.

Let me say right off that being a disciple, getting down to the essentials of the Christian life, is a lot different than just going to church once or twice a week. To get excited because the preacher moved you and the choir inspired you is nice, but it's not enough.

To be part of the family of God is to enter a whole new world. It's a whole new orientation to life. Unless we understand what that means and what it involves, we will never arrive at God's intended will for His people.

The goal and the cornerstone of our activity, that which brings God the most glory, is for us to become disciples. God's goal is not salvation; that's just the introduction to God's goal. His desire is that those who are saved become disciples.

It is not enough simply to say, "I'm on my way to heaven." The issue is, are you becoming like the One who is taking you to heaven? That's discipleship, and that's what Christ wants from us.

Let me give a working definition for discipleship that will undergird everything we talk about in this book: "Discipleship is that developmental process of the local church that progressively brings Christians from spiritual infancy to spiritual maturity so that they are then able to reproduce the process with someone else."

Notice that this brings discipleship around full circle. Disciples are to turn around and make other disciples. Ultimately, that's how we fulfill the mandate of Matthew 28:18–20.

THE CONCEPT OF DISCIPLESHIP

Discipleship was not a new idea in New Testament times. It was a well-established concept in the Greek world in the centuries before Christ. The word *disciple* itself means "learner, student," and the Greeks had disciples in the realm of philosophy.

Plato, often called the "father of philosophy," developed a system of thought that dealt with issues of epistemology, or how we gain knowledge, and issues related to the meaning of life. Plato discipled his student Aristotle, who took what he had learned and built "gymnasiums," or academies.

In the ancient world, gymnasiums were not arenas for sporting events. They were training centers to teach students Plato's thought and the system developed by Aristotle, known as Aristotelian logic. The students thus trained were "gymnatized," which is the verb form of the Greek word for gymnasium.

So successful was this discipling process that it allowed the Greeks to influence the whole Greco-Roman world. This process was called "Hellenization," in which people who were not Greek began to adopt Greek thinking, language, and culture. That was all part of this concept of discipleship.

The New Testament picked up this concept and put it in a spiritual context so we would know what it means to be a disciple of Jesus Christ. Discipleship involves an apprenticeship in which the apprentice or student is brought toward a particular goal.

The Right Information

Since a disciple is basically a student, one aspect of discipleship is information. In order to become a disciple, you must acquire and master a body of knowledge. So teaching is always part of discipleship. It's one of the four necessities we are going to study.

Jesus was the master Teacher, of course. He taught

His twelve disciples the ABC's of what it means to follow Him. In God's Word we have the body of knowledge God wants us to know.

The Right Skills

But knowledge alone does not make you a disciple. You also have to know how to take that information and do something with it. Discipleship involves developing your skills. That's why Jesus would teach His disciples, then take them out into situations where they could apply what they were learning.

All of us know brilliant people who have lots of "book sense," but very little common sense. We wonder how these people can be so smart and yet not be able to function well in the situations of daily life.

That's not what a disciple is supposed to be like. A disciple marries the right information with the skill needed to put it into practice. How important is it that we get this picture?

Well, suppose you need open-heart surgery. The doctor comes into your room the night before the operation and introduces himself. You shake his hand and say, "Doc, this is a serious thing. How many of these have you done before?"

"You're my first one," he answers.

You reply, "Excuse me?"

"You'll be my first open-heart surgery."

"Doc, pull up a chair. We need to talk. How do you know you can do this?"

"Well, I went to four years of college and to medical school, and I made all A's. In fact, I graduated at the top of my class. I know the parts of the body, and I know the surgical instruments I need to use. You have nothing to worry about."

You are going to say, "Passing tests does not make you a surgeon. I want someone in there who has done this before."

So does every other patient! That's why a medical student does an internship and residency. He has to come alongside someone who has been in surgery before, who knows what to do when complications arise and things happen that aren't covered in the textbook. That new doctor's knowledge is very important, but it's not enough. He needs to be shown how to do the operation.

That's discipleship. It occurs when a person brings another person or persons along in such a way that the discipler imparts the right information while modeling the right skill.

This is why you cannot be discipled simply by showing up at church on Sunday morning. Worship is an essential component of following Christ, as we will see. But like knowledge, it's not the whole picture. Discipleship demands someone walking beside you.

We have an example of disciple-making right in our communities: the drug pushers. These guys are slick. They will take a young boy and mold him, giving him the body of information necessary to make a quick dollar, letting him walk beside them as they deal, and then sending him on his own to do what they did.

See, the issue is not whether you are going to be discipled. The issue is, by whom will you be discipled? All of us have people and influences in our lives that shape who we are and what we do. Discipleship demands skills derived from a body of information modeled before you.

I want to make four key observations about the process of becoming a disciple, based on the definition I gave above.

A PROCESS OF SPIRITUAL DEVELOPMENT

The first thing you need to know about becoming a disciple is that discipleship is a process of spiritual development. I have already quoted Matthew 10:25, but let me give it to you again in context with verse 24: "A disciple is not above his teacher, nor a slave above his master. It is enough for the disciple that he become as his teacher, and the slave as his master."

Matthew 10 is a crucial passage on discipleship, and we'll come back to it again. When Jesus said disciples are to *become* like their teacher, He was making clear that this business of being a disciple is a process.

You do not wake up the day after you are converted and discover that you are a spiritual giant, a fully mature disciple. Spiritual maturity takes time.

This concept reminds me of the story about the farmer who brought his family to the big city for the first time. They were particularly awed by the mall. As the wife toured the stores, the farmer took his son into a bank located in the mall. He saw a very elderly lady enter a room, then a few seconds later a beautiful young woman left the same room. The man looked down at his son and said, "Boy, run and get your mother fast." Unfortunately we cannot be transformed into disciples in just a few minutes—or a few years, for that matter. It takes time.

No Timetable

But the New Testament does not give us a step-by-step timetable for becoming disciples, nor does it have a list of formal, legalistic steps to be followed.

There's a very good reason for this. Although the process of discipleship involves certain basic necessities that are common to all believers, our spiritual experiences are unique to us. So is our rate of spiritual growth. Thus Paul admonishes us to work out our own salvation in fear and trembling.

Therefore, although you cannot control the fact that it takes time to become a disciple, you have a lot to say about how quickly you become a disciple. There are people who have been saved for twenty-five years who are less spiritually developed than people who have been saved five years.

The problem with older believers like this is that although they have had more time than the new believers, they have not grown as they should. Discipleship has to do with spiritual development, not how long you've been a Christian. You can know Christ for years but never develop properly as a disciple.

The Process of Discipleship

Jesus points this out in a picturesque way in Matthew 11:28–30: "Come to Me, all who are weary and heavy-laden, and I will give you rest. Take My yoke upon you, and learn from Me, for I am gentle and humble in heart; and you shall find rest for your souls. For My yoke is easy, and My load is light."

The word *learn* is the verb form of the word for "disciple." Jesus is saying, "Come and be discipled by Me." This is a wonderful invitation to the process of discipleship.

Jesus also paints a vivid picture of what the process looks like when He speaks of His "yoke." You have probably seen a horse, a mule, or an ox harnessed around the neck and shoulders in order to pull a wagon or a plow. The yoke is put on for three basic reasons.

One reason for wearing a yoke is to bring the animal under *submission,* under the control of the one sitting on the wagon or the plow and holding the reins. A yoke makes control possible. In discipleship, Christ is seeking our submission. He wants to bring us under His control.

The yoke also speaks of *work* to be done. It implies responsibility. God saved you to bring upon you the right kind of responsibility.

In other words, when a person yokes something, he does it purposefully. There is something he wants to accomplish. God saved you because He has something He wants your life to accomplish. But you can only fulfill the responsibility when you are yoked together with Christ, under His control.

Finally, the yoke speaks of *companionship.* When Jesus says, "Take My yoke upon you," He makes clear He is in the yoke too.

It was a common thing in the ancient world, and still is today in some communities, to train a young ox or mule by yoking it with an older, more experienced animal. That way, the young one comes alongside the experienced one to learn how to pull. When the farmer does this, he usually adjusts the yoke so that most of the weight falls on the experienced animal until the younger one gets the hang of it.

When I was a young teenager, my father used to take me with him when he went to preach. He would preach on street corners and give me a fistful of tracts to hand out. Or he would go to a prison to preach and take me with him for the ride.

As far as I was concerned, when it was over, that was it. I didn't realize then that God would later place a call on my life that would necessitate the experiences I had going along with my dad.

When I was in college, I preached on street corners. I preached in prisons. I was the preacher then, but the groundwork of experience was laid for me by my father, who did the work but took me along to show me how it's done.

Jesus says in Matthew 11:28, "If you come unto Me and are weary and heavy-laden, I will give you rest. I will bear the yoke with you, and I will pull the weight" (author's paraphrase).

A Different Level

I said earlier that not every Christian is necessarily a disciple. You can see the difference in verses 28–29. In verse 28, Jesus says, "I will give you rest." But in verse 29, He says, "If you take My yoke, you will find rest" (author's paraphrase). What's the difference? Verse 28 is a *position*. Verse 29 is an *experience*.

Whenever the Bible talks about rest, it means the enjoyment of God's provision. In other words, as a believer you have God's rest. But you may not be experiencing that rest in your daily life because you have not accepted the yoke. You have peace *with* God, but you may not be enjoying the peace *of* God. The same can be said of joy, power, and a lot of other blessings.

It's not that these things aren't available to us. The problem is that we are not yoked to the One who can give them to us. The yoke implies a different level of commitment.

Matthew 11:28 is an invitation to salvation. Verse 29 is an invitation to the fellowship of discipleship.

A PROGRESSIVE MOVEMENT
TOWARD MATURITY

If discipleship is a process of spiritual development, what's the goal toward which we are to develop? It's spiritual maturity: becoming a full-grown, well-developed disciple of Jesus Christ.

Paul wrote to the Christians at Corinth, "I, brethren, could not speak to you as to spiritual men, but as to men of flesh, as to babes in Christ" (1 Corinthians 3:1). The biblical term for a mature Christian is "spiritual." Paul expected the Corinthians to be maturing in the faith, but instead they were still acting like spiritual babies.

What's interesting is that Paul had gone to Corinth and led these people to Christ about A.D. 50. He wrote 1 Corinthians about A.D. 55. He was saying, "You should be spiritual by now, but you have not used your time well for spiritual development."

A Formula for Growth

This passage points up a very simple formula or guideline for spiritual growth: rate multiplied by time equals distance. That is, the rate at which you grow in your spiritual life in the time you have been allotted determines the distance you will travel down the road of discipleship toward spiritual maturity.

A newborn Christian who dives into the Word and the things of God rather than spending his or her time on other things may burst from the starting blocks and arrive at spiritual maturity faster than a person who has been saved for ten years but is still struggling with the ABC's of the faith. It's your pace that makes the difference.

By the way, if you really want to pick up your spiritual pace, run with someone who is faster than you, who can set a brisk pace. That's really what discipleship is all about. You cannot run the Christian life alone and run it with any speed or with much real endurance.

Where You Are

The good news is that even though you may have started off slowly, or started fast and then stumbled, you can get back in the race toward spiritual maturity. And I have even better news. No matter how you may have messed up, you can still cross the finish line a winner. The issue in the Christian race is not how you start, but how you finish (Hebrews 3:14).

The passage I referred to above in 1 Corinthians is important because it helps you determine how far along you are in your progress toward maturity. In 1 Corinthians 2:14–3:3, Paul identifies four categories of people with respect to the spiritual life.

The first category is the "natural man [who] does not accept the things of the Spirit of God" (2:14). This is the non-Christian, a person living by this world's system who has no capacity to receive spiritual truth. If you realize you are in this category as you read this book, the spiritual necessity for you is to come to Christ and be saved.

But chances are that you are already a believer, so one of Paul's next three categories applies to you. The second category is the spiritual man or woman (2:15), the person who "appraises all things, yet he himself is appraised by no man." This is the other end of the spiritual spectrum.

The spiritual person is a mature Christian, a well-developed disciple. The reason that non-Christians can't "appraise" or understand such a person is that they don't have "the mind of Christ" (v. 16). But the mind of Christ—the ability to live life from God's perspective, the capacity to think God's thoughts after Him—is available to every true believer.

A mature disciple is one who is able to make divinely informed choices. Paul is saying, "The spiritual person is able to look at, understand, and figure out life from a divine standpoint because he has the mind of Christ." The third category the apostle identifies in this text is "babes in Christ" (3:1). The baby Christian is someone who is brand-new in the faith. Newborn Christians cannot be mature. That's an impossibility. They can be on fire and growing like crazy spiritually, but they cannot be full grown.

Paul's fourth and final category is the "fleshly" or carnal Christian (3:2–3). The difference between a carnal Christian and a baby Christian is that the carnal believer has had time to mature. He should know how to live with a heavenly perspective, but instead he thinks and acts like a non-Christian. He makes little progress toward spiritual maturity. This person has not responded to the invitation and challenge to become a disciple.

And lest we think progressing toward mature discipleship is a take-it-or-leave-it deal, let me point you to Hebrews 5:

> Concerning [Melchizedek] we have much to say, and it is hard to explain, since you have become dull of hearing. For though by this time you ought to be teachers, you have need again for someone to teach you the elementary principles of the oracles of God, and you have come to need milk and not solid food. (vv. 11–12)

The writer of Hebrews had some spiritually nourishing, "meat and potatoes" stuff to teach these believers about the Melchizedek priesthood of Christ, but they had "become dull." Evidently, these people had been growing, but they were regressing. If you don't go forward you go backward, because there is no such thing as neutrality in the Christian life.

Adults who can't eat solid food are sick. And Christians who still need kindergarten language in order to understand the things of God are not growing. This was the Hebrews' problem, because they had had enough time to be mature.

In fact, the writer says that by the time of his letter the Hebrews should have been mature enough to teach and disciple others. Every Christian has been saved to be an influencer—a teacher, a discipler—of another Christian.

But the Hebrews were regressing, so the writer continues in 5:13–14:

> For everyone who partakes only of milk is not accustomed to the word of righteousness, for he is a babe. But solid food is for the mature, who because of practice have their senses trained to discern good and evil.

The Goal

We are supposed to know which way is up spiritually because we've been trained—which, by the way, is the word "gymnatized" we talked about earlier. We're supposed to be mature because we've been practicing hard.

That's what God does when He sends us trials. He wants to see whether we are willing to implement on Monday what we said "amen" to on Sunday. Spiritual maturity is the goal of discipleship.

ACCOUNTABILITY WITHIN THE CHURCH

Here's a third important fact about discipleship. God has created a specific environment in which discipleship is to occur. Let me say again what I said in the introduction. Here it is: There is no such thing as biblical discipleship outside of the local church.

People who say they are being discipled outside the context of a local church do not understand the nature of either discipleship or the church. In 1 Timothy 3:14–15, Paul says:

> I am writing these things to you, hoping to come to you before long; but in case I am delayed, I write so that you may know how one ought to conduct himself in the household of God, which is the church of the living God, the pillar and support of the truth.

This means that parachurch groups cannot by themselves fulfill this mission.

Some of these groups, rather than strengthening the local church, have become replacements for it. This is illegitimate. Parachurch groups are only valid as they strengthen and empower the local church. Paul makes clear that the church is the context in which the conduct of the saints is measured and critiqued. The church is "the household of God."

The Nature of the Church

Don't misunderstand. I am not saying you cannot listen to the radio or television and benefit from a message or other program. I don't mean you can't go to a conference and be encouraged and helped.

But all of these things are ancillary. They may augment and support the ministry of the church, but they can't replace it. A child can go to school and learn, but school can never take the place of home.

The church is God's context in which discipleship is to occur. The reason for this is the nature of the church. Ephesians 1:22–23 is crucial to understand here because sometimes it's the church's fault, not the people's fault, when discipleship isn't happening. Why? Because sometimes the church either doesn't understand what it is or forgets what it is.

Paul writes in these verses, "And [God] put all things in subjection under [Christ's] feet, and gave Him as head over all things to the church, which is His body, the fulness of Him who fills all in all."

Notice that although Christ is head over all things, He has only been given to the church. So if you and I are going to follow Christ, we are going to follow Him to church!

Notice also that Paul calls the church Christ's "body," a familiar New Testament metaphor. The body only has one job—to carry out the dictates of the head. Whenever your body stops doing what your brain says, get to the hospital quick. You are a very sick person.

So Christ is the head and the church is His body, manifested in each local assembly. The church's job is to execute the commands of its head. It's in this sense that the church can be said to be "the fulness of Him who fills all in all." The way Christ does what He wants to do today is through His body. Christ fills up the church as the church fills up the purposes of Christ. That's what

Jesus meant when He said, "I am with you always, even to the end of the age" (Matthew 28:20).

The Nurture of the Church

Just as a baby needs a family to provide it with a context for nurture and development, so every Christian must be a dynamic part of a local body of believers. Sadly, there are many people who attend church but do not partner with the ministry. That is a sin.

You say, "Why is that a sin?"

For the same reason that if your finger is not attached to your hand, you have a physical problem. The unattached finger, or Christian, is unusable and cannot develop.

It is a sin not to belong to a local assembly of the family of God. Imagine a child who only comes out of his room to eat. That's not family life. Family life is dynamic participation and involvement.

One reason we need the ministry of the church in this matter of becoming disciples is that no one person can give another person everything he needs to become mature in Christ. We need the full body of Christ, so that what is lacking in one person can be made up by another. That way the whole body grows "by that which every joint supplies" (Ephesians 4:16).

Hebrews 10:23–25 underscores this same truth. The Hebrew Christians were going through difficult times, so the writer urged them:

> Let us hold fast the confession of our hope without wavering, for He who promised is faithful; and let us consider how to stimulate one another to love and good deeds, not forsaking our own assembling together, as is the habit of some, but encouraging one another; and all the more, as you see the day drawing near.

The word *assembling* here is from the word for "synagogue." The writer is talking about the believers' place of assembly, the church. But it's not just a building. He's talking about the fellowship of the saints.

We need the gathered body of Christ because it is the context in which spiritual growth occurs. You may grow some without the family of God, but you cannot develop into a fully mature disciple of Christ without the family of God.

The church is like a hospital. If you are sick, you are welcome. Jesus said, "It is not those who are healthy who need a physician, but those who are sick" (Matthew 9:12). However, I know of no hospital that just wants to make you comfortable with your illness.

No doctor is going to say to you, "In here, we're going to let you have all the cancer you want." The hospital's job is to help you get rid of your illness. The hospital has the people and the equipment to do the job. It's the same with the church.

First Corinthians 12 is another passage of Scripture that points up the necessity of the church for spiritual growth. Paul says here that every believer is critical to the spiritual development of every other believer: "For even as the body is one and yet has many members, and all the members of the body, though they are many, are one body, so also is Christ. . . . For the body is not one member, but many" (vv. 12, 14).

Because this is true, Paul goes on to say that no member of the body can say to any other member, "I have no need of you" (v. 21). On the contrary, "God has placed the members, each one of them, in the body, just as He desired" (v. 18). Why? So that "there should be no division in the body, but that the members should have the same care for one another" (v. 25).

The body of Christ is designed to work the same way the physical body works. If I stub my right big toe on the coffee table, a whole series of things will be set in motion.

My brain will send a signal to my left hand to reach down and grab my right toe. My brain will also send a message to my left leg, "Get ready to bear this brother all by yourself." Then my brain will send a signal to my mouth to let everyone else know that I stubbed my right toe.

What is true of the physical body is true of God's spiritual body. We are to show the same kind of care for one another that the body shows for itself. That's why it is selfish to simply come to church and say, "Minister to me. Serve me. Encourage me. Visit me when I'm down. Pray for me when I'm hurting. Disciple me—but don't ask me to be available to help disciple other believers."

People like this are more like "church leeches" than church members, sucking the lifeblood out of the church without making any meaningful contribution to it.

A TRANSFERABLE PROCESS

Here is the fourth and final component of our definition of discipleship. The process is designed to be transferable from you and me to others.

The goal is for every member of the body of Christ to be active in the development of the rest of the body. We are to reproduce the process of discipleship in the lives of others.

You cannot hire professionals to do it for you. Neither I nor the staff at our church in Dallas can disciple four thousand people. It takes a lot of people to develop four thousand people spiritually. It takes the body supporting itself for this to occur.

Satan doesn't want you to become a disciple. He also doesn't want you to teach anyone else how to be a disciple. He would love for all of us to stay baby, immature Christians, because we can't do him any damage that way. People are not afraid of one year olds.

Satan knows you aren't dangerous until you begin to grow. So he doesn't mind your going to church, as long as that's all you do. As long as you don't get involved in this discipleship stuff, as long as you don't start growing in the faith and helping others to do likewise, he's happy to let you go to church.

But, if your faith ever starts growing and rubbing off on someone else, you become a threat to Satan. The one thing he can't stand is disciples reproducing the life of Jesus Christ in other Christians.

God's Imitators

Paul was the preeminent discipler. He could say, "Be imitators of me, just as I also am of Christ" (1 Corinthians 11:1). There's nothing wrong with following people if those people are following Christ. There's everything wrong with following people who are not following Christ.

The real danger for most of us as believers is not that we will suddenly plunge off the deep end and lapse into gross sin, tossing our faith aside. That can happen, of course, and none of us is immune from the downward pull of the flesh.

But I think a more common danger is that we will take in the truth, not do anything with it, then take in more truth, sit comfortably on it, and continue this process until we are so spiritually bloated we can't move.

We must exercise, using what we are learning to change our own lives, change our communities, and help bring other people along in the faith. Otherwise, what we are taking in even stops nourishing us.

We know it's possible to eat so much that food, instead of nourishing and building up the body, actually begins to work against it. This can happen in the spiritual realm, and it happens all the time.

Discipleship is designed to keep the fat off by allowing us to burn spiritual calories as we put into practice the truth of God. What God is looking for is people who imitate Christ; that is, who look and act just like Him.

Teaching Others

I love the charge Paul gave to his disciple Timothy in 2 Timothy 2:1–2:

> You therefore, my son, be strong in the grace that is in Christ Jesus. And the things which you have heard from me in the presence of many witnesses, these entrust to faithful men, who will be able to teach others also.

Paul is telling Timothy to do with the next generation of leaders what Paul did with Timothy: hand on the truth of Christ. Discipleship is a transferable process. The loop isn't closed until you and I are teaching someone else what God has worked into our lives.

Now let me go back to Hebrews 5:12, a verse we talked about above. We saw that the Hebrews had so regressed spiritually that the writer has to say to them, "I had some good stuff to teach you, but you aren't ready" (see v. 11).

The problem was not only that the Hebrews themselves weren't as spiritually mature as they should have been. They were unable to teach others, which they should have been able to do by then. They needed bottle-feeding themselves, in fact. Their spiritual digestive tracts were underdeveloped. As a result, other Christians who needed to know what they knew were being undernourished too.

Our churches are full of people who have been following Christ for ten, fifteen, even twenty years, yet they cannot point to one other person they are bringing along in the faith. Prospective disciples are all around us: in our marriages, in our families, at church, in our neighborhoods, at work.

Finding a candidate for discipleship is not usually the problem. The problem is that too many of the saints are on the sidelines instead of in the game.

It's easy to sit in the stands and call the plays. It's another story to get out on the field and play the game. We have a lot of professional critics in our churches, but not enough disciple-makers. God has not called you to be a critic. He has called you to build His truth into somebody else's life.

Discipleship is a process that involves some basic concepts, what we are calling four absolute necessities. We're going to talk about these necessities, what they involve, and how you can put them into practice in your life and the lives of others.

CHAPTER TWO

THE REAL DEAL ON DISCIPLESHIP

How many times have you heard someone say, "If I had known what I was getting into, I never would have said yes"?

Many times, probably. And I'm sure you've said it yourself more than once. We've all been there. That's why it's important to know what the real deal is before you make a commitment.

It's the same with discipleship. If you are going to do what's necessary to follow Christ as His disciple, you need to know what He expects of you. You need to know the real deal. And that's just what Jesus Christ wants you to know.

So before we go any further, I want to look at some key passages on discipleship and see what it involves. Then in chapter 3 we'll be ready to look at a group of people who put discipleship into action.

THE PRIORITY OF DISCIPLESHIP

The first thing we need to talk about is the priority of discipleship. We have already established how important this is to Jesus, but the issue here is how important it is to us.

For this, I want to examine an interesting passage of Scripture, Luke 9:57–62. What we're going to see here is that Jesus calls disciples to follow Him even though there are no guarantees in advance.

You may say, "Wait a minute, Tony. I thought you just said Jesus wants us to know what we're getting into when we follow Him." Yes, He does. But knowing what discipleship involves is different from having your every question answered. And it's a lot different from cutting your own deal with God.

The three men in Luke 9 needed to learn that Jesus was not offering guarantees or special deals. What He was offering them was Himself, and that was all they needed.

What I'm saying is that in discipleship, the deal is that you and I are called to follow Christ, period. Not follow Christ if we know we're going to have a roof over our heads. Not follow Him as long as we know where our next meal is coming from. Not follow Him on our own terms, when we're ready.

The real deal is that being a disciple has to be such a priority that we commit ourselves to follow Jesus wherever He leads us and whatever He tells us to do. He wants us to follow Him because we love Him, not because we love what we might get from Him.

A Priority of Action

So in Luke 9, as Jesus and the disciples were heading toward Jerusalem (v. 51), a man said to Him, "'I will follow You wherever You go.' And Jesus said to him, 'The foxes have holes, and the birds of the air have nests, but the Son of Man has nowhere to lay His head'" (vv. 57–58).

We know that Jesus had no permanent home. And we know He was on His way to Jerusalem to die on the cross. So He was saying to this potential disciple that if he followed Jesus, he couldn't be guaranteed anything. He would have to follow Jesus and walk by faith.

Look at what this man said. "Jesus, I'll follow You anywhere." Wife, remember when you told your husband that same thing: "Honey, wherever you go, I'm going"? That's a huge commitment.

Was this man serious about being a disciple? We're not told whether he followed Jesus, but Jesus' answer and the context suggest that he was not really ready to be a disciple. He was talking the right talk. But he didn't realize what he was saying.

He needed to understand that discipleship is not a priority of words, but a priority of action (see Matthew 21:28–31a for another example). I believe this man was thinking, *I'll follow You wherever You go, Jesus, as long as I like the destination.* But Jesus doesn't cut those deals. Wherever is wherever.

A Priority of Immediacy

I have a sneaking suspicion that the second man in Luke 9 was listening to Jesus' conversation with the first man. Jesus turned to this second man and said, "Follow Me" (v. 59).

This is a different case right away, because this man did not offer to follow Jesus like the first man did. He answered, "Permit me first to go and bury my father." But Jesus said, "Allow the dead to bury their own dead; but as for you, go and proclaim everywhere the kingdom of God" (v. 60).

When you first read this, it seems a little cold-hearted on Jesus' part. Aren't children supposed to honor their fathers? What's going on here? But the context makes clear that this man's father was not dead yet. If his father were already dead and he merely needed to attend to the funeral, he would have been home. The Jews buried their dead within twenty-four hours of death.

Besides, Jesus' reply about the dead burying their own dead shows that the father was not dead. When was the last time you saw dead people burying dead people? In my neighborhood, they don't do that. Dead people can't bury dead people.

Jesus is telling this guy, "Let the spiritually dead bury the physically dead." Let those who don't know God hang around and take care of the funeral arrangements. Jesus wanted this man to go out and preach the gospel.

What this man was telling Jesus was that he wanted to put off being His disciple for an indefinite period until his father was gone and all the estate and family stuff was settled. In other words, he wanted Jesus to wait until he was free of all distractions.

But Jesus said no deal. Remember, we're talking about the priority of discipleship. Jesus comes first. There will always be distractions.

I see something else here. If this man overheard Jesus say He had nowhere to lay His head, he may have been thinking, *Wait a minute. This could be a bad deal for me economically. Before I start following Jesus, I'd better see to my financial security. I'd better hang around home until I receive my inheritance.*

In other words, he was trying to establish his security, cover his back, hedge his bets. Jesus doesn't mind your taking a few hours out to bury a loved one, but this man was asking for a few years to get his situation secure before he would start going all the way with God. But Jesus said don't wait.

Some Christians aren't ready to become disciples because the business hasn't gotten off the ground yet, the kids aren't raised yet, or they haven't made all the money they need to make yet. They keep telling Jesus, "Lord, after the business is up and running and the bills are all paid, I'll be there!"

But God says no deal. He doesn't want our leftovers. He doesn't want to wait. He's Daddy; He doesn't have to wait! Besides, you and I know Satan has a unique ability to get us to put off the really important things. As soon as we get one thing fixed, something else breaks.

So we say, "Lord, I'll follow You later. I'll start living for You later. But just give me a little more time." No deal. Discipleship demands immediate obedience.

A Priority of Relationships

Now let's look at the third man in Luke 9:61–62. Like the first guy, he takes the initiative. "I will follow You,

Lord; but first permit me to say good-bye to those at home."

That seems fair. You're getting ready to go away for a long time. You don't even know if you will return. So you want to go home, pack your suitcase, and say bye to the folks.

But Jesus said, "No one, after putting his hand to the plow and looking back, is fit for the kingdom of God" (v. 62). This is the issue. The man wasn't just wanting to go home. He was looking back. In New Testament days, if you were going on a long journey, you just didn't shout a quick good-bye. That party could have lasted a long time.

What Jesus is objecting to here is not a good-bye kiss. He's talking about family making a potential disciple look back, think twice about giving everything up to follow Jesus.

I can imagine this man's family saying to him, "You are going to do *what?* You are going to follow this Man you barely know to places you've never been? You don't know how He is going to take care of you. He can't even promise you a hotel room! This is not a good idea."

But Jesus says anybody who looks back after starting out on the path of discipleship is not fit for His kingdom. Why is that? Because you can't plow looking over your shoulder. If you are going to plow a straight furrow, your eyes have to be focused forward. Jesus is saying that if we try to plow looking back, we are going to mess up His program.

Do you remember Lot's wife? She left Sodom, but Sodom had not left her. She heard all that fire and brimstone raining down from heaven behind her, and she began to think, *My friends are back there. All the stores I like to shop at are back there. The bank where I have my money is back there. Everything that is important to me is back in Sodom.*

So she looked back despite the angel's warning (Genesis 19:17), and God stopped her right there (v. 26). She became the answer to a Bible trivia question. She was judged unfit to go any farther.

What a difference with Abraham in Genesis 22. God

asked for and received Abraham's son, Isaac. The good news is that when you give God your first and best, He gives you His first and best. If you make God a priority, He knows where the rams caught in the thicket are located.

THE COST OF DISCIPLESHIP

Becoming skilled in whatever you do requires paying the cost. You don't just wake up in the morning as a professional. You have to be willing to pick up the tab.

In the same way, you do not suddenly wake up one morning as a mature disciple with the power of God fully operative in your life. There is a price to be paid for following Jesus. Discipleship costs.

Many people want to come to church and say, "Don't expect anything of me. I don't want to pay any price. I'm just here for you to serve me."

If that is how someone thinks, he or she is not going to be very comfortable in church—or at least, he or she ought not to be. That is not how this thing works.

The Cost in Relationships

We can see that in Luke 14:25–33, where Jesus spells out the cost of following Him:

> Great multitudes were going along with Him; and He turned and said to them, "If anyone comes to Me, and does not hate his own father and mother and wife and children and brothers and sisters, yes, and even his own life, he cannot be My disciple." (vv. 25–26)

A lot of people cringe when they hear that. This text has been twisted and misinterpreted in all kinds of crazy ways. Is Jesus overstating the case for discipleship? Do we really have to *hate* those closest to us?

Wouldn't it have been less harsh if Jesus had just said, "Love Me more than anyone else"? But He didn't say that, so we have to ask what He means by hating our family.

The key to this is that Jesus is not talking about our affections. He's talking about our decisions. He is saying that when we come to a decision in life and momma or husband or wife or brother says go left and Jesus says go right, we go right. It's as simple as that.

The issue on the floor here is authority. You and I must be willing to renounce the most precious people in our lives if we really want to follow Christ. He will not be number two in anyone's heart.

Someone may say, "That's not right." Well, suppose a man said to his wife, "If another woman comes into my life, you'll have to step aside." Do you think his wife would nod sympathetically and buy that deal? I don't either!

She shouldn't have to, because she deserves to be the only woman in her husband's life. He made that decision when he married her. If another woman says go left to a man while his wife is saying go right, and he goes left, that brother is in trouble!

The nature of the marriage commitment means that everybody else is number two. Sometimes your loved ones will think you hate them for not choosing them over Jesus. Sometimes a family member will say, "If you loved me, you would." And God is saying, "If you love Me, you will not."

There is to be nothing in my life that deserves my commitment, my determination, and my passions more than my love for Jesus Christ. It is to be so high above my love for my wife and children that sometimes it may look like I hate them.

One reason our prayers aren't being answered, our marriages aren't being healed, and our problems aren't being solved is that too many of us just want the "goodies" of the Christian life. We don't want to hate everything else and come to Christ.

The Bible tells us to love our spouses and our children. But Christ is talking about what happens when it comes down to the issue of authority. If you have to make a choice between Christ and anyone or anything else, you choose Him every time.

I knew I wanted to marry Lois when she told me Christ would always be first in her life. That's how I felt too. I wanted to marry somebody for whom Christ would be number one, not me, because she in turn would never be number one in my life.

But I can tell you that anyone who puts Christ first in marriage will never lose. Putting Him first means I will love my wife the way Christ loves the church. You don't lose by "hating" your mate in comparison to your love for Christ, you win. But it means paying the cost. If you want to follow Jesus, He demands priority over the closest human relationship you have.

The Cost in Suffering

Discipleship also demands a willingness to suffer. Jesus said, "Whoever does not carry his own cross and come after Me cannot be My disciple" (Luke 14:27).

We know that crucifixion was a favorite method of execution for the Romans. They would tie the condemned man's arms to the heavy horizontal bar of his cross and make him carry it through town to the place of crucifixion. Jesus had to carry His cross through the streets of Jerusalem to Calvary.

The Romans made the criminal carry his cross publicly to put him on display, to say Rome was right and this man was wrong. The convicted man's cross was his indictment, saying to the people who lined the path that this man was worthy of death because the Roman government had found him guilty.

Jesus is saying to us, "I want you to carry your cross through town." He wants us to so identify with Him that when we are accused of being a Christian, we say, "I'm guilty." When we're accused of loving and following the Lord Jesus Christ, we acknowledge the charge. "You're right. I'm one of His. You caught me!"

That's what it means to take up your cross, to be a disciple of Jesus Christ. It means to be on public display, to be identified with Jesus Christ in every area of your life.

It means that if your family and friends don't want to be identified with you anymore, it's all right. You will still identify with Christ. It means that if your standards cause people to walk the other way, that's all right.

Jesus is not going to turn around and follow you the other way if you follow them. He says to you, "Follow Me."

There's one other thing you need to know about the cross. When a man carried his cross through town, it was a one-way journey. He was going to die. No matter how much he wanted to turn around and go the other way, he couldn't. He was on his way to the place of execution.

Earlier, Jesus had said, "If anyone wishes to come after Me, let him deny himself, and take up his cross daily, and follow Me" (Luke 9:23). Jesus was not talking about physical death, since you can't die physically every day. He was talking about a day-by-day orientation to life.

Denying yourself doesn't mean just giving up something you want. It means saying no to your desires and plans for your life. It means you deny yourself anything God doesn't want for you. You lay your life down daily for Christ.

Denial hurts, doesn't it? But that's part of the cost of discipleship. Jesus says, "Love Me so much that you will deny yourself anything I don't want for you." But we love ourselves, and we love satisfying our cravings.

Giving Up Your Claims

That brings us to a third cost of discipleship: relinquishing all claims on every aspect of your life. This is a further development of the concept of self-denial.

Jesus gives us two illustrations of what He means in Luke 14:28–32. The first is that of a builder who has to calculate the cost of his project (vv. 28–30). No builder wants to put down the foundation of his building and then discover he underestimated his costs so badly that he has to stop building.

Jesus is saying that being His disciple involves some planning, some calculations on our part. You must plan to follow Jesus. I could preach on discipleship at my church, and someone could say, "Amen, Pastor. I'm with you. I'm excited about being a disciple."

Jesus says, "Just a minute. Pull out your spiritual

calculator. Add up the cost. Make sure you understand what you are saying. Make sure you have the spiritual capital it takes to finish, not just start. Evaluate whether there is anything in your life hindering you from being My disciple."

The Lord's second illustration is of a king who is on his way out to fight another king (vv. 31–32). If this king has ten thousand soldiers and the other king has twenty thousand, the first king is smart to pause and consider whether this battle is a good idea. If he decides he's going to get wiped out, he sends a peace delegation. He says, "Let's make a deal."

The point is that there is no neutrality. The king either has to fight or make a deal. He can't just sit staring into space, or his army is going to be obliterated.

If you are a believer, Satan is coming after you whether or not you decide to become a disciple. Satan is going to throw his army against you no matter what you do, because we are in a war. Since that's true, you'd better make a decision. Look before you leap—but after you look, make sure you leap.

In verses 33–35, Jesus brings home the cost of being His disciple. He can't really use people who aren't willing to love Him supremely, who aren't ready to carry their cross daily, who have counted the cost and said no thanks, who aren't willing to give up all they have for Him (v. 33).

People like this are "saltless salt." They are in the kingdom, but they don't enhance the program and plan of God.

Once you decide to follow Christ no matter what, you are going to discover the other side of discipleship, which is the reward of being Jesus' disciple. We'll talk about that at the end of this chapter and in the four main sections of the book.

But before you begin adding up the rewards, you need to add up the cost. Jesus doesn't want you to start with Him and then turn back, quit building, or give up the battle.

THE MARK OF DISCIPLESHIP

In the Upper Room on the night before His crucifixion, Jesus spoke these very familiar words:

> A new commandment I give to you, that you love one another, even as I have loved you, that you also love one another. By this all men will know that you are My disciples, if you have love for one another. (John 13:34–35)

Jesus established a permanent relationship between being His disciple and love. Love is the mark, the identifying badge, of a disciple as surely as a police officer's badge identifies him.

The Bible says two basic things about love. First, we are to love God with all of our heart, soul, mind, and strength (Deuteronomy 6:5; Matthew 22:37). No matter whether you use your mind, your body, or your innermost being, love for God must burst forth.

The second basic biblical fact about love is that we are told to love our neighbor as ourselves (Leviticus 19:18; Matthew 22:39). According to Jesus, these two concepts are so all-inclusive that the Scripture hangs on them (Matthew 22:40). If you can fulfill these two commands, you have the Bible in a nutshell.

A Commanded Love

Biblical love is a commanded love. This is very important. Because biblical love is a command, that means we can love when we don't feel like it, even when it's inconvenient.

The love that marks us as Jesus' disciples is *agape* love, which involves serving others even if it's at my own expense. Biblical love means I will do the will of God for you, whether you deserve it or not and whether I feel like it or not.

Discipleship love is more of a command than a feeling. It certainly may include our feelings, and it often does. But we can love people we may not even like, because we are commanded to love them. They may not be the people we would choose for our dream dinner, but we can meet their needs as we know them because a disciple loves as an act of obedience to Christ.

Do you know why so many of us believers are in pain over our relationships? Because we have adopted the world's way of responding. Rather than acting on the command and will of God, we act out of our own will. Therefore, a bad relationship keeps us up at night and gives us ulcers and headaches.

We can't get that person we can't stand off our minds because we refuse to respond in obedience. But if we will love that person and seek his or her best no matter what it takes, we will find the burden of our bad feelings rolled away. What a freedom biblical love is.

A New Love

Jesus called this command to love a "new" commandment in John 13:34. Since we know the Old Testament commands us to love others, in what ways is Jesus' commandment new? What's new about the love of His disciples?

First, it's new with regard to purpose. The purpose of the believer's love is to be a testimony before the world. In the Old Testament, Israel's entire sacrificial system was to be a witness to the world of the true God. But now, we believers are told that our love is to be our testimony before the world.

Second, this love is new in regard to identity. In the Old Testament, the way you identified yourself as a true Israelite was by getting circumcised. In early New Testament days, people got baptized by John the Baptist to show that they were followers of John and of God.

But Jesus says these outward criteria are no longer the defining characteristics (although New Testament baptism is still a mark of obedience to Christ). The new identifying mark of the disciple is *agape* love. You probably know a lot of people who love. But you probably don't know a lot of people who love when they aren't being loved in return. This kind of love is the mark of the disciple.

Third, this love Jesus is talking about is new in regard to degree. "Greater love has no one than this, that one lay down his life for his friends" (John 15:13). Disciples are to have such a dynamic love for one another that we would be willing to put our lives on the line for each other. That's love to the fullest degree.

Fourth, this love is new in regard to power. It is provided through a supernatural infusion of the Holy Spirit. "The love of God has been poured out within our hearts through the Holy Spirit who was given to us" (Romans 5:5).

Now you're thinking, *Tony, I can't love like that.* You're absolutely right! I can't love like that either. It takes the supernatural work of the Holy Spirit to love like that.

Fifth, this love is new in regard to its effect. It determines how close you get to God. John wrote years later:

> By this we know that we have come to know [God], if we keep His commandments. The one who says, "I have come to know Him," and does not keep His commandments, is a liar, and the truth is not in him. . . . The one who says he is in the light and yet hates his brother is in the darkness until now. The one who loves his brother abides in the light and there is no cause for stumbling in him. But the one who hates his brother is in the darkness and walks in the darkness, and does not know where he is going because the darkness has blinded his eyes. (1 John 2:3–4, 9–11)

If you refuse to obey Jesus' "new commandment" to love one another, God will keep you blinded so you won't know which way you are going in your life.

Imitating Christ's Love

What we are talking about is imitating Christ's love. He is our model. Embedded in John 13:34 is the key phrase, "even as I have loved you." What is Jesus' love like? It would take another book to describe it fully, but let's look at a few characteristics.

For one, Jesus' love takes the initiative. John writes,

"We love, because He first loved us" (1 John 4:19). God didn't wait until we were lovely to love us. He didn't wait to be asked. He loved first.

We often put conditions on our love. "Well, when you start doing your part, I'll start doing mine." "You go first."

But when we imitate Christ's love, we say, "Even if you never respond, I still love you." "Even if you never change, this is what God would have me do for you." "Even if you never repay me, this is how God wants me to love you."

Imitating Christ's love also means meeting the needs God confronts us with. Again, John explains what this involves:

> Whoever has the world's goods, and beholds his brother in need and closes his heart against him, how does the love of God abide in him? Little children, let us not love with word or with tongue, but in deed and truth. (1 John 3:17–18)

If we love, we cannot close our hearts to a need God has given us the ability to meet. The reason for having "the world's goods" is to meet needs. Paul instructed us "to be generous and ready to share" (1 Timothy 6:18; see also 2 Corinthians 9:6–11; Galatians 6:10). Disciples are ready to help, even as they may need help sometimes. This love works both ways.

Christ's love is negative too. It does not skip over or tolerate sin. The Bible says, "He who spares his rod hates his son" (Proverbs 13:24). Why does love spank? Because love wants to keep a child from hell. Love wants to keep God's discipline off the child's back. So love disciplines and judges.

A Powerful Witness

Finally, our love for one another will also identify us to the world as Jesus' disciples. We will have a powerful public witness when we love each other (John 13:35). What Jesus is doing here is giving the world the right to examine our credibility.

Husbands and wives, can people tell you are Christians by the way you love your spouse? Parents, can people tell you are Christians by the way you love your children?

The love we're talking about is not just natural human love. Only the Holy Spirit can produce Christlike love in us. It can't happen otherwise. Non-Christians can certainly love, but they cannot display the love Jesus is talking about.

Non-Christians ought to look at us and ask, "How can you love like that?" The question ought to be raised. That means our love is supposed to be public, supposed to be visible. Jesus says the world should be able to tell we belong to Him. But the only way they can know that is if they see our love, the mark of Jesus' disciples.

THE PRODUCTIVITY OF DISCIPLESHIP

A fourth reality I want to show you about discipleship is its productivity. God's will is that every disciple become a maximum contributor to the purpose and program of God in the world. Jesus calls it bearing fruit. The classic passage on fruit-bearing is John 15.

God's Initiative

Jesus says in John 15:1, "I am the true vine, and My Father is the vinedresser." Like everything else in discipleship, God initiates the process. A disciple's productivity is initiated and stimulated by God's care and pruning.

Jesus may have said this as He and the disciples were crossing the Kidron Valley on the way to the Garden of Gethsemane. The Kidron Valley was known for its luscious grapevines. So Jesus may have pointed to one of those vines and said, "Gentlemen, that's Me. I am the true vine."

The Greek word translated "true" means "real." Jesus is saying, "I am the real vine. Anyone else who comes along talking about being the vine is an impostor."

Jesus is the vine, and it is the Father's responsibility to take care of the vine. God is the Gardener, Jesus is the vine, and we are the branches. "Every branch in Me that does not bear fruit, He takes away; and every branch that bears fruit, He prunes it, that it may bear more fruit" (v. 2). I want to save the idea of "takes away" for last, because that's an important concept. But here I want to consider the all-important words "in Me."

In John's writings, the phrase "in Me" indicates an organic relationship; that is, these are true believers who are at various stages in their spiritual development. Christ's concern is to move His children from just a relationship to an intimate fellowship with Him through the process of discipleship.

For example, the relationship of marriage does not necessarily produce intimate fellowship. You may have signed on the dotted line. You may be married, but that doesn't mean sparks of love are shooting around your living room. The goal of marriage is more than relationship. It is intimate fellowship.

That's what Jesus is saying here in John 15:2. Notice the progression when this intimate fellowship is being developed. The disciple first "bears fruit," then "more fruit," then "much fruit" (vv. 2, 5).

Finally, in verse 16 Jesus says His will is that "your fruit should remain." Our intimate fellowship with Christ should produce lasting fruit.

The Character of the Tree

What else should we know about fruitfulness in the spiritual life? One thing is that fruit reflects the character of the tree or vine of which it is a part. When you go to an apple tree at harvest time, you expect to find apples. If you find the tree barren, or if you find pears, something is wrong.

Apple trees are designed to produce apples. Pear trees are designed to produce pears. Grapevines are designed to produce grapes. And Christians are designed to produce Christlikeness. We reflect the character of the vine of which we are a part.

The Fruit of the Tree

Here is another truth about spiritual fruitfulness.

The purpose of being fruitful is so that you can impact others for Christ. To put it another way, you produce fruit so that somebody else can take a bite of you and be blessed.

Non-Fruitful Branches

Now let me go back to John 15:2, where Jesus said, "Every branch in Me that does not bear fruit, [God the Gardener] takes away." I want to give a word of encouragement to you here.

Any gardener is very concerned about unproductive vines. Please notice that these branches are "in Me," that is, in Christ. I take it that they are in fellowship with Christ, but they are not producing fruit yet.

So what did Jesus mean by "takes away"? This word can literally be translated, "lifts up." Oftentimes in the vineyards of the Middle East, some vine branches would lie on the ground not getting enough sunlight, being covered by too much dirt.

When the gardener made his daily rounds, he would look for such branches and "lift them up"—tie them to a pole or a post. That way they wouldn't languish on the ground, subject to being stepped on, any potential fruit being stifled. Lifting these branches up allowed maximum sunlight to reach them so the fruit-bearing process could begin.

Every branch in fellowship with Christ, lying on the ground, He lifts up so it can produce fruit. How does God lift up these branches?

One way is by encouraging the branches. God does this especially with new Christians. A new believer may be facing a dead-end problem. God makes a way out of no way. He comes out of nowhere and delivers that Christian. He answers prayer in an amazing way, and the believer finds himself saying, "Thank You, Jesus."

Things like that can get the fruit-bearing started because the Bible says that the praise of our lips is fruit produced for God (Hebrews 13:15). This is part of the "lifting up" process that stimulates fruit-bearing.

This gets the process started. But once a disciple

begins bearing fruit, God really goes to work. He starts pruning us so we will bear "more fruit."

God is not satisfied with no fruit. But neither is He satisfied with some fruit. Once you move from no fruit to some fruit, God now says, "I want to see more fruit." So He starts pruning.

Pruning is that horticultural art of clipping off unwanted distractions from a branch. These are intruders that make their way onto the branch and suck out the life that ought to be going to the branch.

In grape-growing, these distractions are called, appropriately, "sucker shoots." These are tiny shoots that appear where the vine and branch intersect. Sucker shoots siphon away the life-giving sap of the vine that is meant for the branches. If sucker shoots are not pruned, the branch becomes malnourished. It doesn't get all of the life it's supposed to receive from the vine. So the gardener comes along with his clippers and prunes off those shoots. He gets rid of them.

Now in case you didn't know, pruning hurts—just like self-denial hurts. Whenever God starts clipping away at your life, it's going to hurt a little bit.

But once you understand that the pruning is designed to produce more fruit, you can bear the pain. God prunes His branches, His disciples, but not to stunt our growth. He prunes us so that we may be more productive than ever.

THE REWARD OF DISCIPLESHIP

This is the fifth and final point I want to make about discipleship. The call to discipleship is a costly priority, but it brings with it great reward:

> He who receives you receives Me, and he who receives Me receives Him who sent Me. He who receives a prophet in the name of a prophet shall receive a prophet's reward; and he who receives a righteous man in the name of a righteous man shall receive a righteous man's reward. And whoever in the name of a disciple gives to one of these little ones even a cup of cold

water to drink, truly I say to you he shall not lose his reward. (Matthew 10:40–42)

There is great reward in being Jesus' disciple. There is no reward in just being a church member. One day, Peter watched Jesus turn away a rich man who said he wanted to join up with the disciples but who wasn't willing to give up his possessions. Then Peter heard Jesus turn to the disciples and say, "How hard it will be for those who are wealthy to enter the kingdom of God!" (Mark 10:23).

So Peter said, "Hold it, Jesus! You've asked us to do a lot. You've asked us to leave our mothers and fathers and sisters and brothers. We gave up our fishing business for You. What do we get out of this deal?" (v. 28, author's paraphrase). Jesus responded in verses 29–30 by saying:

> Truly I say to you, there is no one who has left house or brothers or sisters or mother or father or children or farms, for My sake and for the gospel's sake, but that he shall receive a hundred times as much now in the present age, houses and brothers and sisters and mothers and children and farms, along with persecutions; and in the age to come, eternal life.

What Jesus is saying is that if your mother rejects you because you are following Him, God is going to give you new mothers in the body of Christ. If your father has turned away from you, God will give you new dads in the kingdom.

God is nobody's debtor. If you give Him all of you, He will give you all of Him. One reason many of us seem to have so little of God is that He has so little of us— maybe two hours on Sunday morning and that's about it.

There is no shortcut to discipleship. It's hard and it's costly. But the rewards are incredible both in this life and the next! Are you ready to go? Let's get after it!

CHAPTER THREE

THE FOUR NECESSITIES IN ACTION

I enjoy microwave popcorn, particularly while watching a good movie or football game. It is intriguing to watch the complete transformation of hard, coarse seeds into soft, delectable treats. This metamorphosis occurs because the microwave heats up the moisture resident in every corn seed until it turns to steam. Once it becomes steam, the pressure becomes so great that the shell can no longer contain the moisture and an explosion occurs. What was once inedible and indigestible is now quite tasteful, edible, and digestible. The point is that environment is everything. When the microwave performs as it was intended to, the seeds of corn are transformed.

What a microwave is to popcorn, the local church is to the Christian. The local church is the context and environment God has created to transform Christians into what we were created and redeemed to be: followers of Christ. Since all true believers possess the Holy Spirit, we already have the internal moisture necessary for the transformation process to occur. Therefore, if the transformation does not happen, we can conclude that either the seeds are not in the proper environment, positioning themselves for transformation, or the microwave of the church is not functioning properly, producing spiritual heat so the pressure of the Holy Spirit gets hot enough to "pop" the believer into something different. How else can we explain the existence of so many defeated, joyless, powerless, angry, bitter, empty Christians today?

I believe that the church's failure to produce disciples is largely to blame for the failure of so many churches. This failure has led to the rise of contemporary, secularized pop psychology with a Christian veneer, which charges exorbitant prices to do what the church should be providing as a natural outgrowth of its ministry. This thesis certainly does not exonerate individual believers from their personal responsibility to follow Christ down the road to discipleship. It does, however, recognize that in addition to personal responsibility, God has created a context for this process to occur. Just as microwaves that don't work are of little use to the seeds of corn, so churches that don't get sufficiently "hot" and don't perform properly won't see much success in producing disciples, authentic followers of Christ.

It is my contention that the road to discipleship is not nearly as complex as we make it. I believe that the church that supplies the four vital experiences that God expects each Christian to pursue and each church to provide will experience the wonder of leading its members into the life of discipleship and will assist them in becoming authentic followers of Christ.

Few people would disagree that the greatest church in history was the first church, the church at Jerusalem in the early chapters of Acts. This church was on fire, possessed by the Holy Spirit, exploding on the scene on the Day of Pentecost.

One reason this church was so dynamic is that it got off to a great start. Jesus had told the disciples in Acts 1:8, "Don't have church until the Holy Ghost shows up" (author's paraphrase). They obeyed Him, and the Spirit showed up in great power at Pentecost.

Acts 2 shows that this church got moving in a big way when it came to living out the reality of being Jesus' disciples. It did this through four vital, Spirit-inspired experiences that are necessities for those who would follow Christ in discipleship.

You know by now that a believer's witness is one of the four necessities that must be present if we are to be Christ's disciples. It's not necessarily the first thing the Spirit cultivates in a disciple's life, since I don't think there is a hierarchy among the four essential experiences of discipleship. Instead, they are meant to operate simultaneously in our lives as we grow and develop. But since witness occurs first in Acts 2, we'll consider it first here. You'll see that when we deal with each necessity in detail in the next four sections, I have switched the order around.

DYNAMIC WITNESS

When the Holy Spirit came on Pentecost to give birth to the church in Acts 2, a number of things happened. One thing was that the church (especially Peter) stood up in a dynamic, bold witness for Christ.

Boldness for Witness

The most obvious event of the church's witness in Acts 2 was Peter's great Pentecost sermon. This is the same Peter who, just a short time earlier, was too scared to admit he knew Jesus when Jesus was being condemned before the high priest.

"I don't even know the man," Peter had said at Jesus' arrest and crucifixion (see Luke 22:57). But when the Spirit took over on the Day of Pentecost, Peter was ready to take his stand and proclaim Jesus boldly. All of a sudden, scared Peter became fearless Peter.

What was the difference? The Spirit of God. The Holy Spirit had taken control of Peter, and Peter was about to take off and soar in his spiritual life. He was going to experience things he had never experienced before because now he was going to be a faithful witness for Jesus Christ.

One of the things you must ask God to do if you're going to grow as a Christian is to help you open your mouth and be a witness. You say, "But I'm not bold. I'm inhibited. I'm a private person."

Well, the fact is that most of us are only private when we want to be. I've met a lot of "private" people who become very public and vociferous when their favorite team takes the field or the court. In other words, when something exciting enough happens in your life, you will talk about it without a whole lot of prompting.

One reason a lot of us Christians don't tell others about Christ is that we've lost our excitement about Christ. When He is exciting to you, you can't keep Him to yourself. When something dynamic occurs internally, you want to express it externally.

If you are a reserved person, if discussing Christ with others is difficult for you, turn over to Acts 4. The Jewish authorities had ordered the apostles to stop preaching and teaching about Jesus, and they backed the order with threats (vv. 18–21).

So the apostles went straight to the church and reported exactly what the authorities had said. The church immediately went to prayer, reminding God of His power and the fact that all this was happening in His predetermined plan (vv. 23–28).

Then notice the church's prayer request in verse 29: "And now, Lord, take note of their threats, and grant that Thy bond-servants may speak Thy word with all confidence."

That's a prayer you can pray too. Ask God to give you the boldness not to be intimidated by this Christ-rejecting world, because there are people all around you waiting to hear the good news you've heard. And you are God's translator to bring it to them.

The Results of Witness

If you're going to follow Christ as His disciple, you must be a witness. The believers who were in the upper room and who received the Spirit on Pentecost became witnesses. The result of their witness and Peter's sermon on that special day was the addition of three thousand new believers to the body of Christ.

Now that's a witness! And please notice that these three thousand people did not come because of an evangelistic program. They came because God's people were overwhelmed by the experience of the presence of His Spirit. They were excited about Jesus. Their excitement erupted in a great outreach and many people were saved.

Their witness also went beyond their words. "And everyone kept feeling a sense of awe; and many wonders and signs were taking place through the apostles" (Acts 2:43). God not only witnessed in word through His disciples, but He also witnessed in deed. They demonstrated the truthfulness and authenticity of the gospel in their works.

In other words, there was not only a message to be heard, but there was also the power of God to be seen. You and I may not work miracles, but we can display the power of God. Maybe that's why a lot of us believers keep quiet about Christ. We have no real power to show anyone. Nothing is happening in our lives.

So in those first days of the church at Jerusalem, there was a strong witness going out in word and deed. This thing was so dynamic that people were getting saved every day (v. 47). The Spirit of God had so filled the people of God that they couldn't keep the faith to themselves. The result was salvation every day. This ought to be happening in our churches as we scatter out each week to witness for Christ wherever we go.

So let me ask you, who is the last person you shared Jesus Christ with? If you can't remember, you need to consider whether you're growing as a disciple the way you should. One mark of a person who wants to follow Christ, one absolute necessity for being His disciple, is to be His witness.

GROWING IN THE WORD

Along with their dynamic witness, the early believers were growing in their knowledge of God's Word. In Acts 2:42 we read, "They were continually devoting themselves to the apostles' teaching." How often were they doing this? This passage says it was "day by day" (v. 46), just as people were being saved day by day.

Desiring the Word

This is what we might call the education of the disciple. It's the process by which the Word of God gets off the page and into our hearts and lives. For a disciple of Jesus Christ the Word of God is as necessary and desirable for the spirit as food is for the body. And although a person can overeat physically, a person can't get too much of the spiritual nourishment of the Word.

In fact, when it comes to spiritual food, some of us are losing weight rapidly. Some of us are losing weight we can't afford to lose. Some of us have become emaciated. Why? Because we are receiving no nourishment.

The Word of God is designed to nourish the believer. It is the Scripture that equips us to live the Christian life. Your mind is key to becoming a disciple, because you are what you think (Proverbs 23:7).

If you have a messed-up mind, you're going to have a messed-up life. The body reflects the thought processes of the mind, and many of us have come into the Christian life with warped minds, contaminated by an ungodly system.

We have minds that need to be renewed (Romans 12:2). Only then will our lives be transformed. I've discovered that trying to change people's actions without changing their thinking only does a temporary, patchwork job.

If you want to fix what you do, you must first fix how you think about what you do. A transformed mind comes through the study and practice of the Bible. All of us know about brainwashing. It's repeating certain data over and over again until a person absorbs that information into his brain, believes it wholeheartedly, and begins to act on it.

A lot of children are the victims of brainwashing in their formative years. If you tell a child long enough, "You're no good. You can't do anything right. You're never going to amount to anything," that child will develop such a poor self-image that he or she will come to believe that negative data.

These are the kids who are programmed to say "I can't" when faced with any challenge. What they need is positive reinforcement, some positive brainwashing. They need something to change their old way of thinking.

That's exactly what the Word of God is designed to do. Many of us have habits in our lives that we want to get rid of. But we say, "I can't," because we've been brainwashed to say that. We've been brainwashed by the enemy to believe we will never have victory in that area.

But God's Word can change that, if we will feed on it regularly the way we feed our bodies. The believers in Acts 2 devoted themselves to the apostles' teaching, or doctrine. This was firsthand Scripture. The New Testament had not been written yet. So the apostles' doctrine was the authoritative Word of God.

Erasing the Old Tapes

If you are going to become a disciple, you must have a dynamic experience with the Word of God. God must begin to erase the old tapes in your mind, your old ways of thinking. One way to erase an old tape is to record new material over the old. The data God wants recorded in your heart and mind is His Word. That's why memorizing portions of the Bible is such a powerful teaching tool. Those verses are stored in your memory bank.

When it comes to our spiritual education, we have a divine Teacher. The Holy Spirit's job is to reveal the Word to you. Jesus said the Spirit would remind us of all that He taught (John 14:26).

Paul gives us a powerful word about how to overcome the devil and his attempts to destroy our spiritual lives:

> For though we walk in the flesh, we do not war according to the flesh, for the weapons of our warfare are not of the flesh, but divinely powerful for the destruction of fortresses. We are destroying speculations and every lofty thing raised up against the knowledge of God, and we are taking every thought captive to the obedience of Christ. (2 Corinthians 10:3–5)

Notice the words and phrases Paul uses here. Satan attempts to raise up speculations and other things "against the knowledge of God." What's the best defense against Satan's attempt to take your thinking processes captive? To "take every thought captive" for Christ. Imprison your thinking to the knowledge of God, which is found only in the Word of God!

This is crucial because the moment you begin thinking the way the world thinks, like everybody else thinks, at that moment you begin thinking defeated thoughts. Many believers are being defeated because of the way they think. They have allowed Satan and the world, instead of Christ, to capture their thinking.

There used to be a time when if you didn't get straight thinking at home, you might get it at school. And if you didn't get it at school, more than likely you got it at church. Today, you're fortunate if you get the straight scoop at even one of those places.

What has happened? The knowledge of God has been systematically removed from the culture. God is now out on the loop of the city instead of downtown. This means that if you are going to become a mature disciple of Jesus Christ, you must make a conscious effort to partake of His Word. You aren't going to get much if any help or encouragement from the culture.

Obeying Christ

Paul says the goal of taking our thoughts captive is that we might be obedient to Christ. You need to know God's Word that you might *live* God's Word. You don't study and learn the Bible so you can pass tests. It is only in applying the Word that it becomes a part of your experience.

You can study a driver's handbook all day long, but that won't make you a good driver. You need to know what's in the manual, but to learn how to drive you eventually have to get into the car with an instructor and take off.

Jesus said in the Great Commission that we are to make disciples by going and teaching and baptizing.

What do we teach? "To observe"—do—"all that I commanded you" (Matthew 28:20).

Therefore, every time you and I open the Book, our prayer should be, "Lord, show me what You want me to do"—not just, "Show me what You want me to know." Every Sunday you come to church, your prayer should be, "Lord, open up Your Word and speak to me."

Developing the Desire

When the two discouraged disciples were on their way home to Emmaus that first Easter, the resurrected Jesus Christ joined them on the road and taught them about Himself from the Word (Luke 24:27).

Later, when Jesus had disappeared, they said, "Were not our hearts burning within us while He was speaking to us on the road?" (v. 32). Then they got up and ran back to Jerusalem to tell everyone that they now believed in the Resurrection. Jesus had changed the way they thought by teaching them the Scriptures.

You say, "Sure, Tony, if Jesus would come and teach our Sunday school class next Sunday, our hearts would burn. We would get excited about the Word."

Well, I can tell you two things. One, that isn't going to happen. And two, you have something even better! You have the indwelling Holy Spirit to make God's Word come alive. In fact, He is eager to set your heart on fire!

So if you want to follow Christ, if you want the necessities of discipleship to become real in your life, you need to develop an insatiable hunger for God's Word. You must cultivate a love for the Word.

If you don't have that love, that hunger, right now, don't fake it. Go to the Lord and pray sincerely, "Lord, give me a taste for Your Word. Make it more precious and valuable to me than the food I eat to keep my body healthy."

I'm not a big vegetable person. But unlike former president George Bush, I have acquired a taste for broccoli. I'm still working on squash and okra. I haven't graduated to that level yet. But I have moved from a hatred of to a tolerance for broccoli. I'm still working on love.

I knew I had to eat some vegetables, so broccoli was the choice. Now every time I eat out, I order broccoli if I can.

Of course, the first few times I ate broccoli I had to have it covered with as much cheese as possible, to hide the broccoli itself and help enhance the taste. But now I'm to the point where I eat broccoli without cheese. Broccoli is an acquired taste of mine. It took repeated servings of the stuff to get me to this point.

A similar thing is true of developing a taste for the Bible. You can't chew on the Book once a year and then wonder why it doesn't taste good. You have to feed on it day in and day out. That's how it becomes sweet to your taste.

People open up their Bibles and say, "I don't understand it." Just reading it once a year, you won't. "It's too hard to read." That could be because you haven't acquired a taste for God's Word.

To acquire a taste for Bible study, you will have to discipline yourself to sit down and read, whether you feel like reading or not. The more time you spend in the Word, the more you will understand. And the more you understand, the more you will want to read.

You know you're becoming a disciple when day by day you're in the Word. You're not just waiting until Sunday so somebody else can feed you. You know you're maturing when you learn to feed yourself. When the Word of God is precious to you, you're on your way.

LIFE-CHANGING FELLOWSHIP

The third experience in following Christ is found back in our foundational verse, Acts 2:42. Along with devoting themselves to the apostles' teaching, the believers were devoted to fellowship.

More Than Coffee and Donuts

Biblical fellowship is not just coffee and donuts in Sunday school or a meal in the fellowship hall. Fellowship is the sharing of our lives with other believers. You'll never grow to full maturity in Jesus Christ all alone. You cannot become a disciple of Jesus Christ independently of others.

That's why the church is so important. It is the "fire-place" where one log touches another and the fire is maintained. In fact, the church at Jerusalem did not only share their lives with one another. They shared their possessions too, meeting any needs that arose (Acts 2:44–45). That's part of fellowship too.

Keeping the Fire Going

If you are getting dull in your spiritual life, you need to be in proximity to others who are on fire so their fire can ignite you. If you are losing your spiritual fire and you're alone, you're going to become ashes.

So the question we must ask is, are we connected with other believers who desire to be on fire too? Fellowship is designed to keep the fire burning. There was no such thing as a non-churched Christian in the early church. They were in dynamic fellowship with each other.

We need each other because the best of us can get spiritually dull. The best of us sometimes want to throw in the towel. The best of us sometimes fall flat on our faces. "Let him who thinks he stands take heed lest he fall" (1 Corinthians 10:12), because falling is right around the corner.

You and I must be in vital relationship to other saints who can hold us up. But we've been slipped a "mickey" here. We have traded relationship for entertainment. See, when you're being entertained, you don't have to do anything. You just sit back and let someone else amuse you.

Relationships are hard. They take work. Entertainment is easy. All you need is a chair and a remote. That's why so many individuals and families are hiding out in front of the television, the great relationship-killer.

I think television is the greatest hindrance to building dynamic relationships, because it absorbs so much time. Whole families never talk to each other because everybody is in a different room watching a different program. At least in the old days, there was one television and everybody watched it in the same room. But now there are televisions all over the place, and family members aren't even in the same room.

That's what happens within the church family, as well. Fellowship doesn't just happen. You have to plan fellowship, set aside time to cultivate friendships with other believers.

Focusing on Christ

Here's something else about biblical fellowship. Fellowship isn't fellowship if Jesus Christ is not part of the conversation. If you invite me over to watch a football game and all we do is watch the game and eat, we did not have fellowship. Fellowship is always designed to spur one another on spiritually, build each other up in the faith, edify one another. True fellowship always has a spiritual goal.

That doesn't mean there cannot be food involved. Acts 2:46 makes it clear there were a lot of fellowship meals in the early days of the church. We're going to have a great meal of celebration and fellowship in heaven (Revelation 19:9).

But the point of it is not simply to get together and eat and call that fellowship. A meal just presents a natural context for fellowship. The question is what happens and what we talk about when we are together. We should leave a time of fellowship strengthened and encouraged in the faith.

Back in the days of slavery, Sunday was a very important day. It was the day the slaves didn't have to work. But more important, they would come together for worship, then devote a major part of the day to fellowship. One sister would bring the potato salad, another the fried chicken, and still another the corn. They would enjoy a meal together.

That Sunday fellowship was so important to those slaves because they all had to go back to slave work on Monday. Monday was painful, with heartaches and headaches. So the reinforcement of Sunday was critical.

But as we have become more affluent and more independent, we've lost our need for one another. Fellowship in the Bible was designed to show us that we need other believers. You can't make it on your own. Neither can I.

DYNAMIC WORSHIP

The fourth necessity in following Christ is worship. Again in Acts 2:42, the believers devoted themselves to "the breaking of bread [celebrating the Lord's Supper] and to prayer." In verse 46 we see that they were going to the temple every day, and "praising God" continually (v. 47).

Our Spiritual Furnace

Worship is the furnace of the spiritual life. Worship is basically the celebration of God for who He is and what He has done. God is the focus of worship.

Therefore, as we will learn in the next section, the issue in worship is not necessarily what you get out of it. The most important thing is what God gets out of it. Worship does not start with what God did for you today. It starts with what you did for Him.

Praising God, worshiping Him, and celebrating Him for who He is and what He has done is the way to get God's attention. God responds to our worship. In fact, we're going to see that God invites us to worship Him. He has taken the initiative. You will be surprised at the way the Spirit of God will ignite your Christian life when worship becomes not an event, but an experience; not a program, but a way of life. That includes both public and private worship, because both are crucial for growing disciples of Jesus Christ.

A Reason to Worship

Many of us want to throw in the towel when something goes wrong. But our foreparents didn't throw in the towel when their whole world went wrong. Why? Because many of them had what we don't have, a worshiping lifestyle.

No matter what is wrong in your life, there is always a reason to worship, to praise God. Don't get me wrong. Praising God doesn't mean denying your problem. If it's there, it's there. But what does Paul say? "Be anxious for nothing, but in everything by prayer and supplication with thanksgiving let your requests be made known to God" (Philippians 4:6). If you want God's power in your life, then worship must be part of your daily operation; celebrating God, exulting in Him for who He is and what He has done.

THE RESULT OF THE NECESSITIES

What happens when you become a witnessing, learning-the-Word, fellowshiping, and worshiping kind of Christian? If those four experiences are a part of your normal Christian life, I guarantee you that you will be progressing in your discipleship. Watch out for the believer who is falling away in one or more of those areas.

When a Christian doesn't show up for worship on a regular basis, something is misfiring in his life. When he has no desire to be with other Christians, something is wrong. When he neglects the Word and when he is silent about Jesus Christ week after week, something is wrong.

But when we submit to the Spirit of God that He might cultivate these things in us, we are going to see exciting things happen. Those early believers had the four necessities going strong, and at least two things happened. They had spiritual power, and they saw spiritual results.

Acts 2:43 says, "Everyone kept feeling a sense of awe." These people were amazed at the work of God that was going on in their midst. This doesn't mean all of them were miracle workers. The apostles were doing the miracles, but everybody was awed. Everybody had a sense that God was at work in a mighty way.

What were the results? We've already looked at Acts 2:44–45, which shows that selfishness began to fall by the wayside. They got concerned about one another. They began to share with one another. Then in verse 47, we saw that people were getting saved every day as a result of this church's dynamic ministry.

And let me reiterate that none of this came about because of a program. These were the results, the overflow, of their experience with God. Things were happening so fast there wasn't time to develop programs. I'm not against programs. But programs can never replace the experience of the Spirit.

My burden and vision for our church in Dallas is that we move more toward experiencing God than doing programs for God. The church is like a marriage. You can't just program a marriage and expect to find happiness. You and your spouse can go out every Friday at the same time, but without any dynamic interaction in the marriage you can program yourselves into boredom.

We can structure the church so tightly that even the Spirit of God can't break through and find a slot on the program. My desire for you as you go through the four sections that follow in this book is that you will not approach the four necessities of God's discipleship process as just a formula; mix this and that, throw in a pinch of the other, and out comes a mature disciple.

Instead, I hope the Spirit of God will enable you to make these things a living reality as you seek to follow Christ and become His disciple.

Also, don't try to make someone else's experience or spiritual routine yours. God is not trying to make us all act alike. We have a common goal, to be fully mature disciples, but we don't all get there exactly the same way.

As you read this book, I want you to enter into an experience with God through your witness, the Word, fellowship, and worship. When these four essentials are in operation in your life, you'll have discovered what matters most.

WORSHIP

CHAPTER FOUR

THE CONCEPT OF WORSHIP

We're now ready to begin looking at the four necessary experiences in following Christ. I want to begin with worship, for at least three reasons: first, because worship has become a popular buzzword in Christian circles; second, because for many believers, worship is still a distant concept; and third, because worship is foundational to everything else in the Christian life.

I'm afraid too many people come to church because it's Sunday, rather than coming on Sunday to worship. Too many come to find out what the "entertainment" for the day is, rather than to give praise to God's holy name. And far too many of God's kids come to be blessed, rather than to bless.

One big reason for this is that many Christians don't know how to worship the rest of the week, so they're not prepared for worship on Sunday. This is a problem we're going to tackle in this section on worship. I hope that when we are finished you'll be a better worshiper, because what the church needs today is purer worship, more focused worship, more biblical worship.

Sometimes, worship gets lost in the pile of other things, and the result can be tragic. I'm reminded of the true story of the mother who gave a party after her baby had been christened at church.

She invited friends and family over after church to celebrate the big event. The baby was laid on the bed, sound asleep, in the parents' bedroom. As the guests arrived, they took off their coats and placed them in the bedroom.

Later, one of the people asked, "Where is the baby?" The mother realized she had forgotten about the baby amid the festivities. When she went into the bedroom, she discovered that the guests' coats had been placed over the baby's head and the baby had suffocated.

I can't imagine anything more tragic for a family. And I can't imagine anything more tragic for the family of God than to smother true worship by burying it underneath all the other stuff we do. When we smother worship, we simultaneously smother our development as Christ's disciples.

So as we try to get a handle on this concept called worship, I want to turn to one of the most concentrated passages on worship in the New Testament. It's found in John 4, the familiar story of the Samaritan woman at the well.

My purpose here is not to retell the details of this story. You can read the first fifteen verses of the story, which recount Jesus' conversation with this woman. She's really interested in His offer of living water until He tells her, "Go, call your husband, and come here" (v. 16).

What Jesus was doing, of course, was confronting the woman with her sin. She did what any sinner does when confronted with the holiness of God—she dodged the issue. But in verses 17–18 Jesus set the record straight concerning her marital and moral status. She responded, "Sir, I perceive that You are a prophet" (v. 19). I guess so!

This brings us to the heart of our subject. In five short verses (20–24), we learn a boatload of truth about worship. I want to make several observations about worship from John 4, beginning with a general observation that I think is critical for us to see if we are going to grasp the centrality of worship.

THE PRIORITY OF WORSHIP

Notice the real-life setting in which God is going to teach us about worship. This wasn't a temple service; it was a well outside of nowhere. This woman, the disciples, and the rest of the Samaritans were real people, as human as they come. Worship has to do with real people.

There were also real needs and problems here. Jesus was hungry. This woman needed salvation. And Jesus' disciples were standing there stunned that He would talk to a Samaritan. The woman herself brought up the age-old hostility between Jews and Samaritans. So there was racial conflict here.

In the midst of this real-life madness, Jesus talked about worship. Why? Because if we ever get worship right, the other stuff we spend so much time trying to fix will get fixed a lot quicker.

This Samaritan woman got the real deal on worshiping God, so she stopped prostituting herself. Because Jesus gave His disciples the right view of God, they were able to fellowship with their former enemies, the Samaritans.

It's interesting that later, Jesus told the disciples, "Lift up your eyes" to see the harvest fields (v. 35). Guess what they saw when they looked up? Samaritans coming out to meet Jesus! When Jesus stayed two days in the town, the disciples must have ministered to them too (v. 40). And the Samaritans themselves laid aside old prejudices to receive Christ.

What I'm saying is that if we get worship right, a lot of things that are "eating the lunch" of believers right now will take care of themselves.

So let's move into verses 20–24, a section I call "worship concentrate." You can get a lot of sweet "juice" out of these few verses, because the word *worship* is used in one form or another ten times. This is very concentrated truth.

THE SPHERES OF WORSHIP

The first thing we learn about worship is that it happens in two spheres: public and private.

The woman said to Him . . . "Our fathers worshiped in this mountain, and you people say that in Jerusalem is the place where men ought to worship." Jesus said to her, "Woman, believe Me, an hour is coming when neither in this mountain, nor in Jerusalem, shall you worship the Father." (vv. 19–21)

The Samaritans had built their own temple on Mount Gerizim to rival the temple in Jerusalem, and they had established their own worship. But Jesus was saying to this woman that worship is not first and foremost a place. It is a state of heart and mind. Worship is not so much where you are. Worship begins with *who* you are.

If you have not learned to worship as a way of life, then showing up in a building with a steeple on top won't change anything. The Bible says your body is a temple—the church—of the living God (1 Corinthians 6:19). So if you are a Christian, you are in church all the time. You don't only come to church. You *are* church. I'm not talking about radical individualism here. We have a responsibility to worship corporately too. Public and private worship are meant to complement each other.

If the Spirit of God is living in you, you can't get out of church. So the question God asks is, "What kind of church are you having when you are not in the church building? What kind of church are you having at work, at home?"

You and I are always in church, because our bodies are God's temple. Many believers are messed up because the only time they are in church worshiping is on Sunday.

If we could learn to be in church just by being the people God wants us to be, then we would always be worshiping Him. The result is that we would always be growing spiritually and thus become better followers of Christ.

Obviously, worship is supposed to take place in the house of God. The church has pastors and teachers and choirs and all of that to lead God's people in worship. The church is one sphere of worship. But when you get

the other sphere of worship going, when worship is part
of who are you, you come alive.

Public Worship

People who have a problem with public, corporate
worship are usually revealing the fact that no authentic
private worship is happening in their lives. Public worship is crucial for a number of reasons.

First, public worship reminds us that God is "our
Father who art in heaven" rather than just "my Father."
That is, public worship demonstrates that you recognize
you are not an only child in the kingdom, but part of a
bigger family. Isolated believers are contrary to the concept of family. To ignore and neglect public worship is to
insult God as the Head of a family of which you are only
a part.

Second, there are things God will do for you in public worship that aren't necessarily available to you in private worship. It was in the context of public worship that
the early church experienced certain miraculous activity
of the Holy Spirit (Acts 2:42–44; 12:1–12).

Third, public worship is designed to benefit others
as well as yourself. God wants to use you and your worship to encourage others (Hebrews 10:24–25). It is the
height of selfishness for us to think only of ourselves
when it comes to worship.

Just as the people at a sports event feed off one
another's enthusiasm when the home team scores, Christians are to feed off each other when we celebrate the
glory of our great God, the "scoring king" of the universe.

Fourth, and most important, God expects us to worship and He awaits His people in the place of public worship (1 Corinthians 11:18–24).

So failing to worship corporately as the body of
Christ is an affront to the God who invites us to His
table—just as it would be an affront for kids to refuse to
come to the table when the head of the household calls
them to dinner. No amount of private spiritual "dining"
can replace our need to join with the rest of God's family
at His table.

Private Worship

If the only time God hears your songs of praise is on Sunday; if the only time you interact with His Word is on Sunday; and if the only time you fellowship with other believers is on Sunday, then your spiritual life is going to be anemic.

In the words of Jesus in John 4, worship is not just in Jerusalem. Worship is in you because the Spirit of God indwells you. That is why Psalm 113:3 says, "From the rising of the sun to its setting the name of the Lord is to be praised."

That is, praise and worship are to be the daily routine of life. Every day the birds sing and the bees buzz as part of creation's praise to God.

I'm talking about devotion to God. Having devotions is not reading a verse a day to keep the devil away. It's not just blurting out a prayer you don't even think about, or saying grace in a mechanical way over your meal without the words meaning anything. No, it is worship. It is saying, "God, I adore You."

When you understand that the meat on your plate came from an animal God made, you understand that He deserves to be praised. When you understand that the water you drink is from the rain He supplied, you understand that His name is to be praised. When you understand that the table you eat on is carved from the wood of a tree that God made, you are ready to praise Him.

God deserves our praise. He wants our worship, privately and corporately with the body of believers. These are the spheres of worship, and they are interconnected. Anyone who is worshiping privately will have no problem worshiping publicly with other believers and becoming the disciple Christ saved him or her to be.

THE VALUE OF WORSHIP

If God is seeking for something, it must be very valuable. According to Jesus, "An hour is coming, and now is, when the true worshipers shall worship the Father in spirit and truth; for such people the Father seeks to be His worshipers" (John 4:23).

Seeking Worshipers

Why is worship so valuable? Because God is looking for it. Jesus' statement is really astounding. He says His Father is looking for authentic worshipers. The implication is that they are hard to find.

Don't misunderstand this. God is not looking for worshipers because He needs them. God does not seek worship because somehow He will be less than God if He does not get it. God is not seeking worshipers among us because if we don't worship Him, nothing else in creation will.

Not at all. In fact, the whole universe worships God. Check out the first ten verses of Psalm 148 and you'll see that the psalmist covers just about the whole created universe when it comes to the things that praise God.

It's all there. The heavenly beings, including the angels, worship God. The heavenly bodies—the sun, moon, and stars—worship Him. Every kind of animal from the "sea monster" (v. 7) to the insects (v. 10) worship God. Even inanimate things like water, snow, wind, fire, and hail praise the Lord.

So God isn't hurting for worship. The entire universe has been constructed to praise Him. The Bible never speaks of God going ant-hunting looking for worship. He doesn't go whale-hunting or mountain-hunting for seeking out praise. These things already praise Him. The only hunting God does for worship is human-hunting.

Deserving of Worship

Why is God looking for human worshipers? Because He deserves them. He knows He deserves worship, and He wants to know who understands that. So God is seeking worshipers, people who will praise and adore His name.

Does that make God self-centered? Absolutely! Does that mean God is focused on His own glory? Correct! The reason is that there is nothing or no one greater than God to whom *He* could appeal, or to whom we could give our worship.

Since there is no being greater than God to give glory to, God claims all glory and worship for Himself. So Paul says that God does everything to the praise of His own glory (Ephesians 1:6, 12). Anyone that glorious deserves to be worshiped. So God is looking for worshipers.

THE CHOICE TO WORSHIP

I said above that the only group in the universe among whom God is seeking worshipers is you and me, the human race. We're the only category of creation that has to think about whether or not we are going to worship God.

We are the only group in the universe that has to decide when we get up in the morning, "Am I going to give God the worship He deserves this morning?" We're the only ones who have to ask ourselves, "Do I feel into worship today?"

For the rest of creation, worship is automatic. For us human beings, worship must be a conscious choice. God created you to be His worshiper, but He wants to see whether you will fulfill the purpose for which you were created. Worship is your choice.

Don't misunderstand. Worship is a choice for human beings now, but all people who were ever created will someday worship God for all time. The Bible says that someday, "every knee [will] bow," and "every tongue [will] confess that Jesus Christ is Lord, to the glory of God the Father" (Philippians 2:10–11).

The choice we have is to worship willingly, out of love. But every person will worship God for eternity, even the people in hell. There are no atheists in hell. People in hell know full well who God is.

WORSHIPING FOR ETERNITY

See, if you are a Christian, God did not save you simply to deliver you from the wrath to come. He saved you to be His worshiper. One hundred million years from now, you will be worshiping God. Throughout all eternity, as a matter of fact, you will be worshiping God.

If the universe lives to worship God, and you were made to worship God, then you need to know something. If you are not worshiping God as a way of life, you cannot really be living. You can *exist* without worship, but you cannot live without worship because that's the reason you are here.

Like the heart in the body, worship is the internal pump that keeps our spirits alive. That's why one of Satan's great tricks is to keep us from worshiping God as a way of life.

So worship is valuable because God is looking for it and because it is why you were made. If you don't worship, you lose. God does not lose. Our lack of worship does not diminish Him. He is going to get His glory. The question is, do you want to get in on the action? I do!

THE MEANING OF WORSHIP

What is this thing the Bible calls worship? The word itself has to do with paying homage or ascribing worth to something or to someone. Worship, then, is the celebration of God for who He is and what He has done.

Recognizing God as God

To put it another way, worship is all that I am paying homage to all that God is. It is my joyful reflection of God's worth, my recognizing God as God. When God is not recognized as God, He is not being worshiped.

The Old Testament book of Malachi brings this out powerfully. In Malachi 1:6–7, God entered into a dialogue with Israel:

> "'A son honors his father, and a servant his master. Then if I am a father, where is My honor? And if I am a master, where is My respect?' says the Lord of hosts to you, O priests who despise My name. But you say, 'How have we despised Thy name?' You are presenting defiled food upon My altar. But you say, 'How have we defiled Thee?' In that you say, 'The table of the Lord is to be despised.'"

God then explains in verse 8 how the people were

dishonoring Him. They were bringing diseased and deformed animals to the temple to offer them in sacrifice to the Lord. He was getting their leftovers.

So God asked the priests a pointed question: "Why not offer it to your governor? Would he be pleased with you? Or would he receive you kindly?" (v. 8). They were offering God sacrifices they wouldn't think of serving for dinner to human officials.

Giving Honor

What's the point? Coming to church does not equal worship. The priests were in the temple, doing their thing for God. But they were not showing Him the honor and respect due Him. Worship has to do with honoring God for who He is.

Chances are that most mornings when you get up, you go to work and honor your boss. You jump out of bed, get dressed, and head off to your job to pay him homage. You honor your boss by showing up and doing a day's work.

You will honor your boss, not necessarily because you like him, but because your money is in his pocket. He holds the purse strings. He is the boss. Your honor of him is based on his position.

God says, "If you give people something better than what you give Me, then you aren't honoring Me as the Lord of hosts." So God said to the priests of Malachi's day, "Try offering your leftover stuff to your earthly rulers. If they won't accept your leftovers, what makes you think I will accept such offerings?" (see Malachi 1:8).

When we talk about worship, we are talking about "ascrib[ing] to the Lord the glory due to His name" (Psalm 29:2). Worship is giving God what He deserves and nothing less.

What many of us call worship is really just our left-over energy, leftover time, leftover resources. We find it easy to stay up Saturday night and then think that because we showed up Sunday morning, we worshiped. That is not worship.

Let me tell you what worship is. Just about everyone

who lives in Dallas has witnessed true worship on the human level. It occurs on most Sundays during the fall and winter. Some people might call it a football game, but Dallas Cowboy fans know it as worship.

At the time for worship, thousands of people will go to the house of worship called Texas Stadium. Or they will enter the room in their homes set aside for worship. In their "holy of holies" they will sit and worship before a pulpit with a TV on it.

This worship is so important that these people have served notice that they don't want to be disturbed during the worship service. They also don't want to be late for worship. They not only want to catch the opening song, they want to be there for the call to worship, the pre-game show. And they won't complain that the worship service lasts for three hours. They are even willing to offer "overtime" worship if called upon to do so.

Countless thousands of people all across Dallas will behold the glory of the Cowboys. And when the team does something worthy of praise, they jump up and shout.

When it is all over, when the post-game benediction has been pronounced, these people will then reflect on the worth of the ones on the field and praise them for their goodness. The players will be glorified for who they are and the great deeds they have done.

I'm being a little facetious, but not too much. If a sports team can demand that kind of worship, can't the God of the universe demand much more?

THE OBJECT OF WORSHIP

Look at what Jesus says in John 4 about the object of our worship:

> But an hour is coming, and now is, when the true wor-shipers shall worship the Father in spirit and truth; for such people the Father seeks to be His worshipers. God is spirit, and those who worship Him must worship in spirit and truth. (vv. 23–24)

People say, "I'm going to church today to worship

God." But the question is, "Who is the God you are worshiping?" Jesus answers that question in these two verses.

He Is the Father

The God we are called to worship is defined as our "Father." First of all, He is our Father by virtue of creation. That is, He made it all, and He owns it all.

God deserves to be worshiped because "the earth is the Lord's, and all it contains, the world, and those who dwell in it" (Psalm 24:1).

If you are a Christian, God is also your Father because you are a member of His family. That means worship is a family affair. We do not only worship God because He is the Creator, but because He is "Daddy," the loving Head of our household whom we follow. We worship Him out of relationship.

The God we worship is also the "Father of our Lord Jesus Christ" (Ephesians 1:3). That means that you cannot worship God if you leave out Christ.

That's why many groups who report for worship each week are not really worshiping. The God they are worshiping is not the Father of the Lord Jesus Christ. The problem with the Jehovah's Witnesses, who want to get to Jehovah while denying Christ, is that you can't come to the Father except through Christ. He is the only Mediator between God and man (1 Timothy 2:5).

He Is Spirit

Jesus goes on to say that God is spirit. That means you cannot worship God with your body alone because in His essence God is not corporeal. That is, He is without a body. When we say that God is spirit, we are saying that He is immaterial. He is invisible, yet He is a Person who possesses intellect, will, and emotions.

So if you are going to worship this immaterial, invisible God, Jesus says your worship must arise from within the invisible part of *you*. See, it is possible for your body to show up at church while your spirit is still at home. You can have the body of a worshiper, yet not have the heart of a worshiper.

Because God is spirit, He deals primarily with the invisible realm, not the visible realm. You may go to church having the look of worship and the smell of worship. You may have the hairdo of worship or the makeup of worship. Most of us fix ourselves up physically for worship.

Many Christians also have the movements of worship. When the choir sings, they have the hand wave and the head shake of worship. Some wipe away the tears of worship. But if all God gets from our worship is our bodies, we are not worshiping Him. For He is not body. God is spirit, and those who worship Him must worship Him in spirit.

This means that true worship is not conjured up by what happens physically. Some people don't think they have worshiped unless their bodies are moved. But the real deal is, unless your spirit is moved, it doesn't matter what your body does.

Don't get me wrong. God does not ignore the body, but He does not start with the body. God always starts with the spirit because that is who God is. This is the problem with artificial aids to worship, whether it's a cross around someone's neck or a picture of Jesus.

God asks, "To whom then will you liken God?" (Isaiah 40:18). You probably have a photograph of yourself on your driver's license. Most of the time these are so bad we are embarrassed to show them to anyone. We apologize and say, "This is really a terrible picture." Anyone can see that you look a lot better than that! Any picture you come up with for God is going to be a bad picture because He looks a lot better than that. God cannot be likened to anything except God. When you worship God, you are worshiping an invisible Being who can only be "seen" and known by the spirit.

Of course, God manifested Himself in human flesh in the person of Jesus Christ. Jesus sat and talked to the woman at the well. She could see Him, but she could not see that He was God in the flesh. Only her spirit could discern that as the Holy Spirit made a spiritual connection.

He Is the Audience

Because God is the object of our worship, the issue is not how good we feel when we worship. There is nothing wrong with feeling good about our worship, but that is not the primary issue. The issue in worship is, how good did *God* feel about it?

The congregation stands up to sing, and we don't sing because we don't like the song. God's comment is, "I thought you were singing to Me. If you came to worship Me, whether or not you like the song is not what matters." That doesn't mean you will sing every word to every song. Perhaps you don't agree with the theology, or you cannot sing the song honestly. But that's different from not singing because you happen to dislike the style. Worship is not for your benefit; it's for God's glory.

Many of us come to church with a backward mentality. We come and say, "Choir, sing to me." The choir is not supposed to be singing to us. The choir is supposed to lead us in giving praise to God. The purpose in preaching is to give the people the Word of God, to hear the voice of God in His Word.

If you come to worship only for what you can get out of it, then what you are saying is, in essence, "God, adore me. Pay attention to me. Focus on me. Enhance me. Glorify me." But that's not the invitation. The invitation is to worship God. When the benediction is given, if God doesn't applaud, we have failed.

If God doesn't clap when we worship, it doesn't matter if everybody else applauds. When the choir sings, if God doesn't applaud it doesn't matter whether we stood up. When I preach, if God does not applaud, it doesn't matter whether the people like the sermon. Unless God says, "Well done," we haven't worshiped.

He Is Glorious

We come to worship God, not to have God worship us. We come to make Him feel good. Yes, we feel good when we worship in spirit, but that is a side benefit. It's not why we come. We come to worship God because of His intrinsic glory.

That means God's glory is bound up in His person. It's part of who He is. The opposite of intrinsic glory is ascribed glory. All human glory is ascribed glory. For example, put a black robe on a man or woman and the person becomes "Your Honor." Put a white coat on someone and the title is now "Doctor." The same glory or honor is ascribed to a police officer.

But once these people lay aside their robes or coats or uniforms, they are just ordinary people. I don't mean they are not worthy of our respect. What I'm saying is that their glory is ascribed to them by the position they hold. It's not an essential part of their makeup as human beings.

God's glory is not like that. You can't take it away from Him. What wet is to water and blue is to sky, glory is to God. It is intrinsic. You can't mess with it, but you can recognize it. You can praise it. You can glorify it, but you can't change it. That's the God we worship. He has intrinsic glory.

THE ESSENCE OF WORSHIP

The final observation I want to make from John 4:12–24 concerns the essence of worship. Jesus identifies this when He says, "God is spirit, and those who worship Him must worship in spirit and truth" (v. 24).

The essence of worship is that it must be both *authentic,* coming from the inner man, the spirit, and *accurate,* reflecting the truth about God. True worship engages the emotions and the mind. It must include both heart and head.

If you and I are going to follow Christ as His disciples, we must learn to worship God with the right attitude and the right information. That is what it takes to worship God.

The Right Attitude

We have already talked about what Jesus means by worshiping in spirit because God is spirit. Here is where the Holy Spirit becomes active in worship. His job is to be the liaison between your human spirit and the God who is spirit. That's why Jesus told Nicodemus, "That which is born of the Spirit is spirit" (John 3:6). The Holy Spirit links our inner spirit with God.

But in order for the Holy Spirit to do His job, you must have a heart that is pursuing God. You must be willing to yield your life to God and let God be God. You cannot transform God into something other than what He is and expect Him to fellowship with you. He only fellowships with you on His terms. We are talking about following Christ, not Christ following us.

Your spirit is engaged in worship when you deal with sin, yield to the Holy Spirit, and praise God. These are the raw materials the Holy Spirit needs to connect your human spirit with God in authentic worship. This is the attitude, or the emotion, of worship.

The Right Information

But the emotion of worship must also be mixed with truth (John 4:24b). The more you know about the God you are worshiping, the better your worship is going to be. Ignorance is not bliss when it comes to worship.

Many of us Christians worship little because we know little and, therefore, we grow little. If you only have a thimble-full of knowledge about God, you are going to run dry really fast. That's why some Christians run out of things to say after thirty seconds of prayer— and why some people pray for thirty minutes without saying anything. They don't know how to talk to God because their knowledge of Him is so small.

The bigger your knowledge of God, the deeper your worship goes. The more you know about God, the better your worship is. So Jesus says our worship must be according to truth.

Which truth? Some people claim there is no such thing as truth. Others would say truth is whatever you want it to be. But as Christians, we have a standard of truth that is objective, independent of and above human opinion.

Jesus Himself claimed to be truth: "I am the way, and the truth, and the life" (John 14:6). That same night, He prayed to the Father, "Sanctify them in the truth; Thy word is truth" (John 17:17). So we have a living Person and a written Word that are absolute truth, in perfect agreement with each other.

When your heart goes after God based on the truth of His revelation, then God the Holy Spirit fans the flame of your human spirit. That's worshiping in spirit and in truth.

Avoiding the Extremes

There are two extremes when it comes to worship. One is spirit without truth. These are the people who want their worship to move them and excite them and get them all shook up. But they really don't want to deal with the revelation of God. What results is empty emotionalism.

The other extreme is truth without spirit. These are the guys with all the rules for everybody to follow. These are people who mouth the truth, but it doesn't mean anything. We call that dead orthodoxy.

It's like the comment a former seminary professor of mine made about one of the state churches in Europe. He said you could get saved reading their doctrine, but no one cared. The cathedrals were literally cold and empty.

Dutiful Desire

Jesus said our worship needs to include both spirit and truth. The goal is not to worship out of duty alone, but out of dutiful desire. Worship is not something you do just because you are supposed to do it as a Christian, but because it is the greatest thing you can do.

Suppose a husband goes to his wife on their anniversary and says, "Honey, it's that time of year again, and it's my job to get you flowers. Here are a dozen roses. I have fulfilled my anniversary responsibilities."

He is likely to get those roses back in his face! Why? Because while being a faithful husband involves duty, a wife also wants to know that being her husband is his greatest joy.

What God wants is for you to worship Him because it is your most joyful duty. He wants to hear you say, "Dear God, I want to know You. I want to love You. I want to serve You."

If you don't have the desire for worship, I urge you to do the duty while you beg God for the desire to do the duty. God wants your heart so that you will be transformed into the right kind of disciple.

BECOMING A WORSHIPER

The reason so many Christians can be so sanctimonious inside the church and so totally un-Christian in the parking lot is that they don't understand worship. They think that somehow when they walk into church, something magical will happen. They think there is magic in the pulpit or the pew. No, the secret is in the believer. It's called the Holy Spirit.

See, if you have not been worshiping God all week long, a heart for worship is not going to suddenly swoop down from out of nowhere and fall upon you on Sunday. Some people get all excited in church, then when the benediction is pronounced they return to normal.

What happened to them? Nothing. That's the problem. Nothing happened because they didn't worship God the way He wants to be worshiped, in spirit and truth. The fuel of worship is the truth of God. The furnace of worship is the spirit of man. The fire of worship is the Holy Spirit. When those three come together, you have worship.

You can fool the crowd. I can fool the crowd. But the Bible says that God looks on the heart (1 Samuel 16:7). You can make people think you are worshiping, when in your spirit you know that God doesn't have your undivided attention and the undistracted devotion of your heart.

Sure, Satan tries to divert us from worship, as we said earlier. But he cannot rob you of your passion for God. Deep down, you know whether you have a passion for God or not.

"Tony," you say. "I know I need to worship God from the heart as a way of life. But I'm not there yet." Then the issue is, do you *want* to get there? Are you on the way?

If you really want to worship God, nothing can stop you. Nobody can keep you from fulfilling this necessity for following Christ and becoming His authentic disciple!

CHAPTER FIVE

THE CONTENT OF WORSHIP

In Psalm 34:1, the psalmist wrote, "I will bless the Lord at all times; His praise shall continually be in my mouth."

That's the kind of worship God wants from you and me. He wants us to put worship in our mouths as often and with as much delight as we put food in our mouths.

In fact, our desire to worship should be like our drive to eat. If the need for food goes unmet, we feel pain. When we go for an extended time without eating, the body shrinks—which is not all bad for some of us! But when we go for an extended time without worshiping and we shrink spiritually, that's a disaster.

The reason this is true is that we are made to worship. God created you and me for Himself. When we are not fulfilling that drive, or when we are using that drive to worship something or someone other than God, we shrink and become spiritually anemic.

The writer of Hebrews said, "Let us continually offer up a sacrifice of praise to God" (13:15). Worship is not a place or an event. It's an orientation to life.

As we saw in the previous chapter, God is seeking those who will worship Him. Don't misunderstand that. God is not just seeking worship. He has plenty of worship. Angels worship Him. Nature worships Him. The animals worship Him. But He is seeking people to worship Him.

Why? Because God wants to see how many of the creatures He made in His image will voluntarily worship Him continually, the way His heavenly creation and the unconscious earthly creation worship Him. You can't follow Jesus Christ without developing a lifestyle of worship.

So we need to ask, what makes up worship? What is its content? We have a good picture of worship's content in Exodus 24:1–11, the description of a great worship service in which God's covenant with His people was ratified. Let's look at it and notice the ingredients of worship.

DIVINE INVITATION

Worship begins with a divine invitation. "Then [God] said to Moses, 'Come up to the Lord, you and Aaron, Nadab and Abihu and seventy of the elders of Israel, and you shall worship at a distance'" (Exodus 24:1).

God's Call to Worship

Worship is always at God's invitation. The preacher doesn't call you to worship. It's not the choir calling you to worship. It is God calling to you, "Come up to Me." So when you don't worship, you turn God down. When you don't worship, you say to God, "Meeting with You is not really that important to me."

I am not just talking about your Sunday worship, but the everyday experience of worship that God desires from us. God's people ought not be turning down His invitation to worship. The Psalms are replete with calls to worship, invitations to meet with God.

If your boss were to say, "Come up to me. I want to meet with you at 9:00," you would be there at 8:55 because of who called. What about God's invitation to us to worship Him? He bids us come into His presence — individually, as a family, and then as a congregation.

I want to spend some extended time on this matter of the divine invitation to worship because it is so foundational. So I'm going to leave Exodus 24 for a while and consider Psalm 95, a great psalm that also begins with an invitation or call to worship:

> O come, let us sing for joy to the Lord; let us shout joyfully to the rock of our salvation. Let us come before His presence with thanksgiving; let us shout joyfully to Him with psalms. For the Lord is a great God, and a great King above all gods. (vv. 1–3)

The Invitation to Sing

Singing is simply putting the truth of God to music. But notice that we don't just sing. The psalmist says, "Shout." Get excited! It's not just a song, it's a mood. It's something we feel. It's something that penetrates to our emotions.

Notice who the audience is: "the Lord" and "the rock" (v. 1), "His presence" and "Him" (v. 2). This is not just the choir singing to the congregation, or the congregation singing to the preacher. It's the Lord who wants to hear our voices. If God does not hear you sing, it doesn't matter who else hears you sing.

Why should we sing heartily to the Lord? Because He is a great God. He is the King of all kings, "In whose hand are the depths of the earth; the peaks of the mountains are His also. The sea is His, for it was He who made it; and His hands formed the dry land" (vv. 4–5).

That's greatness! Do you know anyone else who can do what God can do? The psalmist says God made the mountains. Anybody you know who is a mountain-maker? We are walking around on the earth He has made. Do you know any earth-maker other than God? I don't either.

In verse 7 we are called "the people of His pasture, and the sheep of His hand." I like that because it means that we are not the owners of the earth. We are simply grazers on God's land.

Because our God is a great God, we ought to shout for

joy. There ought not be any mumbling and moaning in His presence. The church building ought to quake when we raise our voices to God. After all, He Himself asks, "To whom then will you liken Me?" (Isaiah 40:25). If we can make a sports stadium rock and roll, we ought to be able to shake a few walls with our worship.

But too often we're like the boy who was praying by his bed. "Lord," he prayed, "thank You for church today. It was a wonderful service. I wish You could have been there!"

I'm afraid that many times God doesn't show up at our services because we are not coming to our great God at His invitation. We are coming to do our little religious thing, not to meet with the One who is unlike any other and who bids us come. Part of His worship invitation to us is to raise our voices in joyful praise.

Should you sing with joy because of your circum-stances? Not necessarily. Is there joy because everything is perfect at home? No. Joy because there are no prob-lems in your life? No. The joy is because you are bringing all that mess to a great God!

If your banker invites you to meet with him to work out a solution to your financial problems, your joy is not that you have the problems. The joy is that you have somebody who can help you pay the bills.

When a great thing happens in your life, you want to express it with your lips and with your body. There is nothing wrong with getting excited in worship, because nothing demands your excitement more than God. He is worthy to be praised. He is worthy of the full expression of your worship.

The Invitation to Move

The Bible says that when God delivered Israel out of Egypt, Miriam and the women of Israel took their tam-bourines and danced to God (Exodus 15:20–21). They danced and sang of God's greatness in opening the Red Sea and delivering His people, then drowning Pharaoh and his army in the sea.

When David brought the ark of the covenant to

Jerusalem, he was so overwhelmed with joy that he "was dancing before the Lord with all his might" (2 Samuel 6:14). But when David's wife Michal looked out the window and saw him dancing, she said, "Look at that fool I married" (see vv. 16, 20).

But David said to Michal, "I wasn't dancing for you. I was dancing to my great God. When He allowed me to bring the ark of the covenant home, my feet couldn't keep still. My hands couldn't keep still. He is too great a God" (v. 21, author's paraphrase).

Because Michal condemned David for his worship, God closed her womb and she was barren the rest of her life (v. 23). I believe it was because she dared to do what the Bible declares we are never to do: quench the Holy Spirit. She tried to keep David from praising the Lord for His greatness.

The Invitation to Bow

But worship includes more than joyful noise and movement. In Psalm 95, we are also told, "Come, let us worship and bow down; let us kneel before the Lord our Maker. For He is our God" (vv. 6–7a).

God invites us to a worship that involves the expression of a whole range of emotions. You can see this in the Bible itself. One moment the worshipers may be dancing and shouting in celebration, and the next moment they are kneeling in quiet humility. One moment they are celebrating how great God is. The next moment they are humbling themselves before His face.

The point is that bodily movement in worship is always associated with heart attitude. So in times of joy, we sing and celebrate. In times of dependency, we bow down. The Israelites would prostrate themselves because they were bowing before God.

When the immoral woman came to Jesus, she bowed before Him, broke "an alabaster vial of perfume" on Jesus' feet, then wiped them with her hair (Luke 7:37–38).

The Pharisee who was hosting Jesus said to himself, "If this man were a prophet He would know who and what sort of person this woman is who is touching Him, that she is a sinner" (v. 39). Jesus had to explain that when a person is forgiven much, he or she loves much (v. 47).

The reason we don't bow down more in worship is that we don't remember what God has done. We don't remember what He has brought us from. The psalmist calls God "our Maker" (Psalm 95:6). He is our Creator. And He is our Redeemer.

Although Psalm 95 invites us to worship, it closes with a warning: "Do not harden your hearts, as at Meribah, as in the day of Massah in the wilderness; when your fathers tested Me, they tried Me, though they had seen My work" (vv. 8–9).

The Lord goes on to say through the psalmist that the people who were indifferent and rebellious toward Him would not enter into His rest (vv. 10–11).

God wants us to take Him seriously. In other words, don't just come to Him because you want to shout. Don't just come because you want to feel good. Come because you understand how great and awesome He is.

One of our problems today is that we don't take God seriously. We don't really believe that He is God. If we did, we would turn pale at our sin and be in pain over it. We wouldn't act like nothing had happened. We would run to the altar, take hold of those horns they used to tie up the sacrificial animals, and say, "Have mercy on me, for I am a sinner."

The Invitation to Silence

Another part of the invitation to worship is silence. I like the call to worship that the prophet Habakkuk issues: "The Lord is in His holy temple. Let all the earth be silent before Him" (Habakkuk 2:20).

Every now and then when I was growing up, my father and I would start talking at the same time. He would be trying to tell me something, and I would be talking. My father would say, "Hush, boy. Can't you see I'm talking?" When your father is talking, you need to shut it down.

There are times in worship when we say nothing. In

the midst of the silence we think with awe about the grandeur of God, and there is nothing left to say.

When I went to the Grand Canyon for the first time and stood on the precipice of that big hole in the ground, I was awestruck. I couldn't get any words out of my mouth. My tongue was stuck to the roof of my mouth because of the grandeur of the place. When I went to India and saw the Taj Mahal, all I could say was "Ooh!" because of its grandeur.

When you see who God is, there is nothing to say, because our great God sometimes overwhelms us. All you can do is clam up. Zephaniah 1:7 commands us, "Be silent before the Lord God!" Zechariah 2:13 says, "Be silent, all flesh, before the Lord."

It's like a presidential press conference. The press corps is there, and everyone is talking. But when the president comes into the room, all of a sudden it gets really quiet. The leader has arrived. Everyone gets quiet to hear what he has to say. When God is in the room, sometimes you have to be silent.

So the invitation to worship includes celebration and shouting and dancing and reflection and silence. Our God demands and deserves all such expressions of worship. He invites us to join the rest of the universe in praising Him. "Come up to [Me]" was His invitation to Moses and the others in Exodus 24.

DIVINE REVELATION

The content of worship includes not only divine invitation, but also divine revelation. Let's go back to Exodus 24, where God issued His invitation:

> Then Moses came and recounted to the people all the words of the Lord and all the ordinances; and all the people answered with one voice, and said, "All the words which the Lord has spoken we will do!" And Moses wrote down all the words of the Lord. Then he arose early in the morning, and built an altar at the foot of the mountain with twelve pillars for the twelve tribes of Israel. . . . Then he took the book of the

covenant and read it in the hearing of the people; and they said, "All that the Lord has spoken we will do, and we will be obedient!" (vv. 3–4, 7)

The "words of the Lord" are His revelation, His declaration of Himself. You see, the only things you and I can learn about God are the things He decides to tell us. I get tired of people going around saying, "Well, I think God would want this or want that."

The only way you know what God wants is when He tells you. You can't just make up what God wants. He is big enough to speak for Himself. Let's look at three areas related to this issue of revelation.

Reading the Word

First, there is the reading of what God has said. Paul told Timothy to give careful attention to the public reading of Scripture to the congregation in Ephesus (1 Timothy 4:13). In Nehemiah 8:1–8, Ezra the priest stood and read the Word as the covenant was renewed. The people stood while Ezra opened "the book of the law" (v. 1), and they wept as he read God's commands.

Moses reviewed the covenant with the people, then wrote the words down and read them. In the Scripture, reading the Word of God commanded the people's attention because they understood that the message being delivered was the truth of God.

Simply reading the Bible has power in our lives. If we never read the Word, we are missing out on something. You say, "But I don't understand it all."

That may be true, but it doesn't mean you won't understand it the second time around. The reason we read the Bible in worship services is that hearing the Word can add to our understanding. Many believers never get around to understanding the Bible because they don't even read it. But there is power in the reading of God's Word.

Proclaiming the Word

Next comes the proclamation of the Word; that is, declaring what God has said.

Moses declared the covenant to the people (Exodus 24:3). He explained its meaning, its sense. That's why a major part of worship is the proclamation or preaching of the Word of God.

Don't get me wrong. Preaching is not the only part of worship. Some churches use music simply as an introduction to the sermon. That's not the idea. Worship includes the Word, but the sermon is not the sum total of worship.

But proclamation is crucial to true worship. It is through the Word that God speaks. The test of any man who gets behind the pulpit is, "Is he true to the Word?" God forbid that I or any other pastor would distort what He has said. Moses delivered to the Israelites what God had said.

Our church in Dallas gets a lot of requests from people who want to come and use our pulpit to promote politics or social movements. God is certainly concerned about these things, and the Bible speaks to political and social concerns. But worship is about declaring what God has said, not about someone giving a particular viewpoint.

Sermons are not designed just to give information. The proclamation of the Word, unfolding its meaning and its application to our lives, is designed to call people to respond to God. A person could go to church every Sunday and take notes on the sermon, yet not be helped one bit.

There is nothing wrong with noting things that capture the hearer's attention. But God is not trying to fill notebooks. He is trying to change lives. The purpose of a sermon is to challenge people with the truth of God. That's why the third aspect of the divine revelation in worship is the response that God demands.

Responding to the Word

The response called for is a commitment to obedience. When Moses had finished recounting God's covenant, the people responded immediately with a pledge of obedience (Exodus 24:3). Then when he read the book of the covenant, they responded again, adding, "We will be obedient!" (v. 7).

The only thing God wants to know at the benediction of a worship service is how our lives are going to be different because we accepted His invitation and showed up to worship Him. If you can't answer that question, then you are at a religious ceremony only. Worship is responding to God as well as hearing from God. No response means no discipleship.

That means at the end of every sermon, we should ask the question, "What am I going to do differently because I was in the presence of God and heard His expectations of me?" We need to ask that question every day, in fact, as we make worship a way of life.

If you want to grow in your faith, the fastest way to do it is to ask yourself, "What will change in my life because I heard the voice of God?" I'm not saying that every time you open your Bible, you will make radical changes in your life. Sometimes the change may be very small. But God's Word is designed to change and reshape us into the image of Christ, so we need to be ready to obey what He says. God always responds to the statement, "We will do," not just, "We will hear."

DIVINE PRESENTATION

The third element that goes to make up the content of our worship is the divine presentation.

In Exodus 24:4–5, we are told that Moses built an altar and then "sent young men of the sons of Israel, and they offered burnt offerings and sacrificed young bulls as peace offerings to the Lord." Moses wasn't about to enter God's presence without an offering to present to Him.

Our Offerings

God deserves our offerings because of who He is and what He has done. You don't come before a king without a gift. When we worship, we have to ask ourselves, What do we offer God when we come into His presence?

When you and I come before God, we must come

with an offering. We saw above that we come with a "sacrifice of praise" (Hebrews 13:15), an offering from our lips and hearts.

But we also come with a tangible offering, our gifts that represent the work of our hands. You hear a lot of church people, and outsiders too, asking why in the world the church has to take an offering at every service.

The basic reason is the one I mentioned above, that God deserves our offerings. He has also commanded us to bring our gifts to Him. He wants us to acknowledge that all we are and all we have come from Him. Our offerings are one way we can show God we understand that truth.

When you come before God without the offering He deserves and asks for, you are saying to Him, "I don't really need You. I got this job on my own. I got the energy to do this job on my own. So this is my money. These are my resources. You ought to be happy I'm here."

The Best We Have

Not only did Moses send out these young men with an offering, but it was not just any offering. We know from the Law that the animals brought to God for sacrifice had to be the best: no spot or blemish at all. Israel's offerings had to be pure and clean. They had to be real offerings, cheerfully given. They had to be the best, the "firstfruits," of what the people had.

One of the most critical passages in the Old Testament, and one I referred to in the last chapter, is Malachi 1:6–10, where God indicted His people for bringing Him their leftovers.

This was a stinging rebuke, because it was such an insult to God's greatness to bring Him leftovers. Our offerings are supposed to say to God, "You are a great God to meet my needs like this. You are a great God to give me a place to live, a car to drive, clothes to wear, and food to eat. You are a great God!"

See, you don't tip a great God. You don't give Him the crumbs from your table. You give Him what He deserves.

A family sat around the dinner table one day, complaining about the church service. The son said, "Boy, that preacher stutters when he talks. I couldn't understand him. What a horrible sermon."

The daughter said, "That choir can't sing. They are all out of tune."

The mother added, "Yes, that was a horrible service, and it lasted far too long."

The father got frustrated hearing all of these complaints. He looked at his family and said, "Be quiet, all of you! What did you expect for a quarter?"

That is what we do so often. We want the best from God, but we tip Him. We want all of His power, but we give Him our "chump change." We want all of His glory, but we give Him offerings He can't use.

God said to Israel in Malachi's day, "Don't bring your diseased sacrifices to Me. Try giving them to your earthly leader and see if he accepts them. Don't give Me your leftover lambs, your blind sheep. I am a great God. Present Me a great offering, or shut the doors of the temple and lock it up."

Three Kinds of Givers

Someone has said there are three kinds of givers: the flint, the sponge, and the honeycomb. To get anything out of a flint, you have to hit it with a hammer. Then all you get are little chips and sparks.

To get water out of a sponge, you have to squeeze it. The more you squeeze the more water you get, but you still have to squeeze it.

But a honeycomb drips with sweetness. The honey comes out in an overflow. When God's people understand what He has done for them, no one will have to prime them or plead with them to give. They will give out of the overflow of their gratitude that He is such a great God.

In fact, sometimes we ought to jump to our feet during the offering and applaud the privilege we have to give. We ought to shout with joy that we have been blessed with strength enough to work so that we might have something to give.

DIVINE CONSECRATION

Consecration is the fourth component to worship, following in logical order from the invitation, the revelation, and the presentation:

> Moses took half of the blood and put it in basins, and the other half of the blood he sprinkled on the altar. . . . So Moses took the blood and sprinkled it on the people, and said, "Behold the blood of the covenant, which the Lord has made with you in accordance with all these words." (Exodus 24:6, 8)

Moses took the blood from the sacrifices the young men offered and divided it in half. He sprinkled half on the altar and the other half on the people. Blood is always a means of consecration because it makes possible fellowship between sinful people and a holy God. Whoever wants to worship God must come by the blood.

The Blood of Christ

Fellowship with a holy God has always come by blood. For Moses, the blood of animal sacrifices mediated between men and God. But now, the blood of Jesus Christ has made Him the "one mediator" between God and us (1 Timothy 2:5).

When we gather at the Lord's table in an act of worship, it's all about Jesus' body and His blood. It commemorates His one, final sacrifice for sin. We don't come to worship anybody but Jesus Christ. He alone is worthy because He was slain, and with His blood He purchased our salvation (see Revelation 5:9).

It may seem odd to us that Moses sprinkled blood on the people. But when you accepted Christ, God sprinkled His blood on you. Christ's blood has already cleansed the heavenly mercy seat, so now you can have fellowship with God. The blood of the covenant shed at the ratification ceremony in Exodus 24 looked forward to the blood of Christ.

Jesus Christ has consecrated us with His blood and

has brought us close to God. We ought to worship God just because of Jesus. He reached down and caught you with one hand, reached up and caught the Father with His other hand, and brought the two of you together. No wonder the only song in heaven is, "Worthy is the Lamb that was slain" (Revelation 5:12).

Our Consecration

The church observes communion because it is the symbol of the new covenant, the symbol of our consecration. When we eat the flesh and drink the blood of Christ, we are saying, "Jesus is my life. He is my purpose. He is my reason for living."

You and I have been made children of God by the blood of Jesus Christ. We can pray because Christ is our Intercessor. His blood keeps on cleansing us from sin (1 John 1:7) so that we will never have to worry about the sin question.

Jesus has consecrated us to God, making us acceptable to the Father by His blood. In return, we ought to consecrate ourselves to Him every day as our "spiritual service of worship" (Romans 12:1). When we get up in the morning, we need to say, "Dear God, because of Jesus, I am Yours today."

We used to say the Pledge of Allegiance every day in school. The pledge is a reminder that you are a citizen of the United States. Consecrating yourself reminds you that you are a citizen of heaven. You belong to heaven. Consecration is a crucial component of worship.

DIVINE ILLUMINATION

Here's a fifth component that goes with the other four to make up the content of worship. When you have all the other pieces in place, then you will experience divine illumination. Let's pick up the story in Exodus 24 again:

> Then Moses went up with Aaron, Nadab and Abihu, and seventy of the elders of Israel, and they saw the God of Israel; and under His feet there appeared to be

a pavement of sapphire, as clear as the sky itself. Yet He did not stretch out His hand against the nobles of the sons of Israel; and they beheld God, and they ate and drank. (vv. 9–11)

I like that. When they got their worship straight, they got to see God. And instead of being consumed by His awesome presence, they had a feast!

What It Takes to See God

Our problem today is that we have a bunch of people looking for God who don't want to worship. We have a bunch of people saying, "Lord, I did not see You last week." But did you worship last week? "Lord, I didn't feel You today." Did you worship today?

Moses and his companions saw God when they worshiped. Some of God's people are too "polite" to worship, too self-conscious to go down on their knees, too reserved to call on Him in song. Others are too busy to worship, too tied up with the job or with the television. They just can't get around to worship.

Let me tell you, if you can't get around to worship, then don't be surprised if you don't see God. Don't be surprised if you don't see His hand moving in answer to your prayers and His power working in your life. If you don't have the time or the desire to worship, don't be surprised if God stays invisible.

But when Moses and the others worshiped, they saw God. They did not see just a hazy old outline of something. We're not sure in what form God appeared to them, but they saw God over a pavement of sapphire! It was like the noonday sky shining bright. They saw God in His true splendor. They saw the glory of God.

Lifestyle Worship

Do you want to see the glory of God? Learn to worship Him! If you want to see His glory continuously, then commit yourself to continuous, lifestyle worship.

Every now and then won't do it. One church service a week won't get you the glory of God as these men saw it. But when you make your life a life of worship; when you "present your [body] a living and holy sacrifice, acceptable to God" (Romans 12:1); when worship is your commitment, then God will illuminate Himself to you.

Worship is key because it's the only thing you can give someone who doesn't need anything. Think about it. What do you give the person who has everything? Well, people always seem to come up with some kind of gift because in reality, nobody on earth has everything.

But God does. "The earth is the Lord's, and all it contains, the world, and those who dwell in it" (Psalm 24:1). God owns it all. He needs nothing. So what can you give Him that He really wants? Your worship!

God wants to hear you say, "I will bless the Lord at all times; His praise shall continually be in my mouth" (Psalm 34:1). Are you ready to worship God? Do you desire above all to praise Him, to give Him the glory due His name? Worship is an absolute necessity if you and I are going to follow Christ.

CHAPTER SIX

THE CONTEXT OF WORSHIP

I hope you are getting the idea by now that worship is not just a private experience between God and yourself. Neither is it a once-a-week event in which you go to a service, worship for an hour or two, and then pick up life where you left off as if nothing happened.

Instead, worship is both private and public. It is personal and corporate. You not only need to worship God in your own life, but you also need to worship Him with other people in His body, the church. Corporate worship is one of the essentials for following Christ.

The church, in fact, is the primary context for our worship. That is because the church is God's new entity through which He is doing a new work. So in this chapter, I want to talk about the context of worship.

I've always said that anyone who is worshiping God personally and privately will be serious about worshiping Him corporately as well. We've all heard people say, "I can worship God at home. I don't need to go to church."

You may have said it, or at least thought it, yourself. But God always calls His personal worshipers to be His corporate worshipers. As we are going to see, the church (the people, not the building) is the context in which we find our identity as worshipers.

The idea of God's people as a worshiping community goes back a long way. When Moses went to Pharaoh, the first thing he said on behalf of Yahweh was, "Let My people go that they may celebrate a feast to Me in the wilderness" (Exodus 5:1).

God was saying, "Let My people go that they may worship Me." When Israel finally came out of Egypt, God assembled the people as a community of believers in and worshipers of Yahweh (Exodus 13).

We live in a world where people want their worship the way they get their fast food. They want to be customers participating in McWorship, who can leave as the same people they were when they arrived. They want "drive-through" worship where they pull up and call out their order, then drive ahead, pick it up, and go home. The idea of coming and sitting down to dine with God is getting lost.

But God's stated will is that His people come together regularly as His body to worship Him. In the earliest days of the church, the believers met every day. Then it became a weekly experience as they set aside the Lord's Day for worship based on the resurrection of Jesus Christ (Acts 20:7).

The idea of setting aside one day in seven for the Lord was established early in Scripture. The fourth commandment instructed Israel to keep the Sabbath (Exodus 20:8–11). It was a day to focus on God, to recognize that He had provided for them the six days before. It was also a declaration that God's people were depending upon Him to provide for them in the week ahead.

For the church, that special day of worship is the Lord's Day, the first day of the week. It's the day we come together to celebrate the new life and new covenant we enjoy by virtue of Christ's death and resurrection.

And, by the way, the corporate worship of God's people is not just here on earth. The book of Revelation contains several scenes in heaven where myriads of angels and people are gathered around the throne in worship, coming together in eternity to worship God (Revelation 5:13; 7:9–17; 14:1–3; 15:1–4; 19:1–10).

The scene in Revelation 19 is that of the redeemed church coming to the "marriage supper of the Lamb" as Christ's bride. What I'm saying is that the church as the context for worship is not a temporary idea. We will worship God for all eternity as His bride.

So you can worship God privately, and you ought to. I don't want to take anything away from what we have said about worship as a way of life. If you are only worshiping God on Sunday, your spiritual life is going to be undernourished.

But if you *aren't* worshiping Him in the context of His body, your spiritual life will also be anemic. Why? Because God has constructed the Christian life in such a way that there are certain things He will do because you worship Him privately. And there are other things He will do because you worship Him corporately.

So there is a balance between individual and collective worship. You and I will not fully develop and mature as Christ's disciples until both of these aspects of worship are active in our lives.

A NEW ENVIRONMENT

One reason the church is God's primary context for worship is that when the church gathers together, we are brought into a brand-new environment in a way we don't experience in private worship.

A New Audience

In worship, God is the audience and we are the actors. You should not come to church just to see your friends or to hear the choir or the preacher. Of course they have a place in worship. But when we gather for worship, we are coming to meet God, to bless and glorify Him, and to hear from Him.

The choir matters because it is singing about God. The preacher matters because he is preaching about God. The saints matter because they have come to meet God as a united people. That is a new environment, different than anything else on earth.

See, if you take God out of the picture, a worship

service ceases to be anything special. Take God out of the sermon, and it might as well be a motivational talk to a civic organization. Take God out of the music, and it could be just another concert. Without God, the saints getting together could be like a fraternity or sorority or any other group with shared interests.

But when we come to worship God as His people, it's supposed to be a very different story. We are common partakers of the work of Christ. We come to meet Him. If anybody asks you why you are going to church, tell him, "I'm going to meet Somebody." Part of the new environment of worship is the new audience.

A New City

According to the author of Hebrews, our corporate worship also transports us to a new city. In Hebrews 12, he writes:

> You have not come to a mountain that may be touched and to a blazing fire, and to darkness and gloom and whirlwind, and to the blast of a trumpet and the sound of words which sound was such that those who heard begged that no further word should be spoken to them. For they could not bear the command, "If even a beast touches the mountain, it will be stoned." And so terrible was the sight, that Moses said, "I am full of fear and trembling." (vv. 18–21)

There's a worship service no saint would sleep through! This is what it was like when God gave the Law to Moses on Mount Sinai (Exodus 19:16–25). Read the story for yourself and you'll see just how solemn and frightening this event was.

The people of Israel were warned not to come near the mountain. God did not want even the priests to "break through" the barrier around the mountain. The people had to consecrate themselves and stand by while this awesome scene unfolded. Even Moses was scared out of his wits.

If you had been there that day and disobeyed God's instructions, His holiness would have scorched you. You would have been burned to a crisp. God told Moses to tell the people not to touch the base of Mount Sinai lest they fry. The holiness of God prohibited the people from intimate contact with Him.

This is not the case when we come to God as His church to worship Him. That's because we come to a new city:

> But you have come to Mount Zion and to the city of the living God, the heavenly Jerusalem, and to myriads of angels, to the general assembly and church of the first-born who are enrolled in heaven, and to God, the Judge of all, and to the spirits of righteous men made perfect, and to Jesus, the mediator of a new covenant, and to the sprinkled blood. (Hebrews 12:22–24)

In the Old Testament, the city of God was Mount Zion, Jerusalem. It was the holy city, the place you went to worship God. When we come together to worship God, we come to a new city, "the heavenly Jerusalem."

Your body may be in the city where your church meets. But in your spirit, your inner person, you are transported to a heavenly city when you come to worship God. Paul called it "the heavenly places in Christ" (Ephesians 1:3). It is the place of spiritual activity.

In worship, we are transported to a whole new city. So you are in two places at once when you worship. Your body may be in a church pew, but if you are sincerely worshiping, your spirit is in the heavenly Jerusalem, the new city of God.

A New Crowd

When you are transported to God's new city, you are going to find a new crowd of people. According to what we read above in Hebrews 12:22, when you worship God, you are hanging out with the angels. Why would the writer say that? Because guess what the angels in heaven do twenty-four hours a day? They worship God!

In Isaiah 6, the prophet saw the angels worshiping the Lord on His throne. They called out, "Holy, Holy,

Holy, is the Lord of hosts, the whole earth is full of His glory" (v. 3). When you worship, you join the angels around God's throne, bowing before Him and declaring His greatness.

But we benefit too, because Hebrews 1:14 says that angels are ministering spirits sent to minister on our behalf. The beauty of going to the heavenly Jerusalem and hanging out with the angels is that when you come back to earth, angels come with you.

There is a provision of God that as we join in His worship, His angels serve us. It's invisible. You can't see it. But when we believers collect for worship, the angels are very much involved with us because we are where they are.

This new crowd also includes "the general assembly and church of the first-born" (Hebrews 12:23). We not only engage with the angels in corporate worship, but we also engage with every other believer who is worshiping. In the same way that a computer network can link people all over the world, we are vitally linked with every other believer in the world who is worshiping God.

Also in this new crowd are the Old Testament saints, called "righteous men made perfect" (v. 23). When we worship, we are in spiritual company with Abraham and Isaac and Jacob—and also with Paul and Peter and all of the saints who have gone on before.

But it gets even better. In worship, we are also connected to God Himself (v. 23). As we saw in the previous chapter, God issues the invitation to worship. We worship Him because He asks us to worship Him.

When you worship, you are also participating in the same activity as people like Peter and Paul. So, in a sense, worship is more than cross-cultural. It brings the "dead in Christ" and those still alive together in one pursuit.

Finally, Hebrews 12:24 says we also hang out with Jesus when we worship. We learned in chapter 4 that He is the mediator of the new covenant. When we worship, we connect with Christ and get plugged in to the benefits of the new covenant.

When we worship, we are also sprinkled with His

blood. We talked about the importance of the blood in the previous chapter, so I won't restate that here.

Do you know why Satan wants to keep you from worshiping with the body of Christ? He wants to make you a "Lone Ranger" Christian because when you come to the new city, the heavenly Jerusalem, you are whisked away into a whole new realm.

A NEW IDENTITY

When we worship as the body of Christ, we not only enter into a new environment, but we also take on a new identity. The apostle Peter addresses this transformation in 1 Peter 2:4–10, where he lists five aspects of our new identity as the people of God.

A New Building

First of all, Peter says we are a new building:

> Coming to Him as to a living stone . . . you also, as living stones, are being built up as a spiritual house for a holy priesthood, to offer up spiritual sacrifices acceptable to God through Jesus Christ. (vv. 4–5)

God is building Himself a new house of worship—only it doesn't have walls and doors and windows and a street number on the outside. God's house of worship is located in the people who come into the church building each week.

For a number of years, our church in Dallas met for worship in the gymnasium of our family center. But if someone were to ask our people where they were going on Sunday, they didn't say they were going down to the gym. They said they were going to church.

How could they say that? One reason is that they were coming there to meet God, not to shoot hoops. Another reason is that they were coming as part of a group of people with a similar relationship to God. They were coming as part of the living "brick and mortar" that make up God's new house of worship.

Worship can transform a gym into a sanctuary

because the worshipers bring the sanctuary with them when they come. This is why Israel could worship God in a portable tabernacle or in a permanent temple. When God's spiritual house gathers, it doesn't matter whether the physical structure has stained-glass windows or glass backboards.

We are living stones because we are linked to *the* "living stone," Jesus Christ (v. 4). Jesus is the Builder, and He is building only one house. His design is that all of us as living stones fit together into His one building.

Nobody ever built a house out of just one brick. Individual bricks are important, and if you get enough of them you can build a house. But one brick can't make a house. You can be a good disciple, but you can't be the gathering of the body of Christ. You can only be your brick contributing to the whole.

Look at the implications of this truth for worship. Peter makes a direct connection to worship in verse 5 when he calls the church "a holy priesthood, to offer up spiritual sacrifices acceptable to God through Jesus Christ."

What are the sacrifices we offer up? The Bible gives us a number of them. One is the offering of your body to God as a "living and holy sacrifice" (Romans 12:1).

I wince when people tell me, "I wasn't at church last Sunday, but I was with you in spirit." It's hard to worship with spirits. Worship always includes your body. God wants to do His thing through your body as you yield the members of your body to Him.

Another sacrifice we are called to make is a "sacrifice of praise to God . . . the fruit of lips that give thanks to His name" (Hebrews 13:15). We give testimonies, we pray, and we sing in worship as offerings of praise and thanksgiving to God.

The next verse in Hebrews says, "Do not neglect doing good and sharing; for with such sacrifices God is pleased" (13:16). One reason corporate worship is important is that it connects you with brothers and sisters in the spiritual house whose needs you can help to meet —and who can help you when you're in need.

The Bible also says that giving is a sacrifice we are to offer up to God (Philippians 4:18). Paul calls giving "an acceptable sacrifice, well-pleasing to God" because it is sharing what God has given you so that it can benefit the program of God to others.

When Peter says this spiritual house is "being built up" by Christ (1 Peter 2:5), he uses the verb that means "to edify." This word means to build, to encourage, to strengthen. When the New Testament talks about building up the church, the focus is on people, not buildings.

One key purpose of worship is that believers might come together to build each other up in the faith and encourage each other. Our main focus in worship is the Lord Himself, but the overflow of our worship should touch other people.

I often use the analogy of logs in a fireplace. One log alone in a fireplace will quickly burn up and not produce much of a fire. If you want a big fire, you have to get a pile of logs touching each other. It is essential that the logs connect. The more logs, the bigger the fire.

If you want to see a spiritual flame ignited in your church, you had better be touching other believers and have other believers touching you.

This is why the Bible has so much to say about the church edifying itself. Paul says in Colossians 3:16, "Let the word of Christ richly dwell within you, with all wisdom teaching and admonishing one another." The word *you* here is plural. God dwells in you richly when you come together with other believers in worship to teach and admonish and encourage one another.

Have you ever noticed that you can go to church in a dark or down mood, and leave in an entirely different mood? One thing that brought about that mood change was the fact that you were in touch with other people of like mind.

It's something like what happens at a ball game. You can watch a game on TV and cheer a good play. But when you are in the stands, your reaction will be entirely different. Why? Because you are not cheering alone. You are shoulder-to-shoulder with other people who are also standing and cheering, and electricity passes between you.

You may prefer to stay home and watch the game on TV, because it takes less time and effort to do that than to get up and make it to the stadium. But the effect on you will not be the same. Something will be missing.

When we come together to worship as God's spiritual house, we are transformed by the Spirit of God. The Spirit begins to do things among us that are different from what He does when we are by ourselves.

A contractor was having trouble with the second floor of a building. The first floor had gone up fine, but nothing seemed to fit on the second floor. Then the contractor discovered he was following the wrong set of plans for the second floor. If we are going to follow Christ, if our discipleship is to be effective, we have to be following the same blueprint. We must all be following the same plan in worship. That's why we have to stick to the Word of God.

First Corinthians 14 probably has more to say about corporate worship than any chapter in the New Testament. In verses 24–25, Paul says that when the church is gathered in worship and the whole body is edifying one another by speaking the Word of God, an unbeliever who comes into the service may be struck by the power of God and fall on his face in worship.

This is why worship is never defined just by what happens on the platform. As we said earlier, you don't come to church to watch other people perform. Worship is participatory.

One week, a visitor came to me after church to express her joy at the service. "I have never been in anything like this," she said. "Can I get to know God like these people do?"

That is what worship should do. It's good to worship by yourself. But when we all gather in one place, worshiping God in spirit and in truth, lifting our voices to God and edifying one another, something is supposed to shake. Something special is supposed to happen.

You are not supposed to leave worship yawning.

When all of this energy and power comes together, some heat is going to be generated. That is why the issue in worship is not just whether you feel like worshiping, but whether your brothers and sisters need you to worship with them.

The reason you and I as believers can be cemented together as a spiritual house is that the church is built on the cornerstone of Jesus Christ. In 1 Peter 2:6–8, the apostle reminds us there is only one cornerstone that God is using to build His worshiping church.

That Stone is Jesus Christ, and if He isn't your cornerstone, He will be your "stone of stumbling" (v. 8). Those who reject Jesus will trip over Him and tumble right into judgment. This matter of knowing and worshiping Jesus is no small thing!

But if Jesus is of "precious value" to you (v. 7), you can't help but come and worship Him with His body. You can't help but worship Him all week long in your heart. You carry pictures around with you of people who are precious to you and you show them off proudly. You tell other people about your precious ones. That's how we will be about Jesus when we are worshiping Him the way we should.

A Chosen Race

We spent a lot of time on Peter's first aspect of our new identity, God's spiritual house, because Peter devoted a lot of space to it.

But then in verse 9 of our text, Peter gives us, in rapid-fire succession, four more truths about the new identity we have in Christ as His worshipers. We know Peter is speaking collectively and not just individually because the word *you* is plural. Let's see what he says about us as the body of Christ.

Part of our new identity is that we are "a chosen race." That means you and I didn't get into the body of Christ because of anything we were. We got here because we were selected, "chosen," to be here.

That's why in Jesus Christ, there are no racial or class distinctions (Galatians 3:28). That does not mean you cease being a Jew or a Gentile. You do not have to deny being black or white or Hispanic or Asian or whatever. God recognizes races. He created them.

But what the Bible means is that all of us in the church are part of a bigger agenda. When the United States goes to the Olympics, the country goes as one nation. Black Americans, Hispanic Americans, white Americans, Asian Americans all go to make up the team. But when an American wins a medal and the U.S. flag is hoisted, only one national anthem is played.

When you go to the Olympics, you are part of a bigger group. You are not just out there to represent your group. Your group may be legitimate, but it is narrow. That's the way it is in the body of Christ. We are a new race in which all of the old distinctions are irrelevant to our unity in Christ.

So you and I can never let our narrow view control our Christian decision making. We cannot let our culture control our relationship to Jesus Christ. We are a chosen race, selected by Christ to carry out a whole new agenda. Worship is a wonderful way to express that unity.

All who know Christ and walk through the door of our church in Dallas are "accepted in the beloved" (Ephesians 1:6 KJV) regardless of color, class, or culture. They belong to our race. That does not negate their racial or cultural identities, but it means these categories are subservient to the bigger international category of the children of God.

A Royal Priesthood

Peter also says we are "a royal priesthood." I like that word *royal*. It has got a "king ring" to it. I don't care who people think you are out there in the world. In the church, you are both nobody and somebody. Let me explain.

In the church, you are nobody in the sense that you are not greater than the next person because of your worldly status. A well-to-do man in our community once came to me and said he wanted a position of leadership in the church.

I told him that at our church, people get leadership the old-fashioned way. They have to earn it. He was a little bit offended. He said, "You don't know who I am."

I said, "No, but I'm beginning to find out." I explained to him that a person has to prove himself spiritually to be a leader. He was offended because he thought he was somebody. But God is not privileged to have us. We are privileged that the grace of God was open to us. There are "not many mighty, not many noble" by the world's standard among us (1 Corinthians 1:26).

But having said that, in Christ we are somebody because we are His royal priesthood. Back in the days of slavery, the slaves were nobodies. Grown men were called "boy" and had to say "Yes massa'. No massa'." They were nobody until Sunday morning.

But on Sunday morning, "boy" became "Deacon Jones." "Girl" became the mother of the church. What happened? They understood that when they came into the presence of God to worship Him, they were royalty. The King's blood was running through their veins. They knew they could get to God.

The beautiful thing about being a Christian is that you don't need anybody else to bring you to God. Jesus has already brought you there. People can pray and intercede for you, of course. But through Jesus Christ, God is accessible to you directly because you are His priest.

So when we come together in worship and raise our voices to God, we get through to Him because we are His priests. You'll remember that in Acts 12, Peter was arrested and jailed by Herod. But the church went to fervent prayer for Peter (v. 5), and a light came on in his cell as an angel delivered him.

God's royal priests went to Him in prayer. Back in verse 5 of 1 Peter 2, Peter called us a "holy priesthood," meaning we are set apart to God for His use.

That's an unbeatable combination. Being holy makes us fit to serve a holy God. And being royal makes us fit to serve the King of Kings. So we are somebody when we come to the house of God to offer up our sacrifices as priests.

A Holy Nation

Peter isn't finished yet. He calls the church "a holy nation" (v. 9). This is the other side of our identity as a chosen race. We come together as a new race to form a new nation.

Holy does not mean perfect. We will never achieve perfection in this life, but our passion should be toward holiness.

Being a holy people means we feel pain over our sin. We are hurt when we rebel against God and disobey Him. We confess rather than trying to hide our sin. We bring our sin to the cross that it might be crucified.

Peter is saying that when we come together, we need to define ourselves as a holy people, a people whose passion is to please God. Holy worship is the only kind God accepts.

God's Possession

Peter's final description in 1 Peter 2:9 of us as believers is "a people for God's own possession." We are special people because of who we belong to.

Many of us have family heirlooms, possessions that have been handed down over the generations. Some of those have real value, whereas other things are of no value to anyone but us. But even the heirlooms that aren't very valuable are worth a million dollars to you because that was your mama's brooch, your daddy's watch. Those things have no price tag on them.

On our own, we are not worth very much. But to God, we are priceless because we are His. He holds us dear, and He won't let us go for anything.

A NEW LIFESTYLE

Peter has a closing word for us in 1 Peter 2:9, 11–12. Because we are brought into a new environment in worship and take on a new identity, we should live a new lifestyle when we go home. Peter says the purpose of all this is "that you may proclaim the excellencies of Him who has called you out of darkness into His marvelous light."

Several metaphors can serve to show how that new lifestyle is lived out in daily life.

"Advertising" God

Simply stated, God wants us to advertise Him. You know what an advertising agency does. It markets something, highlighting its strongest qualities. God says that we ought to show forth His qualities, His nature.

Why must we advertise Him? Because He is the invisible God. People can only see what God looks like by watching us. We're like the guys who used to walk up and down the sidewalk wearing those old sandwich signboards. We are supposed to be walking advertisements for Jesus.

Does your church advertise God well? If someone wanted to find out what God is like and what heaven is going to be like, he or she should be able to visit our churches and see.

Waging War

Look at verse 11 of our text, where Peter describes our new lifestyle as a warfare: "Beloved, I urge you as aliens and strangers to abstain from fleshly lusts, which wage war against the soul."

Why should you resist the flesh rather than yielding to it? Because every time you please your flesh, you hinder your spirit. If you satisfy the flesh, your flesh is going to feel good.

The bad news is that your spirit is going to feel bad. Your flesh can make you feel good temporarily, but your flesh can't take you anywhere spiritually. You can't be pleasing the flesh and following Christ as His obedient disciple.

You can't be pleasing the flesh, for example, and still say you want God to answer your prayers. You can't be pleasing the flesh and still say you want God to intervene in your circumstances. If you are pleasing the flesh, you are actually fighting against what God wants for you.

Going Public

Instead of indulging our fleshly lusts, we need to go public with our acts of faith:

> Keep your behavior excellent among the Gentiles, so that in the thing in which they slander you as evildoers, they may on account of your good deeds, as they observe them, glorify God in the day of visitation. (1 Peter 2:12)

I like that. Peter says to go public. Stop being a "secret agent" Christian. This is not strutting or showing off. This is practicing authentic Christianity in a way that no one can argue with.

Why shouldn't we go public for Christ? Every other group has gone public for their cause. Since every other cause has "come out," God's people need to come out too and display Christ to a watching world. Let people see your good deeds and your Christlike spirit.

The best way to show that Christianity is real is to be a real Christian. It's time to be like Paul, who was "not ashamed of the gospel" (Romans 1:16). This is what happens when we worship corporately as the body of Christ. We enter a new environment and we receive a new identity, that we might live a new lifestyle.

CHAPTER SEVEN

THE COMPENSATION OF WORSHIP

Is there a payoff for those who follow Christ in worship? That's the question I want to consider with you as we close this section on the first of four essentials in following Christ. What will be different in your life if you begin making worship a way of life instead of a two-hour extravaganza on Sunday morning? What benefits can you expect from becoming the kind of worshiper Jesus says the Father is seeking (John 4:23)?

I want to show you at least six benefits, six "paychecks," if you will, that you will enjoy if you develop a lifestyle of worship. Whether we are talking about individual worship, family worship, or the corporate worship of the church, there is incredible compensation awaiting worshipers who are authentic disciples of Christ. Of course, authentic worshipers do not approach God asking the question, "What do I get out of this?" Worship is for God's glory, not ours, and God deserves our worship whether or not we get anything out of it for ourselves. But God has determined to bless those who worship Him in spirit and in truth.

INTIMACY WITH GOD

The first thing worship will do for you is bring you

into intimate contact with God. The psalmist writes, "Thou art holy, O Thou who art enthroned upon the praises of Israel" (Psalm 22:3).

Some versions say that God "inhabits" the praises of His people. No matter how you translate the concept, if you want to get God's attention, worship. If you want to hear from heaven, worship. If you want to get God involved with your life, worship.

Carrying Your Altar

The Old Testament saints understood this. They understood it so well, in fact, that they carried their altars around with them! The Bible records that Noah, Abraham, Jacob, and Moses all built altars and worshiped God at critical times in their lives.

Moses, for example, built an altar in the middle of the wilderness after the defeat of Amalek (Exodus 17:15). It didn't matter whether it was the Sabbath or not. The tabernacle for formal worship hadn't even been built yet. The only thing that mattered was that God moved, and Moses worshiped.

We saw in the previous chapter that the church is the primary context for worship. But, as we said, this does not negate personal worship at all. If you have a mess on Monday, you can't just say, "Boy, I can't wait until Sunday to bring this to the altar!"

It's a long time from Monday to Sunday. You had better carry your altar with you, because the Lord inhabits the praises of His people.

See, whenever worship takes place, God shows up. That's why worship is critical not only for us as individuals, but as families. If you are the head of your household, you ought to be gathering your family together for worship. Take time to sing and read the Scripture and pray about the things that are on your hearts.

That's what my dad used to do when he did not have enough work and we did not know where our next meal was coming from. He would call the family around the "family altar" and say, "Let's worship." I didn't know where those beans came from, but they showed up on the table!

Now I know it's because God inhabits the praises of His people. When we worship, He enthrones Himself right in the midst of our praise and adoration. Wherever true worship takes place, God comes.

Worship brings the God who seems to be "way out there" in close to you. It closes the perceived distance between you and God. If God seems a long way off, one reason could be that you are not worshiping. Long intervals between our times of worship lead to a long-distance relationship with God.

Drawing Near

In Hebrews 10:19–22, the writer makes this invitation:

> Since therefore, brethren, we have confidence to enter the holy place by the blood of Jesus, by a new and living way which He inaugurated for us through the veil, that is, His flesh, and since we have a great priest over the house of God, let us draw near with a sincere heart in full assurance of faith, having our hearts sprinkled clean from an evil conscience and our bodies washed with pure water.

He is saying, "Come close to God. Because of the blood of Christ, you have no reason to be far from God anymore."

This is really God's invitation to us to enter His presence in worship. You say, "What will I find when I get there?" The writer of Hebrews answers that for us:

> Since then we have a great high priest who has passed through the heavens, Jesus the Son of God, let us hold fast our confession. For we do not have a high priest who cannot sympathize with our weaknesses, but one who has been tempted in all things as we are, yet without sin. Let us therefore draw near with confidence to the throne of grace, that we may receive mercy and may find grace to help in time of need. (4:14–16)

You say, "I've got a mess. I have a need. Things are falling apart." Draw near to God in worship and you'll find a sympathetic High Priest waiting to meet you.

There's a big difference between drawing near to Jesus and drawing near to anyone else. As a pastor, I seek to understand and sympathize with my people when they are hurting. I can set up an appointment and invite them into my office, or I can pick up the telephone and say, "I understand."

But sometimes, that's the only thing I can say. When the doctor says there's no cure for the illness, I can sympathize with the person, but I can't fix the problem. I can't supply "grace to help in time of need." That believer needs to draw near to Someone who can supply all the mercy and grace needed.

See, the trouble with only drawing near to other people is that they have weaknesses and problems too. But the thing I love about our awesome God is that we can all draw near to Him simultaneously, and He does not miss a beat with any of us.

This does not mean every problem will disappear and every illness will be healed when we worship. God never promised that. What He does promise is all the mercy and grace we need.

But let me warn you about something. When you draw near to God, you are coming to "the Holy One." You are drawing near to Someone who has an entirely different standard.

Drawing near to God is like putting yourself under an X-ray machine. He is going to look behind the external and penetrate the soul. You are drawing near to Someone who is going to expose and deal with your sin.

That's why in worship we need to pray, "God, search me and show me what I really am." Until God does that, He can't help us with our need because He is the Holy One. Your doctor isn't interested in relieving your symptoms without treating the cause of your problem.

God's cure is simple. "If we walk in the light as He Himself is in the light . . . the blood of Jesus His Son cleanses us from all sin" (1 John 1:7). As we draw near to God, He is going to show us the real deal.

You know what it's like to walk into a dark kitchen at night and suddenly flip on the light. The light is going to reveal whatever is there, whether it's a clean, picture-perfect location or a room that has tall stacks of dirty dishes, scurrying roaches, and an overflowing trash can. If you want to draw near to God, you have to come clean with Him.

The reason many of us don't hear from God when we come to worship is that we fail to come with a "sincere heart" (Hebrews 10:22). We don't come clean. We try to hide our sin as though God can't see it. We try to cover it up, just in case He blinked when we did it.

But we must understand that drawing near means coming to God on His terms and His turf. That's why those Old Testament saints often prostrated themselves in worship. They knew who they were dealing with. They felt the pain of their sins. They understood that they were drawing near to a holy God, in whose blazing light we see ourselves as we really are.

You can't come to God and say "I'm OK" if you are not OK. The reason some of us say the same prayers all the time is that we don't want to tell the truth. If we told the truth, we would be on our knees all day.

But when you are ready to come clean before God, when you come to Him with a sincere heart, His word to you is, "Come up close, child. Snuggle up to Me and worship."

A RESTORED FAITH

I know there are believers who have thought about throwing in the spiritual towel. They've considered quitting, backing up, going the other way.

Why? They go to work every day and it looks as if the sinners get the promotions. They try to serve God and it seems like they are going nowhere. They try to do right, but it's the folk doing wrong who are getting ahead.

Things like this sometimes tempt God's people to think, *Is the Christian life worth it? What good is doing right when doing wrong gets you ahead?*

Envying the Wicked

If you've ever been tempted to think that way, you

need to do what the writer of Psalm 73 did. You need to go to the house of God, because worship reminds you that what you see is not all there is. A second benefit of worship is that it restores your faith.

In Psalm 73 we meet a believer who was wondering if serving God was worth it. He knew how things were supposed to work: "Surely God is good to Israel, to those who are pure in heart!" (v. 1). But it wasn't working for him. He was standing on a spiritual banana peel (v. 2), ready to slip at any minute.

What made the psalmist consider throwing in the towel when it came to being righteous? He got his eyes off God and onto the wicked. He became envious of "the prosperity of the wicked" (v. 3). He saw their bank accounts and their cars and their houses. It seemed to him that they had no pains, their bodies were sleek, and they did not have trouble like other people.

As bad as that was, what really bothered the psalmist was that these wicked people were proud of their evil ways. They wore their pride like a necklace (v. 6). They decorated themselves with arrogance. They thumbed their noses at God.

So the psalmist concluded, "I'm wasting my time keeping my heart pure. All it's got me is trouble" (vv. 13–14, author's paraphrase). This didn't sound right to him, so he knew he had to get another perspective. And he knew where to get it.

That's why I love the end of verse 16 and verse 17: "It was troublesome in my sight until I came into the sanctuary of God; then I perceived their end." In other words, he went to worship. Then everything changed. He saw something he hadn't seen before—the end of the story.

What worship did for the psalmist was show him that it's the wicked, not the righteous, who are standing on the banana peel (v. 18). He saw that he didn't have to worry about slipping because God was holding him by the hand (v. 23). Then he confessed that God was all he needed (vv. 25–28). His faith was restored.

A New Perspective

In worship, God lets you see things you would not normally see. Have you ever come to worship down on life or confused about what you ought to do, only to have God show you the answer through something you see or hear or read? When that happens, you leave worship saying, "I'm ready to go on."

What happened? You entered into a new environment. You saw a different program. Worship changes your perspective. That's what happened with the three "Hebrew boys," Shadrach, Meshach, and Abednego, in Babylon (Daniel 3).

The story is familiar. King Nebuchadnezzar ordered everyone to worship his golden image. But the complaint came back to him: "These three Hebrews won't worship it" (see v. 12). They had decided they were going to worship the God of Israel only, so they were ready to handle the fire of a hot furnace (v. 21).

You may be going through the fire on your job. You've talked to your supervisor. You've been to your supervisor's supervisor. If you could, you would go to the president of the company.

But have you gone to the God of the universe? Have you worshiped? Because these Hebrew boys insisted on worshiping God, when "Nebby" put them in the fire, a fourth Person showed up who looked like the Son of God (v. 25).

See, God did not deliver them from the fire. But He joined them in the fire, and they didn't burn. I don't know what you are going through now or will go through tomorrow. But if you will worship, even if God lets you go into the fire, He will show up with fireproofing!

In worship, God has a way of restoring your faith. David testified, "He restores my soul" (Psalm 23:3). Worship gives you a pick-up. But we turn to everything else to give us a lift. Some may even have a bottle of pills in one hand and a bottle of alcohol in the other. These things alter your perspective, no doubt about that. But they give you a distortion, an illusion, not a new perspective. Worship restores your faith.

Worship and God's Provision

Genesis 22 shows us just how crucial worship is to our faith. God told Abraham to do the hardest thing any human being has ever been told to do: "Take your only son, Isaac, and offer him to Me as a burnt offering" (see v. 2).

Do you realize what God was telling Abraham? He was saying, "Abraham, I want you to worship Me. I know this is hard, but I want you to build an altar and hold a worship service to Me." Abraham understood what God wanted. He told his servants, "I and the lad will go yonder; and we will worship and return to you" (v. 5).

What Abraham did not say, but what he meant, was, "I don't know what is going to happen up there. I don't know how God is going to pull this off. All I know is that I am going to worship Him, and when we are finished Isaac and I will return" (see Hebrews 11:17–19).

Remember we said that the patriarchs built altars whenever they wanted to worship God. That's exactly what Abraham did here (Genesis 22:9). He was prepared to follow God's command to kill Isaac because he knew how to worship! Abraham's ability to worship God changed his whole perspective.

As Abraham raised the knife over Isaac, the "angel of the Lord called to him from heaven." What was the verdict? "Now I know that you fear God." Then Abraham saw the ram caught in the thicket (vv. 11–13).

Worship will lead you to God's ram in the thicket. Worship will lead you to where God wants you to be. No matter what you are looking for—a mate, a new job, a new perspective, a ram caught in the thicket—you don't go looking for it to the exclusion of your worship or your relationship with God.

You say, "Excuse me?" That's right. You don't go husband- or wife-looking. You go "worship-looking." Can you imagine Abraham beating the bushes on Mount Moriah, trying to scare up a mountain goat or a ram for a sacrifice so he wouldn't have to offer Isaac?

If Abraham had done that, you wouldn't be reading about him in Genesis 22—or in Hebrews 11. God had the ram tied up. That animal wasn't going anywhere.

This is so relevant to where we live. For instance, one of the great problems in our society is the shortage of godly men to marry our godly young women. But if singles start getting frustrated and desperate for a mate, they could make a big mistake.

I told the single women in our church that if God has a husband for them, that guy is caught in a thicket. He's not going anywhere. If our commitment is to worship God, He can show us where the thicket is. That's no problem for Him.

Worship restores your faith. It enables you to hang in there when you want to throw in the towel. If you feel like quitting, worship God.

DEFEATED ENEMIES

A third benefit or compensation of worship is that it takes care of your enemies.

Do have any enemies? Anybody who tries to pull you down or is out to hurt you? The best way to deal with your enemies is to worship. There's a great example in 2 Chronicles 20:1–30.

Word came to King Jehoshaphat of Judah that "the sons of Moab and the sons of Ammon" were getting ready to attack him (v. 1). Jehoshaphat was afraid, but notice what he did. He called an all-Judah fast and worship service (vv. 3–4).

When the people had all come together to seek the Lord, Jehoshaphat offered a powerful prayer (vv. 5–12). God answered through a man named Jahaziel, assuring the king that he would be victorious without firing one arrow (vv. 14–17).

Jehoshaphat heard that, and he and all the people went down on their faces before the Lord in worship, while the Levites stood up to sing praises to God (vv. 18–19). Do you see what was happening here? Jehoshaphat and the people of God won this battle on their faces before Him in worship.

It was only after they went down low in worship that they were ready to get up early the next morning and face the enemy. Actually, the next morning was just a continuation of the worship, because Jehoshaphat put the singers out in front of the army (vv. 20–21).

While the people were having a great time singing and praising the Lord, He took care of Moab and Ammon. God caused them to turn on each other and destroy each other. All Judah could find on the battle-field was corpses (vv. 22–24).

And how did Jehoshaphat and the people of Judah react? They carried their spoil back to Jerusalem and headed straight for the "house of the Lord" to worship (v. 28)!

You say you have done everything you can to fix the problem of your enemies? Maybe if you worship, God will make your enemies your footstool. Maybe you need to believe God when He says, "Vengeance is Mine, I will repay" (Romans 12:19). Maybe the issue is getting God to fight your battles for you rather than you fighting your battles yourself.

Jehoshaphat saw an army destroyed while he was on his face before God. Joshua brought down the walls of Jericho by marching around them. Because they worshiped, neither leader suffered a casualty. Worship saves lives. Worship saves time. Worship collapses your Jericho.

The Bible says that Jesus Christ "appeared for this purpose, that He might destroy the works of the devil" (1 John 3:8). When your spiritual adversary shows up, if you will turn to Christ in worship and get Him on the case, you might see more things finished more quickly.

This aspect of worship is very meaningful to the African-American community. We witnessed this way of dealing with our enemies in the march to Selma, on the steps of the statehouse in Montgomery, Alabama, and in cities all across the Deep South.

When the authorities came, perpetrating a system of ungodliness, the marchers went to their knees. They sang and prayed, and the federal government sent troops to protect the freedom marchers. Every time they came up against a dog, a billy club, or a hate-filled person, they got down on their knees and prayed. They worshiped.

Then the Black Panthers came, not with prayer and hymns, but with bullets. That did not change any laws. The federal government did not send troops to protect that. A Panther's bullet isn't the reason African-Americans are not riding at the back of the bus. It's because marchers got on their knees and worshiped. The reason I can eat anywhere is that men got on their knees and worshiped. Worship changed the laws of the land.

The Bible says, "The king's heart is like channels of water in the hand of the Lord; He turns it wherever He wishes" (Proverbs 21:1). God turned the hearts of our leaders in Washington, D.C., in the 1960s. He told them to do something about the injustice. God spoke because people worshiped. Worship changed the temperature of American culture.

If God can do that for a nation, He can do it for you. He can help you on your job and in your circumstances if you will just worship. Worship takes care of your adversaries.

CONTENTMENT IN LIFE

Here's a fourth benefit of worship. The psalmist put it this way: "In Thy presence is fulness of joy; in Thy right hand there are pleasures forever" (Psalm 16:11).

This is where a lot of Christians struggle. Their problem has little or nothing to do with the person working next to them or the people next door. It has to do with them. Something is wrong inside. As a result of that, many believers are in bad situations they have concocted themselves.

They're like the man who came to work one day with a bologna sandwich. He sat down at lunch, bit into the sandwich, and threw it down in disgust. "I hate bologna!"

His coworker said, "The wife make a bad sandwich for you today?"

"No," the man said, "I made the sandwich myself."

A lot of us are like that. We're eating bologna sandwiches, even though we're sick of bologna. The problem is we keep making ourselves bologna sandwiches.

The beautiful thing about worship is that in worship, God can intervene in your mess and turn it around. He can take the bologna in your life and turn it into a filet mignon. He can take the chaos of your life and bring contentment and peace.

Job is the great example of the contentment that worship can bring. Here was a man whose life fell apart. Amid the loss of his children and his property, "Job arose and tore his robe and shaved his head, and he fell to the ground and worshiped" (Job 1:20). He confessed that everything he had was from God, so God had the right to take it away. "Blessed be the name of the Lord" was his conclusion (v. 21).

You may say, "That's not the kind of contentment I want! That's not the path I want to take to inner peace." I'm not saying Job had no distress. I'm saying that he knew where to turn when everything came apart, and the Lord sustained him.

But if Job had not had the inner peace of a worshiper, he wouldn't have survived his ordeal. Even his wife advised him to curse God and get the mess over with (2:9).

If you know the contentment that only comes from a lifestyle of worship, when you find a pink slip on your desk, you can go on. When the company downsizes, you can get down on your knees and say, "Lord, You gave me this job. The only way I can lose it is if You allow it. I want to thank You that You give jobs, and You take away jobs. Since You give and You take away, I give myself to You. Show me where my next employment is to be."

That's what you do when you worship. You take it to God. Worship gives you contentment and peace in the time of trouble. In a hurricane, while there are heavy winds all around, there is always one peaceful spot, and that is in the eye. When Jesus Christ is the eye of your storm, you can have peace in the midst of the trouble.

That was the difference between Martha and Mary

(Luke 10:38–42). Martha had no peace because she was so busy in the kitchen. She was fussing and fuming and talking about "What goes around, comes around."

But Luke says Mary just sat at Jesus' feet, worshiping Him. Mary was "chillin'." Cooling it, not going through any trauma. And what happened? Jesus said Mary made the right decision. When chaos set in, she knew where to hang out.

If we would take some of the time we spend on the phone telling everybody else what's wrong and tell it to Jesus, we would be a lot farther down the road. When we learn to worship, we find the waters begin to calm.

Worship may not alleviate the storm, but it can change you in the midst of it. That's why Hebrews 12:2 advises us to keep our eyes on Jesus.

SALVATION OF OTHERS

A fifth compensation of worship is one you may not have realized. Worship brings people to Christ.

Remember Acts 2:46–47, one of our foundational texts for this book? We read that as the believers practiced the essentials of following Christ every day, including worship, people were getting saved every day. The more worship you do, the more people you see saved.

For example, I'm convinced some people are believers today because they had mothers who never stopped worshiping. When they went off to college and started to turn from the way of the Lord, their mothers kept on praying, "Lord, bring my lost child home."

Those people are Christians today not because they went looking for God, but because God heard their mamas' prayers and went looking for them. Worship can bring people to Christ and bring wayward people back home.

I wonder how many Christians who are thinking about leaving their mates have worshiped regarding their mates? Someone may say, "Worship?! I just want to get out of this marriage. God doesn't want me to be this miserable."

If a person hasn't worshiped regarding his or her

mate, there is no basis for hope. But when a husband or wife falls on his or her knees and says, "Lord, I just come to worship You. My marriage is so messed up, only You can fix it. Come and bring Yourself glory through my marriage," then God can move. Worship can bring back a mate who has gone astray.

TRANSFORMED LIVES

A sixth and final payoff for worship is the transformation it brings. In 2 Corinthians 3:18, Paul says, "We all, with unveiled face beholding as in a mirror the glory of the Lord, are being transformed into the same image from glory to glory, just as from the Lord, the Spirit."

Paul is referring to Moses, who put a veil over his face after being on Mount Sinai to receive the Law (2 Corinthians 3:7, 13). According to Exodus 34:29, when Moses went up into the presence of God, his face began to glow.

If you've ever been in Texas on a hot summer day, you know how easy it is to start perspiring. If it's hot enough, you don't have to do anything to get a "glow" on your face. All you have to do is be here. The sun will get you. Why? Because you are in the presence of an awesome power that transforms you.

Moses got his glow from worshiping God on the mountain. His glow began to fade, so he veiled his face. But our glow never needs to fade, because we reflect the image of God's glory in our inner person.

How does it happen? By the power of the Holy Spirit. When we worship God, the Spirit carries us into the presence of God, and the "Sonshine" affects us. It makes us glow. Most of us need plenty of things to be transformed in our lives. And we need to see other people around us transformed.

The best foundation for that transformation is worship. Sure, we need other things along with that. But if it is not built on the foundation of worship, we are building on quicksand. We have to worship. As we worship, we are transformed. When we worship, the Spirit of God starts changing things and transforming people—including us.

"THE WINNER IS . . ."

I love to watch the special awards shows on television. As you know, those are always popular shows, and I think I know why. It's because they are all about giving honor.

The master of ceremonies will read the nominations and open the envelope. Then comes the big moment: "And the winner is . . ." The name is read, and the winner jumps out of his or her seat to the thunderous applause of the crowd to receive the honor that's due. Thousands of people gather in the auditorium, and millions more watch, just to applaud the winners.

When you worship, you are saying, "God, I nominate You for honor. There is no other name in the envelope, because You alone are worthy. Nobody can do what You can do."

Who can do the things God can do? Who can take two cells and make a baby? Who can speak and bring a universe into existence? Who can keep everything in perfect balance? Only God. He is the Winner! Give Him the prize.

And when we worship, something amazing happens. God shares the prize with us! When we come to Him to give Him all the praise and glory due His name, He compensates us for our worship.

NECESSITY TWO

FELLOWSHIP

CHAPTER EIGHT

THE CONCEPT OF FELLOWSHIP

When we started our church in Dallas in 1976, I sat down one day to think about what we would call this new work. The term "Oak Cliff" seemed pretty obvious, since that is the area of Dallas where the church is located.

It was important to me to have *Bible* in the church's name, because it would signal to everyone that God's Word was to be the centerpiece of everything we did, the guideline to govern how we were going to function.

That part was easy. But when I got to that last word, I wrestled with it a little bit. My initial thought was simply to add the word *church* and call it the Oak Cliff Bible Church. But that didn't capture what I wanted to communicate. I wanted a term that would highlight what a church is supposed to be, and after a while the word *fellowship* won out.

Fellowship is very important for the people of God. It is the contention of this book that you cannot be a dynamic, growing disciple of Jesus Christ without practicing dynamic fellowship. It's one of the absolute necessities in following Christ as His disciples.

In this chapter, we are going to spend most of our time in the book of 1 John. But before we go there, I want to touch briefly on our foundational text for this book, Acts 2:42–47.

There we read that the early disciples "were continually devoting themselves . . . to fellowship, to the breaking of bread" (v. 42). Then verse 46 tells us they had daily fellowship, "breaking bread from house to house" and "taking their meals together with gladness and sincerity of heart."

Fellowship was critical to their functioning as the church, the disciples of Jesus Christ. Fellowship is critical for us too, so we are going to spend the next four chapters taking this concept apart, examining it closely, then putting it back together.

This is important because when a church stops being a fellowship, it becomes an organization. It may be known for its programs, its music, its preaching, or some unique feature, but it ceases to be known for the quality of its relationships. God designed the church to be not merely an organization, but an organism; a pulsating, breathing, dynamic, living fellowship.

THE PRINCIPLE OF FELLOWSHIP

Let me begin our study of fellowship with a definition of the term. The Greek word translated "fellowship" is *koinonia.* This is an interesting term. It means basically "that which is common." The language in which the New Testament is written is called *Koine* Greek because it was the common language of the day, the language people spoke on the streets.

Now something that is common is something shared. So the New Testament uses this term for commonness to refer to our sharing together, our communion or participation, in the body of Christ. To have fellowship is to have something in common, to enjoy a shared relationship.

If I were to attempt a formal definition of fellowship, it would be this: Fellowship is the intimate sharing of Christians in the uniqueness of the life of Christ. It is a shared relationship.

While you're thinking about that, let me consider a few misconceptions of this concept of fellowship. By far the most common is equating fellowship with a social activity. It seems that when it comes to the church, fellowship will forever be linked with "food and fun."

Christians often say to each other, "Why don't you come over to my house for some food and fellowship?" which, being interpreted, means, "Let's get together to watch the ball game or shoot the breeze, and we'll have something to eat."

There's nothing wrong with doing that, but it does not fit the biblical concept of fellowship.

For other people, fellowship is associated with a place. What does almost every church call the place where people gather for socials and meals? The fellowship hall.

It's possible that true fellowship will take place in the church's fellowship hall, but it's not guaranteed. Fellowship is more than a place where the saints gather for a good time. It takes more than an event and a menu to make fellowship happen.

Fellowship is a potent concept, and if it is reduced simply to a gathering or a place or a menu, it loses its potency. It is robbed of its real significance.

Fellowship and Joy

The first principle of fellowship I want us to see is found in the opening verses of 1 John 1, our main text for this portion of our study. The apostle John begins his letter by saying:

> What was from the beginning, what we have heard, what we have seen with our eyes, what we beheld and our hands handled, concerning the Word of Life—and the life was manifested, and we have seen and bear witness and proclaim to you the eternal life, which was with the Father and was manifested to us—what we have seen and heard we proclaim to you also, that you also may have fellowship with us; and indeed our fellowship is with the Father, and with His Son Jesus Christ. And these things we write, so that our joy may be made complete. (vv. 1–4)

John says there is a direct correlation between the depth of your fellowship and the extent of your joy as a Christian. The completeness of your joy is dependent on the richness of your fellowship.

To put it another way, if you aren't experiencing dynamic fellowship, something is missing in your Christian life. If you feel like a part-time saint with part-time joy, one of the missing ingredients in your life may be fellowship.

There are too many "Lone Ranger" Christians in the body of Christ today. You know people like this. They come to church with their masks on. When they leave, people are apt to say, "Who was that masked man?" "Who was that masked woman?" Nobody really knows, because they are isolated from other believers.

I'm not putting other Christians down, because I am affected by this tendency too. What we have done in our contemporary world is trade togetherness for "toys" we play with. We have substituted television for relationships. Too many of us as God's people find our greatest fulfillment not together, but apart. We're beaten up at work all day and come home tired, wanting someone or something to talk to us without demanding that we talk back. So we plop in front of the TV.

When we do that, we relinquish fellowship. Husbands don't talk to their wives, wives don't talk to their husbands, parents don't talk to their children, children don't talk to their parents. They all just pass each other with a nod, and fellowship, relationship, communion get lost. And when fellowship is lost, our joy gets siphoned off.

Union and Communion

Let me show you a second principle of fellowship, a vital correlation I believe John is making in 1 John 1:1–4. Notice that fellowship has two aspects to it, union and communion.

By union I mean a formal relationship with Christ. We are connected to God the Father through His Son, Jesus Christ, by virtue of our faith in Him. Salvation brings us into union with Christ, the way a marriage ceremony formally unites a man and a woman.

But in addition to our formal union with Christ, there is energetic partnering through communion. Communion enhances union by adding the element of intimacy, closeness, oneness. If you have union without communion, something will be missing, as many married couples can readily testify.

See, you can show up for a wedding and enter into a union that is legal and official. But that does not necessarily a communion make. Most people who get married aren't just excited about forming a union. They are anticipating the communion, the intimacy, of marriage.

This connectedness, the experiential sharing of two lives, should be the result of the formal union of marriage. When you have union tied to communion, you have fellowship.

If all you have is the union, that's all you can talk about. You can take a group of people who belong to the same church and say they have union because they are all identified with the same local body of believers.

But if they are not experiencing communion with Christ and with each other where life touches life, heart touches heart, and there is mutual care and concern, then the union won't be what it could be. The joy that should be part of being members of that local body won't be there as fully as it could be, with the result that their spiritual development is stunted.

Communion is what is lacking in so many marriages. And when communion is lacking, the union is empty. I'm not downplaying the union. You can't skip over the union and try to build communion, or you build on a faulty foundation. I get regular opportunities around the country to speak on racial issues. One of the problems we have is that people want racial communion without the foundation of the right union.

The reason we never seem to solve the racial problem in a significant way is that people are not operating on the same assumptions. They don't have the same foundation. They are starting from different points, so they arrive at different conclusions. Until we solve the union problem, we will never arrive at communion. And until we see union and communion as two essential elements in biblical fellowship, we'll continue to have racial tension, strained marriages, and shallow church relationships.

THE PROCESS OF FELLOWSHIP

There is a process to this matter of fellowship. It has both a vertical and a horizontal dimension. John speaks to both of these in 1 John 1:3 when he says, "What we have seen and heard we proclaim to you also, that you also may have fellowship with us; and indeed our fellowship is with the Father, and with His Son Jesus Christ."

I want to deal with the second of these elements first, the vertical dimension of fellowship. John is saying, "If you want to have fellowship with me and the other apostles, then you have to have fellowship with God, because that's who we are in fellowship with."

Fellowship Begins with Christ

So dynamic fellowship with other believers starts with our dynamic fellowship with Christ. This must be the foundation, the thing that determines the legitimacy of fellowship.

People often get together on purely human or cultural terms. They may be of the same color or ethnic group, they may like the same things, they may live in the same neighborhood. That is fine for the world, but when it comes to the church of Jesus Christ, He is the starting point of our fellowship.

When people who name the name of Christ make their decisions based on race or culture or some other criterion, then fellowship is broken. Our fellowship as Christians has to start with our commonality in Jesus Christ.

Then, if you are committed to Christ and I am committed to Christ, let's hang out with each other. Our commitment to Christ becomes the starting point for this principle of fellowship (see 1 Corinthians 1:9). Trying to build fellowship on any other basis is starting in the wrong place.

That's why the Bible tells a Christian not to marry a non-Christian or enter into any close relationship that binds a believer and unbeliever together (2 Corinthians 6:14). Light and darkness have nothing in common. There is no fellowship between them. Fellowship must begin with Jesus Christ.

A gathering that leaves out Jesus Christ is not true Christian fellowship. It's just a social gathering. Again, there is nothing wrong with that. Just call it what it is: a party, a basketball get-together, a food-and-football bash, a luncheon.

But in order for something to qualify as Christian fellowship, Jesus Christ has to show up. If Jesus never comes up in the conversation, if reference is never made either directly or indirectly to Him being the standard that brought you together, then what you have is not biblical *koinonia*. You have a get-together.

I'm hitting this one hard because it is foundational. First and foremost, you and I have been called into fellowship with Jesus Christ. Peter writes, "For by these He has granted to us His precious and magnificent promises, in order that by them you might become partakers of the divine nature, having escaped the corruption that is in the world by lust" (2 Peter 1:4).

The word *partakers* is from the same root as *koinonia*. Peter is saying we have become "fellowshipers" in the life of Christ through the salvation He has granted us.

Fellowship Flows to Others

When saints are communing with Jesus Christ, the dynamic of this fellowship will automatically overflow into their relationships with other believers. Our horizontal fellowship is simply an overflow of our vertical fellowship.

This means that if your relationship with God does not overflow into caring about God's people, you are not as close to God as you thought you were. If your union with God has not produced a communion with God that overflows to the benefit of other believers, you are not as spiritual as you thought you were.

If a believer comes to church week after week and takes in the Word of God, yet nobody else ever benefits from what God is doing in his life, he is a carnal, out-of-fellowship saint.

How do I know that? Look at 1 John 4:20: "If someone says, 'I love God,' and hates his brother, he is a liar; for the one who does not love his brother whom he has seen, cannot love God whom he has not seen."

If there is a breakdown in your fellowship with Christ, there will be a breakdown in the dynamic of your fellowship with others. If you stop communing with Christ vertically, there will be a loss of fellowship with others horizontally.

Here's how this works. The believer for whom Jesus Christ is no longer everything will get ticked off at other Christians for whom Jesus is everything.

This is when you start hearing people say things like, "He's a fanatic," "She's carrying this spiritual thing too far," or "Sure, I go to church, but you don't have to go off the deep end to be a Christian."

Why does this happen? One Christian is in intimate communion with God, and the other is satisfied with union. What you have is a drifting apart on the horizontal level because there has been a drifting on the vertical level.

Don't let a carnal Christian spoil your fellowship with Jesus Christ. Don't let people who don't want to commune with Christ control you. When they are gone, you're still going to need Jesus in the vicinity.

The great saints of God throughout the Scriptures found that fellowship with Him was essential. In Isaiah 26:9, the prophet cried out, "My soul longs for Thee, indeed, my spirit within me seeks Thee diligently."

The psalmist wrote in Psalm 5:3, "In the morning, O Lord, Thou wilt hear my voice." In Psalm 25:5, David says, "For Thee I wait all the day." And in Psalm 63:6, he confesses, "I meditate on Thee in the night watches." He could not get God off his mind.

These believers understood the power of communion with God. Even Jesus knew the importance of communing with His Father (Mark 1:35). He was God in the flesh, but He knew He needed intimate fellowship with the Father in order to function properly in His humanity.

Too many of us are trying to live successful Christian lives based on union without any development of communion. That's like trying to have a happy marriage without any development or growth after the wedding day.

If the only way you relate to God is based on what happened to you the day you accepted Him as your Savior, if you're counting on that day to keep you close to heaven, you are a defeated saint. Fellowship demands ongoing communion.

When we husbands stop loving our wives as we ought to, something's wrong with our relationship with God. Wives, when you stop relating to your husbands as you ought to, something's wrong with your relationship with God. Yes, there may be something wrong with the other person. But I'm talking about the deeper issue of your communion with God.

When you are right with God, He works things out in your life so that your joy is full despite your circumstances. One reason people so often give up and become defeated in their Christian lives is that they have no reserve of joy to fall back on in times of trial.

These are the believers who derive all of their joy from their circumstances. When circumstances take a turn for the worse, they collapse, because without a dynamic fellowship with God they don't have any spiritual reserves to draw on.

THE IMPEDIMENT TO FELLOWSHIP

According to the apostle John, there is something that breaks our fellowship with God and with others. Let's go back to 1 John 1 and see what it is:

This is the message we have heard from Him and announce to you, that God is light, and in Him there is no darkness at all. If we say that we have fellowship with Him and yet walk in the darkness, we lie and do not practice the truth. (vv. 5–6)

Sin breaks fellowship with God. And you can bank on the fact that if sin breaks fellowship with God, it will break fellowship with others. The way for a believer to avoid sin is to walk in the light of God. God's light gives us the standard by which we can settle conflicts and maintain or restore fellowship with one another.

Light and Darkness

See, if you and I are having an argument, we need somebody to shine light on the situation. You have your view, I have my view. But when God's light is allowed to shine on the issue, what is right and what is wrong become evident.

God's light is His revealed, infallible Word. That's why, as I told you at the beginning of the chapter, I wanted our church's name to include Bible. It was a statement that everything we did would be governed by the Word of God.

Since there is no darkness at all in God (v. 5), we cannot walk in the darkness and have intimate fellowship with Him. And when we are in the darkness, we can't walk in close fellowship with other Christians because we can't see clearly in the dark.

There can be no fellowship when God's light is not allowed to shine on the situation. If we persist in following sin into the darkness, we lose the light of God. And when we lose the light of God, we lose the benefit of communion with Him. We begin to commune with the darkness of sin.

First Corinthians 10 puts this contrast very graphically. Paul asks, "Is not the cup of blessing which we bless a sharing in the blood of Christ? Is not the bread which we break a sharing in the body of Christ?" (v. 16). He's talking about communion, the table of the Lord.

Then he says in verse 21, "You cannot drink the cup of the Lord and the cup of demons; you cannot partake of the table of the Lord and the table of demons."

Paul is saying you can't have it both ways. We would say in our world, "You can't have your cake and eat it too." You cannot seek to have fellowship with God and have fellowship with the devil. You cannot be a disciple of Jesus Christ and be a part-time saint. You cannot be following Jesus and walking in the darkness.

Too Many Counterfeits

This is a problem we have in the church today: too many part-time Christians. We have too many SMOs — "Sunday morning only" Christians—who want to play the religious game. But it's a counterfeit Christianity.

You can go a long way with a counterfeit bill, especially if it's well made. You can buy groceries with a counterfeit bill. You can buy gas with it. You can eat with it and do a lot of other things.

But when that counterfeit bill hits the bank, its true nature is going to be exposed. It will be utterly worthless. We have a lot of Christians like that, people who have nothing to offer anyone else in the way of authentic fellowship because they are not dealing in truth. John says, "Come to the light of God and let's deal in truth, so we can have fellowship with God and with each other."

Genuine Fellowship

If a church is going to be a great church, biblically speaking, it will not be primarily because of the people on the platform on Sunday morning. It will be because of the relationships formed in the pew and continued on Monday morning. It will be because there is a group of people who care for one another and love one another based on their commonality in Christ.

We recently had a living illustration of genuine, biblical fellowship in our church in Dallas. The wife of a dear couple in our church became gravely ill when a blood vessel burst in her head.

We called the whole congregation to prayer on their behalf as this sister hung on a slender thread between life and death. I had prayer with her husband. Some of our members went over to offer help. One family took this couple's two children into their home during the time the wife was in the hospital so the husband could give his full attention to her.

The body rallied around this family. Needs were met as the family of God ministered in the name of Jesus Christ. God mercifully answered prayer, and this sister recovered.

That's fellowship in action. A sermon alone can't do that. A choir alone can't do that. When life collapses, you need the *koinonia* of the body of Christ. You need the ministry of those who are following Christ as His obedient disciples.

Romans 12:15 says, "Rejoice with those who rejoice, and weep with those who weep." In other words, don't let any saint laugh alone or cry alone. Make sure the family of God is there, good times or bad.

Why is it important that you practice biblical *koinonia?* Because God's Word tells us to do so (Galatians 6:2). But there's another reason. One day, you're going to cry. No matter how together your life may be right now, there is coming a day when you will cry—and you won't want to cry alone. You will need the fellowship of the body.

The question is, are you too busy in your own world to become part of the *koinonia?* If so, you are too busy to become Jesus Christ's disciple.

THE PRODUCT OF FELLOWSHIP

When a church is marked by true fellowship, what does it produce? Look back at our foundational text in Acts 2:

> And all those who had believed were together, and had all things in common; and they began selling their property and possessions, and were sharing them with all, as anyone might have need. (vv. 44–45)

Notice the words *together* and *common.* The believers took their commonality seriously. The scene is similar in Acts 4:

And the congregation of those who believed were of one heart and soul; and not one of them claimed that anything belonging to him was his own; but all things were common property to them. . . . For there was not a needy person among them, for all who were owners of land or houses would sell them and bring the proceeds of the sales, and lay them at the apostles' feet. (vv. 32, 34–35a)

Needs Are Met

Their fellowship met the needs of the body. There were no welfare programs or government grants in Jerusalem, just the *koinonia* of the church. When any Christian had a need, it was covered by the family of God because they were sharing.

Unity Is Developed

Another product of fellowship is unity in the body. When the body is at work, when every member sees that he or she is part of something bigger, when the saints understand that the church is a gathering of believers who are knitted together, something dynamic happens.

According to Ephesians 4:12–13, the saints are equipped to do the work of the ministry for "the building up of the body of Christ; until we all attain to the unity of the faith." That is, we are all going in the same direction, believing the same thing about the essentials of the faith.

The result of this unity is maturity, according to Paul. Instead of being tossed around like children (v. 14), we will "grow up in all aspects into Him, who is the head, even Christ" (v. 15).

This takes the operation of the "whole body" (v. 16). Every joint, every ligament, every blood vessel in the body is important.

We all have valves in our hearts. All those valves do all day long is open and close. They may be small, but let those little brothers close and stay closed, and it's all over. They regulate the flow of blood to the heart, and they're absolutely critical. That brother in the pew you don't get along with may very well be a heart valve in the body of Christ!

TIME FOR *KOINONIA*

If you want to be a disciple of Jesus Christ, you have to understand the importance of biblical fellowship. If you are part of the body of Christ and a member of a local church, yet no one else is better off because you are there, you don't understand what the life of Christ in you is meant to do.

The life of Christ is meant to work in you so that His power and blessing might flow through you to others. Too many of us are "cul-de-sac" Christians. We want to take it all in, but there is no outlet.

God wants us to be mature disciples, but that won't happen without meaningful fellowship. This means you must do two things. You must carve out time to be with God and you need to carve out time to be with others.

Don't look for a convenient time in your schedule to practice fellowship, because you will never find it. Like the other necessities we are talking about, fellowship has to be a priority. You and I can't be too busy to be close to Christ and close to each other and still call ourselves His disciples.

CHAPTER NINE

THE CONTENT OF FELLOWSHIP

W e are learning what it takes to follow Christ, to be His disciple. We have seen that a follower of Christ must be a worshiper. In the last two sections of the book, we will see that a disciple is also a learner and a witness. But for now, we need to understand that discipleship involves *koinonia,* authentic fellowship.

If your church is anything like the typical church, it contains people who believe that if they arrive on Sunday morning in time to hear the sermon, they have met their weekly Christian requirement. They showed up, the preacher showed up, God showed up—and everyone went home happy.

People who practice this kind of Christianity fail to understand the nature of the church and the nature of the faith they profess. Being a disciple means far more than listening to sermons or attending Bible studies, just taking in the truth.

The problem with this is that proclamation without fellowship leads to dead orthodoxy. It is truth with no life. On the other hand, fellowship without the proclamation of the truth leads to empty sentimentalism. This is "touchy-feely" religion with nothing to touch or feel.

Some people say, "Our church preaches the Word."

Other people say, "Well, our church loves people." If a church can't say it does both, it is a lopsided congregation. The fact is that when you became a part of God's family, you inherited a whole houseful of brothers and sisters. If you are married, you know exactly what I mean. You didn't just marry your spouse. You married his or her family and inherited a bunch of in-laws, including the good, the bad, and the ugly. They came with the deal.

When you became a member of the household of faith, you inherited some siblings. And by now you know that there are some people in the body of Christ who can make life difficult. Indian leader Mohandas Gandhi is reported to have said he would have become a Christian if it were not for Christians.

Unfortunately, God's people can sometimes have that kind of effect on people. The answer to the problems and challenges of life in the body of Christ is not to refuse Christ, of course. God's answer is *koinonia*—biblically based, authentic fellowship.

This fellowship has a definite content to it, which I want to examine under four key ideas that I believe sum up what our fellowship ought to consist of. These ideas are captured in the phrase "one another," which is used repeatedly throughout the New Testament to express the relational aspect of discipleship.

If you have ever studied the "one another's" of Scripture, you know that there are several dozen of them. I want to list the major ones here and then isolate four of these exhortations that are critical to the concept of fellowship and that embody the rest (the four are in bold here):

John 13:14—Wash one another's feet
John 13:34–35—Love one another
Romans 12:16; 1 Thessalonians 5:13; 1 Peter 3:8—Live
    in peace with one another
Romans 12:10b; Philippians 2:3—Honor one another
Romans 14:13—Stop judging one another
Romans 15:7—Accept one another

Romans 15:14; Colossians 3:16—Teach and admonish
one another

Romans 16:16; 1 Corinthians 16:20; 2 Corinthians
13:12; 1 Peter 5:14—Greet one another with a
holy kiss

1 Corinthians 1:10 (NIV)—Agree with one another

**1 Corinthians 9:19; 2 Corinthians 4:5; Galatians 5:13
—Serve one another**

1 Corinthians 12:25—Have equal concern for one
another

Galatians 5:26—Do not be conceited, provoking and
envying one another

Galatians 6:1—Restore one another

Ephesians 4:2; Colossians 3:13—Bear with one
another

Ephesians 4:32; 1 Thessalonians 5:15—Be kind to one
another

Ephesians 5:19–20—Sing to one another

Ephesians 5:21—Submit to one another

Colossians 3:9—Do not lie to one another

**1 Thessalonians 4:18; 5:11—Comfort and encourage
one another**

Hebrews 10:24—Spur one another to good deeds

James 4:11—Do not slander one another

James 5:9—Do not grumble at one another

James 5:16—Confess your sins to one another

1 Peter 4:9—Offer hospitality to one another

1 Peter 5:5—Clothe yourselves with humility toward
one another

1 John 1:5–7 Fellowship with one another

What I want you to see is that fellowship is not a small thing in God's mind. It is not an afterthought, an addendum to the real stuff, a toss-in to make us feel better. *Koinonia* is one of the four absolute necessities in following Christ. So let's examine the content of fellowship.

LOVE ONE ANOTHER

The first "one another" I want to talk about is Jesus' command in John 13:34–35:

A new commandment I give to you, that you love one
another, even as I have loved you, that you also love
one another. By this all men will know that you are My
disciples, if you have love one for one another.

Paul said in 1 Corinthians 13:1–3 that no matter what
you do in the way of Christian service or sacrifice, even
giving your life, if you don't have love everything else is a
waste of time. You can do any number of things for God,
but if love is not your motivation, God doesn't appreciate
it. "Anything minus love," Paul says, "equals nothing."

The Heart of *Koinonia*

Today, love is sort of like the dollar. It has been devalued so much that it isn't worth its face value. We use
love to describe our feelings for everything from our
favorite food to our favorite sports team. Then there are
the people who say, "I just love everybody and everything."

Love has been so devalued and so misused that most
people don't even know what it is anymore. Love has lost
its significance because we have emptied it of its biblical
definition, which is not primarily emotion but an act of
the will by which we seek the highest good for others.

Love is at the heart of fellowship. Love is to fellowship what chicken is to chicken noodle soup. If you
remove it, what you have left is just flavored broth with a
few noodles but no substance.

Unfortunately, that's what happens in the lives of a
lot of Christians. They don't know how to practice loving
fellowship, so what they are left with is a bland broth
instead of meaty soup.

Truth in Action

I said above that biblical love is an act and decision
of the will. So let me give you three simple words that I
think capture the true meaning of love. Biblical love is
truth in action.

Biblical love requires a body of truth. If you love
what is wrong, then your love is illegitimate, no matter
how good you feel about it. If it's wrong, it's not love.

But even if you know what is right, yet do nothing about it, that's not love either. If you hear the truth of God, but it doesn't change what you do, you don't understand the love that energizes fellowship. Love is truth in action. John spells it out for us:

> We know love by this, that He laid down His life for us; and we ought to lay down our lives for the brethren. But whoever has the world's goods, and beholds his brother in need and closes his heart against him, how does the love of God abide in him? Little children, let us not love with word or with tongue, but in deed and truth. (1 John 3:16–18)

Notice that two things must be operative: the truth and the "deed" or action. To say the right thing and not do the right thing for each other is not enough. John asks, "How can God's love abide in us if we're just love talkers, not love walkers?"

If the movie character Forrest Gump were a pastor, he would say, "Love is as love does." That is, you can measure love by its action. If you know of people in the body of Christ who are suffering or are in need, and you say, "I care," something should happen. The sick should be getting comfort and help; the needy should be seeing their legitimate needs met.

John's illustration of love in verse 17 communicates powerfully. "You have the goods and you see a brother in need, but you don't do anything. How is that love?" For the person who claims to be a disciple of Jesus Christ, love must be translated into action.

Every husband knows it's not enough just to tell his wife, "I love you, honey." She must see it acted out in order for it to be authentic. Love can certainly be expressed in words, but words alone are not enough.

When a husband and wife are trying to restore their relationship, the question in counseling must always be, "What are you going to do?" If a solution doesn't work itself down to that level, it's not authentic. The apostle James asks:

If a brother or sister is without clothing and in need of daily food, and one of you says to them, "Go in peace, be warmed and be filled," and yet you do not give them what is necessary for their body, what use is that? (James 2:15–16)

If your brother is hungry and needs a ham sandwich, don't just say, "I'll pray for you." If he had wanted prayer, he would have asked for prayer. What he needs is some ham and cheese between two slices of bread with mayonnaise.

As I said in the previous chapter, too many of us are "cul-de-sac" Christians. We take it in, but we don't want to let it go out. So God says, "I don't want to come into that neighborhood."

John writes, "If someone says, 'I love God,' and hates his brother, he is a liar; for the one who does not love his brother whom he has seen, cannot love God whom he has not seen" (1 John 4:20). You know you love God by how you relate to the members of His family.

We have too much "love talk" and not enough "love walk." Love is truth in action. The reason a lot of our relationships in the body are not spiritually productive is that we are not right with God.

If there is never any time, energy, or inconvenience given to your brothers and sisters in the body, never any stretching of yourself to help someone in your local family of believers, John says you don't love God. No matter how many Sundays you go to church, you are living a lie.

Affection Among Saints

Loving one another also involves genuine affection among the saints. Read Romans 16:1–16 and you will see the word *greet* over and over again, culminating with, "Greet one another with a holy kiss" (v. 16). This is a greeting born out of relationship, out of *koinonia*. Paul is talking about deep, legitimate affection among the people of God.

There's a beautiful picture of this in Acts 20:37, when the elders from Ephesus repeatedly kissed Paul when he told them they would never see him again. This was authentic love, real *koinonia,* in the family of God. It's the kind of love that recognizes that when we see each other, it's a family reunion.

Peter admonishes us, "Fervently love one another from the heart" (1 Peter 1:22). The word *fervent* means to "stretch" yourself out in love toward your fellow Christians.

Let me give you some good news about this. You don't necessarily have to like the people you are commanded to love. God does not command you to like me. "Like" has to do with our preferential, emotional attachments. No one is going to like everybody else equally. You don't have to like me, but you have to love me.

You say, "But you can't just turn love on and off." Really? Who told you that? That's the world's way of thinking. Biblical love can be commanded because it is controlled by your will, not by your emotions. Biblical love says, "This is the truth, and this is what I will do in light of the truth."

It may take us time to like each other, but I can start loving you right now. That's why Jesus could tell us, "Love your enemies." You may not like your enemies, but biblical love says you can choose to do the right thing even for your enemies, to the glory of God. That's love, and it's a big part of what fills our fellowship with content.

SERVE ONE ANOTHER

The second "one another" I want to look at in relation to fellowship is Paul's command, "Serve one another" (Galatians 5:13).

We can see this concept in action in an enlightening passage, Romans 12:1–8. In verses 1–2, Paul issued his famous call to present our bodies to Christ. In verses 4–8, he talked about ministering to Christ's body by the use of our spiritual gifts.

So verses 1–2 talk about loving God. Verses 4–8 talk about serving others. But Paul dropped a very interesting verse in between these two sections:

For through the grace given to me I say to every man among you not to think more highly of himself than he ought to think; but to think so as to have sound judgment, as God has allotted to each a measure of faith. (v. 3)

An Inflated View of Self

Here's why we don't have more servants in our churches. We have too many people with an inflated view of themselves. They have a wrong self-analysis. They rate themselves higher than God rates them. Most of us need someone in our lives to keep us from getting carried away with ourselves.

My mother called me one day and said, "Boy."

I knew right away she was upset with me. So I said, "What's wrong, Mama?"

"You haven't called in three weeks."

I said, "Mama, I had this to do and that to do."

She said, "Listen, boy. Anytime you are so busy doing all the stuff you're doing that you can't pick up the phone and call your mama, you're too busy. Whenever you're too busy to call your mama, something's wrong with you."

She's right. And whenever you're too busy, too important, or too successful to let the love of God work through you to serve somebody else, something is wrong with you. We need the spirit of humility that God demands and that Jesus illustrated.

Washing One Another's Feet

In John 13, Jesus and the disciples were in the Upper Room for the Last Supper. The disciples were fussing among themselves over who was the greatest, so they were not about to lower themselves to wash each other's feet, as the custom of the day demanded somebody do.

These important disciples, soon-to-be apostles, were looking around wondering, "Who is going to play the part of the servant here?" But none of them moved.

Without a word, Jesus picked up the basin and the towel and began washing their feet. We are talking about the Son of the living God, God in the flesh, serving others in the most menial task imaginable.

When was the last time you picked up a towel or did whatever you had to do to serve someone else? True fellowship demands that we serve each other without waiting to be told. No one told Jesus to pick up the towel and wash His disciples' feet. He did so because He came to serve, not to be served (Mark 10:45).

After He had finished washing their feet, Jesus told the disciples, "If I then, the Lord and the Teacher, washed your feet, you also ought to wash one another's feet" (John 13:14).

I'm not arguing for the ritual of foot washing. I'm saying that fellowship, our sharing in the life of Jesus Christ, involves selfless service.

But continuing with the example of foot washing, let me say that when you wash someone else's feet, watch the temperature of the water you use. Don't wash another person's feet in the cold water of callousness and indifference.

Don't be talking about, "Give me your dirty feet. God told me to wash your stinking feet, and I'm going to do what God says!" When you serve with that kind of a hard heart and a grudging attitude, you are washing the person's feet in very cold water.

Don't wash someone's feet in hot water either, or you'll burn them. A spirit of criticism says, "I told you about this, and if you had listened to me, you wouldn't be in this mess where I now have to serve you. I hope you burn your feet when you put them in the water."

No, when you wash another's feet, use warm water: not too hot, not too cold. You may have to give a little correction and a little instruction, but keep the water warm, tolerable, beneficial. That's what Jesus did.

No Selfish Service

In Philippians 2:3, Paul says, "Do nothing from selfishness or empty conceit." Don't serve others for what you can get out of it. Don't make your service a business deal.

I once had to ask a man to leave our church because he came looking for businesspeople with whom he could cut a deal. He wanted to know what ministry most of the businesspeople served in so he could join it. He was interested in selfish service.

There's nothing wrong with business between believers. But that should not be the motivation for your service. The motivation for service should be to come alongside and help someone else. Romans 12:10 tells us to honor one another; that is, help somebody else look good.

First Corinthians 12:25 is critical to fellowship. God's desire is that "there should be no division in the body, but that the members should have the same care for one another."

When something gets in your eye, your whole body goes into action. One hand reaches for it, the tear ducts begin to wash it, the legs stop so that you can focus on it. The whole body goes into action because one little piece of dust got into one eye.

You wouldn't appreciate your body saying, "Why all this attention? It's only one eye. You still have one good eye on the other side." Your body doesn't react that way. Why? Because the quicker the rest of the body attacks the problem, the quicker it is fixed.

When one member of the body of Christ has a need, other members should be moving in to say, "Let's fix it." That's biblical fellowship. It happens when a member of the body is hurting and others rush in to address the need through service.

If we had more of this kind of body life, we would have far less need for professional secular psychologists, and we would save God's people a lot of money in the process.

RESTORE ONE ANOTHER

The third "one another" that helps us flesh out the content of fellowship is found in Galatians 6. This is a tough one, because it demands that we bear the burden of an erring brother or sister in such a way that he or she is restored:

> Brethren, even if a man is caught in any trespass, you who are spiritual, restore such a one in a spirit of gentleness; each one looking to yourself, lest you too be tempted. Bear one another's burdens, and thus fulfill the law of Christ. (vv. 1–2)

Mending the Broken

Christians need restoring on a number of levels. First of all, we need to restore the brother or sister who is "caught" in a sin. The word *restore* here means to mend a broken net or set a broken bone.

The picture is of a believer caught in a sin the way a bear or some other animal walks into a trap and is snared. That bear wasn't looking or planning to get caught in a trap. He just walked into it and got caught.

There are members of the body of Christ who get caught in sin. They may not have intended to sin, or they may not have realized the full effects of their actions. They are "overtaken" by sin, caught in sin's trap. And, like an animal whose bone is being crushed in the trap, they need someone to set them free and mend the broken bone.

How do believers get caught in sin? Maybe they don't have the right knowledge, so in ignorance they make a bad decision and get stuck. Or maybe they go along with the crowd, not really knowing where the crowd is going. When the crowd gets in trouble, they get in trouble too.

The problem is that these people don't have the strength to release themselves from the trap of sin. Paul says our job is to get them out of there.

But too many Christians don't want to do that. They want to gossip. "Did you hear about John? He got caught." "Bill never should have gone there. If he hadn't, he wouldn't be in trouble now."

That's not what a trapped brother needs. He needs somebody to open the trap and get him out. Notice the qualifications of those who should help a person caught in sin.

First, the helpers should be *spiritual*. These are people who know and walk with God. You don't need "amateurs" to help you when you're caught. You might wind up with two people in the trap!

Second, the helpers ought to be *humble*. The person caught is to be restored in "a spirit of gentleness" (v. 1). If you're hurting, you don't need somebody to jab your sore spot. You need somebody who can bandage the wound, not make it hurt more.

Third, the restoration should be *collective*. These pronouns in Galatians 6 are in the plural.

Fourth, the helpers should proceed with *caution*. They need to keep an eye on themselves, lest they fall into the same temptation. Don't think you are better than the person who is caught, because there's a trap waiting for you around the corner.

When a fellow believer is caught in sin, the church that is practicing authentic fellowship rushes to the rescue. The church is not a firing squad. We are healers who mend broken bones.

I can't teach Galatians 6 without recalling the day in 1970 when my leg bones were snapped in two on the football field. My leg definitely needed to be restored.

I was taken by ambulance to the hospital, where the surgeons cut my leg open and put a steel plate on the bones. Even today that plate is there, holding everything in my leg together.

What I didn't need that day was a surgeon asking, "What was he doing playing football anyway?" Nor did I need a surgeon saying, "I don't feel like doing surgery today. Give me that leg!" I needed a compassionate, skillful restorer who knew what he was doing and could fix my leg.

Restoring the Carnal

Not only are we to restore the caught, we are to help the carnal. The carnal believer is different from the caught believer. The latter didn't necessarily intend to plunge into sin. He or she got stuck and doesn't know how to get out.

But the carnal person knows what he is doing, doesn't care, and is going to keep doing it. The apostle James says:

> My brethren, if any among you strays from the truth, and one turns him back, let him know that he who turns a sinner from the error of his way will save his soul from death, and will cover a multitude of sins. (James 5:19–20)

If you see a believer going the wrong way intentionally, that's a carnal person. You're to go after him and turn him around. Why? Because he's not turning himself around.

The person who is caught wants to get out. But the carnal person doesn't necessarily want to get out, because he is bent on going the wrong way. Your job is to track him down and restore him before God has to take his life because of his sin.

The reason we don't do this is that it is risky. It was risky for Paul. In Galatians 4:16, Paul asked, "Have I therefore become your enemy by telling you the truth?"

If you seek to restore a carnal Christian as an act of genuine fellowship, you risk having your feelings hurt. You risk rejection. Many people say, "Why should I run that risk?"

The answer is in James 5:20: The erring believer runs the risk of death. His loss will be greater than your loss. The essence of fellowship is that we are family, and when it comes to family you don't just sit by and watch someone destroy himself. This is family. Take the risk.

And once you restore the person, you need to forgive him. Let me tell you why by reminding you of a familiar parable Jesus told in Matthew 18:21–35. It concerns the slave who owed his king more than "ten thousand talents" (v. 24), a tremendous sum of money.

The slave could not repay the debt, so the king ordered him and his family to be sold to settle the debt. But the slave threw himself down before the king and begged, "Have patience with me, and I will repay you everything" (v. 26).

The master had mercy on his slave and forgave him the entire debt. But then that slave went out and found a fellow slave who owed him a few hundred dollars.

Even though the king had forgiven this guy a huge debt, he demanded that the other slave pay him on the spot. The second slave begged for mercy just like the first one did, but no deal.

The forgiven slave threw the other slave into prison until he could repay the debt. The problem was that the other slaves told the king what happened.

The king hit the roof and handed the forgiven slave over to "the torturers" until he could pay back the full debt (v. 34).

The point is that if you don't forgive, you'll wind up being worse off than the person who needs the forgiveness. If you fail to forgive, you'll wind up in your own spiritual prison.

If a person repents, he is already bearing the consequences of pain and remorse over what he has done. The man who sinned in Corinth (1 Corinthians 5) had repented, so Paul urged the church to let up because their discipline was threatening to overwhelm him with sorrow (2 Corinthians 2:6–7). They were creating a spiritual prison for this man.

Why imprison yourself and others, when God wants to set you free? That doesn't mean there are not consequences that must be borne. It means that you say to the other person, "I will no longer lay this sin to your account. You may have consequences to bear, but I release you from the debt of this sin."

Breaking Fellowship

What happens when restoration is refused, when the person involved does not repent? This is a hard one, but the Bible is clear. You can no longer have any fellowship with him or her.

In regard to the problem in 1 Corinthians 5, Paul said in verse 11, "I wrote to you not to associate with any so-called brother if he should be an immoral person, or covetous, or an idolater, or a reviler, or a drunkard, or a swindler—not even to eat with such a one."

That means no more lunches with a Christian who won't repent of sin. He or she doesn't get invited over for dinner anymore. There is to be no fellowship on any level with this person. You have to make the point clear. "I will help restore you, but I will not help you disobey God."

This is where Christianity gets tough, but it's necessary to restore the sinning believer to fellowship with God and fellowship with the other members of the body.

ENCOURAGE ONE ANOTHER

The fourth "one another" that I believe gives content to our fellowship is found in 1 Thessalonians 5:11, where Paul writes, "Encourage one another, and build up one another."

The Job of a Comforter

The goal of encouragement is to build other believers up. Why? Because they're torn down. What may have torn them down? Circumstances may have torn them down. Sin may have torn them down. Your job is not to tear them down further. Your job is to encourage, to become their spiritual cheerleader.

My second daughter, Priscilla, was a cheerleader in high school. Amazingly, some of the best cheers she did was when her team was losing. Why? Because the job of the cheerleader is to bring hope and encouragement. That's what we have to do if we are going to follow Jesus by practicing authentic fellowship.

We have an example in 1 Thessalonians 4 of Paul being a comfort to the believers there. Some people in the Thessalonian church had died, and the others were afraid they would never see these brothers and sisters again.

Paul wrote that great passage in verses 13–17 to correct their thinking and give them hope, and then he said, "Therefore comfort one another with these words." Sports teams need cheerleaders. Children need parents who will be their cheerleaders. And members of the body of Christ need cheerleaders.

The Tools of a Comforter

But to be good comforters, good cheerleaders, we need to know the cheers. You're a bad cheerleader if you don't know the cheers.

What do Christian cheerleaders need to know? We need to know the Word of God, because it is the Word we use to comfort other believers. Our comfort must be biblical to be genuine. Ignorant cheerleaders are bad cheerleaders.

See, you don't learn the Word of God just for yourself. You learn it so you can use it to minister to somebody else. That's the essence of discipleship, which is the larger picture we are looking at in this book.

Romans 15:14 says we are to "admonish one another." That word has to do with counseling and guiding another Christian. A good Christian comforter is a good counselor.

We saw this ministry of encouragement in operation recently at Oak Cliff Bible Fellowship. We had a couple in our church that was hurting deeply, in great pain. I sat down with them to counsel and talk with them.

But what they needed most, I could not give them. They needed somebody who had been through what they were going through. So I connected them with another couple who had walked where they were walking.

This other couple was able to do something I was unable to do because I had not been through what this hurting couple was facing. But this second couple in our church came alongside to help, took the hands of the first couple, and walked with them through their struggle.

God used that ministry to begin a process of reversal. This helping couple took the Word of God and put biblical fellowship into practice. Now it's a joy when I look up at church every Sunday or Wednesday and see two people who were hurting deeply but are now rejoicing in the Lord.

That's what true *koinonia* does. It saves relationships and builds lives and gives new hope when people don't think they can make it. *Koinonia* says, "I know where you are. Let's get together around God's Word." It encourages, builds up, and brings hope.

Until the church takes this responsibility seriously, Christians will never know the healing power God's grace was designed to bring them through His church. We must stop turning to others to do what God entrusted to the church.

No False Advertising

You have probably seen yards where the owner has put up a "Beware of Dog" sign. The only problem is, there is no dog. The sign is just a ruse to scare people off. It constitutes false advertising.

The church has a sign hanging on its fence that reads, "Come In for Fellowship." Sometimes, though, there is no reality behind the fence. There is no real fellowship taking place.

I said to our church, "Don't let our name be Oak Cliff Bible Fellowship while we have no fellowship behind the fence. Don't let us say to people, 'Come in for the authentic *koinonia*,' and then offer them no love, no service, no restoration, and no encouragement. If we say we have fellowship, let's deliver."

What I want for our people in Dallas, I wish for every believer who desires to be a disciple of Jesus Christ. If we claim we have a dog, then let's have a bark. When people meet us, may they say two things: "My, how that person loves the Lord," and "My, how that person loves others." When it comes to fellowship, if people say that about us, they have said it all.

CHAPTER TEN

THE CONTEXT OF FELLOWSHIP

One of the most popular television shows of recent years was the sitcom *Cheers*. People by the millions gathered around their TV sets every week to watch a group of lonely people who got together regularly in a neighborhood bar to talk to each other.

The characters on the program shared the good times and the bad together. They talked about death and life and victory and defeat and other matters of daily life and human relationships. *Cheers* was so successful because it documented the pilgrimage of people in search of what the New Testament calls *koinonia:* fellowship.

That's what "happy hour" in a bar is all about. People don't go to happy hour to drink. They can drink alone at home. People go to happy hour looking for *koinonia,* meaningful fellowship. They want to be in an environment where life touches life. They want to talk, to relate, to congregate.

But authentic fellowship will not be found at the local bar or at the hottest club in town. That's because fellowship occurs in a theological and biblical context. If we want to follow Jesus Christ as His disciples, it is essential that we understand the context of fellowship.

THE RELATIONAL NATURE OF GOD

God in His essence is a relational Being. God has never known what it is like to be alone. He is a triune Being: God the Father, God the Son, and God the Holy Spirit. In eternity past, when there were no angels and no creation as we know it, God was in dynamic, intimate, powerful, expressive relationship and fellowship with Himself.

Therefore, we should not be surprised that in His creative genius, God made a world that requires relationships in order to function properly. Fish swim in schools, wolves run in packs, cattle congregate in herds, and bees swarm.

Neither should it surprise us that when God surveyed His creation, He pronounced it all good with one exception: "It is not good for the man to be alone; I will make him a helper suitable for him" (Genesis 2:18). God was saying, "If Adam is alone, he is not like Me, for I exist in relationship."

When God collectivized His people, He created a community and drew up what the Bible calls a covenant, which bonded His people together in vital fellowship as they shared His life. In the New Testament age, the church is God's covenant community, the context in which He designed *koinonia* to function.

The church is more than a classroom for spiritual instruction. It is more than a theater for spiritual performances. It is more than an organization to carry out spiritual programs.

The church is an organism designed to enhance spiritual relationships. When authentic, biblical fellowship is missing, the church becomes a sterile, empty place. But when *koinonia* is occurring, the church is a dynamic, pulsating environment in which people find themselves alive.

THE CHURCH AS A HOUSEHOLD

The Bible has three relational metaphors for the church that I want to consider in this chapter. These metaphors are a household, a body, and a community. I want to look at each in some detail.

As Paul concluded his letter to the Galatians, he gave this word of instruction: "So then, while we have opportunity, let us do good to all men, and especially to those who are of the household of the faith" (Galatians 6:10).

Here in one verse is both a key biblical metaphor for the church and a call to practice fellowship within the church when there is need. Paul further develops this concept of the church as a household in 1 Timothy 3. He was hoping to come to Timothy soon, but he wrote:

> In case I am delayed, I write so that you may know how one ought to conduct himself in the household of God, which is the church of the living God, the pillar and support of the truth. (v. 15)

This adds another dimension to the household. Not only is the church the place where the people of faith live, but it is also the place where God dwells. The church is God's home. As the temple was God's home in the Old Testament, so the church is God's home in the New Testament.

Joining a Family

This means that when you become part of a local church, you are joining a family. What makes us a family? We all have the same Father (Ephesians 3:14–15). We all have experienced the same spiritual birth and have the same spiritual blood flowing through our veins. Our relationship in the church transcends ethnic, clan, or earthly family relationships.

The implications of this truth are staggering. Paul develops them in Ephesians 2, where he says that God took Jews and Gentiles, who were alienated from each other and were far apart religiously, socially, and in every other conceivable way, and brought them together in Christ (vv. 13–14). Jesus Christ did this "by abolishing in His flesh the enmity, which is the Law of commandments contained in ordinances, that in Himself He might make the two into one new man, thus establishing peace" (v. 15).

In other words, Jesus Christ united Jew and Gentile into one new entity, the church, in which people no longer related to one another as Jew and Gentile (Galatians 3:28), but only as brothers and sisters in one family.

Look how Paul summarizes this incredible new reality in Ephesians 2:19: "So then you are no longer strangers and aliens, but you are fellow citizens with the saints, and are of God's household."

If you want to understand *koinonia*, Paul says, you must identify with the family. For some of us, that's hard to do, given the families we grew up in. Some believers had bad family experiences, so the idea of the church as a household doesn't have a positive ring to it.

The church ought to be an alternative to bad family experiences. It ought to be the one family that makes family make sense. It ought to be the one place where authentic family is being realized, because it's not your daddy's household, it's God's household. It operates by a different standard, and the relationships are determined by a different set of criteria.

The Significance of Family

How significant is this family we call the church? I want to show you from Matthew 12 an incident in the earthly life of Jesus Christ:

> While He was still speaking to the multitudes, behold, His mother and brothers were standing outside, seeking to speak to Him. And someone said to Him, "Behold, Your mother and Your brothers are standing outside seeking to speak to You." But He answered the one who was telling Him and said, "Who is My mother and who are My brothers?" And stretching out His hand toward His disciples, He said, "Behold, My mother and My brothers! For whoever does the will of My Father who is in heaven, he is My brother and sister and mother." (vv. 46–50)

This is deep, because Jesus is saying, "My real moth-

er and brothers and sisters are My disciples, those people who are committed to doing the will of My Father."
This ought to be all the motivation you need to become
Christ's disciple. He considers you family when you follow Him!

Some of us have closer relationships with brothers
and sisters in the household of God than we had with
our biological siblings. Some of us didn't find a real
father until we found a man of God who cared about us.
Some of us never knew a real mother until we found a
spiritual mother in the church.

Jesus certainly honored and respected His mother.
But He was saying that His family's biological ties to
Him were not as deep as the spiritual ties He had with
His disciples. The people who chose to follow Him were
His true family.

The church is to be a household. Is it any wonder,
then, that when the church was born, its members not
only met in the temple, but they also went fellowshiping
"from house to house" (Acts 2:46)?

Those early believers understood that you can do a
lot more around a fireplace than you can in a foyer. They
understood that they needed to be together not only on
Sunday, but Monday through Saturday as well, to stimulate, encourage, and motivate one another.

The Ministry of Family

This family atmosphere is prominent in the New
Testament. The material needs of believers were met
because they were family. As we saw in the previous
chapter, John says we know the love of God abides in us
when we open our hearts to the needs of the brethren (1
John 3:17).

Being a family also means we meet spiritual needs.
Two other texts we studied in the previous chapter were
Galatians 6:1 and James 5:19–20. These verses tell us
that when we see a brother or sister falling into sin, we
don't just stand by and watch or say, "Go ahead, get yourself in trouble."

The church is a household, a family. When it comes

to family, everyone has to contribute. The Christian who only wants to come to church week after week and warm a pew is like a child who only comes home to eat and sleep and refuses to relate to the other members of the family.

That's not the way family is supposed to work, and that's not the way the church is supposed to work. The church is to be an environment of *koinonia,* of shared lives.

THE CHURCH AS A BODY

The New Testament does not just liken the church to a household. Paul's most common metaphor for the church, by far, is that of a body. More than fifteen times the apostle says the ministry of the church can be understood in terms of the way the human body functions.

A classic passage that lays out this image is Ephesians 4:7–16. I don't want to quote that entire passage here, since you can open your Bible and read it for yourself. But I do want to make some observations on key verses in this important text.

The Aspect of Development

One aspect of the body imagery Paul teaches in Ephesians 4 is that of development. In verse 13, Paul says the body of Christ is to be built up by service "until we all attain to the unity of the faith, and of the knowledge of the Son of God, to a mature man, to the measure of the stature which belongs to the fulness of Christ."

In verse 15, Paul says the goal is to "grow up in all aspects into [Christ]." That is, the goal for a body is to grow and develop until it reaches maturity. Notice that this maturity is something we are "all" supposed to attain (v. 13). That means every member of the body is to grow, and you can only do that when the parts of the body are connected.

This is where fellowship is so crucial. If you are disconnected from the rest of the body, you won't develop spiritually. No part of the body will grow once it becomes detached. It has no source of life.

God has so constructed the spiritual body that growth and maturity only occur in the context of attachment. God doesn't have any independent agents operating on their own.

Development also requires a context of unity. Ephesians 4:13 speaks of "the unity of the faith" as the first goal of the body's growth. Paul put it this way in 1 Corinthians 12:

> For even as the body is one and yet has many members, and all the members of the body, though they are many, are one body, so also is Christ. For by one Spirit we were all baptized into one body, whether Jews or Greeks, whether slaves or free, and we were all made to drink of one Spirit. (vv. 12–13)

What is the recurring word here? One. It speaks of a commonality of purpose. Every member of the body must be going the same way. You cannot have your right foot going forward and your left foot going backward and expect to get anywhere. In order for the body to progress, there must be unity of purpose. Everybody must be pulling in the same direction as instructed by the head, Jesus Christ.

The Aspect of Direction

The church as a body must receive its direction from the same place that your physical body receives its direction: from the head.

Look at Ephesians 4:15, which says, "We are to grow up in all aspects into Him, who is the head, even Christ." Christ is the Head of the body. The job of the head is to give direction to the body. So if the church is going to follow Christ and have dynamic fellowship, we must take our cues from Christ. See, if you are to be a disciple of Christ, the deciding thing is not what your mother or your father told you. Let's hope they taught you well in the things of God, but for Jesus' disciple the standard for obedience is what the Head tells you to do.

I think this is what Jesus was communicating in the

Matthew 12 passage we studied above. As the Head of the body, Jesus was not under the direction of His earthly family. He gives the directions to the body. It is the will of His Father that His disciples need to pursue, not the wishes of anyone else.

We get our cues from Christ—which means that we won't do things the way the world does them. For example, a disciple of Jesus Christ won't do business the way the world does business. A disciple won't view morality the way the world views morality. Once you become part of Christ's body, you will look weird to the world. I guarantee it.

The Aspect of Diversity

Here's another aspect to the metaphor of the church as a body that we don't often consider: the body's diversity. This is important to an authentic fellowship, because the body only works right when each member is doing the job it was designed to do.

Paul articulates the body's diversity clearly in 1 Corinthians 12:

> If the whole body were an eye, where would the hearing be? If the whole were hearing, where would the sense of smell be? But now God has placed the members, each one of them, in the body, just as He desired. (vv. 17–18)

We also see diversity suggested in Ephesians 4:16, where Paul talks about each joint supplying what is needed and "each individual part" working properly.

This means that our unity does not cancel out our diversity. In fact, unity demands diversity. I'm not sure what you would call a thing that was all one eye, but you wouldn't call it a body. It would be more like a monstrosity. The church becomes a monstrosity when everybody has to be like everybody else.

The beauty of the body of Christ is that it needs eyes and ears and noses and all sorts of parts. The church is a place where people of different races, different colors, different personalities, and different classes can come together to function in beautiful harmony.

Every member of an orchestra doesn't play the same instrument, but they all play the same song. If they were all playing different songs at the same time, that would be another story. But each instrument in an orchestra is needed to fully express the music the conductor has chosen to play.

The body of Christ operates like a good orchestra: different parts doing their work, producing beautiful music under the direction of our divine Conductor, Jesus Christ. There is unity in the music, but diversity in the instruments.

Many husbands say, "My wife and I are so different." Of course you're different. If both of you were the same, one of you would be unnecessary. The problem in many marriages isn't that the husband and wife are so different. The problem is that they are not working toward the same purpose. They are not playing the same song.

When unity of purpose is lacking, diversity can produce strife. The idea is to keep the diversity and develop a plan of unity.

I spoke at a Promise Keepers rally in Charlotte, North Carolina, not long after a black church in the community had been burned. The pastor of the church came to the rally and told how the Christian community had rallied to rebuild his church. He said, "The first thing we did was tear down the old walls."

That statement had a double truth to it. That community not only tore down physical walls, but they also tore down walls of racial and spiritual division.

What happened was that some white people went into a neighborhood they had never been in before. People who were of a different class came over to a side of town they had not been in before. Other people accepted help from people they had never accepted help from before.

All of these people worked together, and the beauty of it is that what they did went far beyond rebuilding a church. These people were doing things together that they hadn't done as a community in a couple of hundred years. It all happened because they put their diversity to work for a common agenda in the name of Jesus Christ. They practiced true *koinonia*.

The church has the ability to do that with every issue of division and strife facing us. If you have unity without diversity you have sameness, and that's boring. If you have diversity without unity, you have confusion and division. The body of Christ must have unity that expresses itself in diversity. There is no conflict between the two.

The Body at Work

In order for all of this to work, all of the body has to work. The saints must be equipped "for the work of service" (Ephesians 4:12). The whole body must be "fitted and held together by that which every joint supplies" (v. 16). Fellowship involves service.

A non-working member of the body of Christ is not contributing to *koinonia*. A non-serving saint is a spiritual leech who drains off the body's blood supply without putting anything back. Anyone who comes to church week after week and does nothing but sit and soak is a spiritual leech, not an authentic follower of Christ.

Suppose you had a hand that said, "I don't feel like working today." Suppose your foot said, "I'm not into walking today." As I have said before, if the parts of your body stop taking direction from the head, put this book down and get to a doctor. You are a very sick person.

Because the body is so intimately connected, the activities of one part have a tremendous effect on the other parts. Let your eyes shut down for a day, and your effectiveness will be curtailed. Let your feet take the day off, and you won't get very far.

The same goes for your ears or hands or just about any other body part you can name. When one part of the body shuts down, it affects the ability of the other parts to function.

When even one member of a local body of believers

decides to become a spiritual leech, taking but not giving, it helps to kill *koinonia*. Something that could be done is not being done, because someone wants the benefits of the body but doesn't want to function in the body. *Every* joint has to do the job for the body to grow.

Two Needs of the Body

Before we go on to the third and final metaphor of the church I want to deal with, let me address two needs the body of Christ has: the need for authentic life and the need for dynamic attachment.

Too many of Christ's followers are what I call spiritual Frankensteins. You remember Frankenstein's monster. He was put together by a man whose dreams produced a creature he could not control. The being was anatomically correct and structurally accurate, but he had no meaningful life. It took a bolt of lightning to zap the monster to life, but it was a pseudo-life.

As Christ's disciples, we don't need a Frankenstein type of life. The church is to be a body with authentic life, growing and developing in order to become like Christ.

So how do you know if you're Frankenstein's monster or not? One way you know is by how you react to someone who is on fire for Jesus Christ. If you think that person is a little overboard, sort of a fanatic, then you may be suffering from a lack of real life.

When someone is sick, he often forgets what it feels like to be normal. If your spiritual temperature is low, someone who has a normal temperature may appear feverish to you. So the person who wants to live totally for Jesus Christ, who is willing to sacrifice for the cause of Christ, may appear to be a little abnormal.

But it ought to be normal for people in the body of Christ to be on fire for Him. It's normal for disciples of Christ to make sacrifices to follow Him. You can measure the authenticity of your spiritual life by how you respond to the call for total commitment and surrender that is demanded of disciples.

The other need of the body is dynamic attachment.

Let me illustrate it this way. My granddaughter sucks her thumb all the time. That's not unusual for a little girl her age. But suppose she was sucking on a thumb that wasn't part of her hand. That would be repulsive. As long as the thumb a baby sucks is attached to the baby's hand, thumb sucking is acceptable.

A person who is a nail-biter doesn't pay any attention to a fingernail he or she has bitten off. Why? Because the nail is no longer attached to the body. It is good for nothing but to be discarded and forgotten. No one gets too upset about a piece of nail that has become detached from the body.

A thumb or a fingernail that is attached to the body is useful. But once a part of the body becomes detached from the body, that part dies.

You get the point. If you are not vitally attached to the rest of Christ's body through authentic, vital fellowship, you will shrivel up spiritually. But when you are a working part of the body, you flourish and grow.

THE CHURCH AS A COMMUNITY

The church is a household and a body. It is also a community. That means the church is a place where you move from "me" to "we."

Although the New Testament does not use the word *community* to describe the church, the imagery of community shows up in a number of places. In the best sense of the term, a community is a group of people who are committed to each other, who belong to each other.

As the community of believers in Jesus Christ, we belong first to Christ Himself (see Romans 14:8). We are also "members one of another" (Romans 12:5). We belong to one another. This is a "one another" passage like the passages we studied in chapter 9. The "one another's" of Scripture speak of community.

A Community of Relationships

According to Galatians 2:9, Paul says that when the Jerusalem council (see Acts 15) recognized his calling to the Gentiles, the apostles in Jerusalem extended "the right hand of fellowship" to Paul and Barnabas. They were brought into the *koinonia* of the church, where they would belong to one another.

The church is the community where we can find positive, influential relationships. This is crucial because the Bible says, "Bad company corrupts good morals" (1 Corinthians 15:33).

In 1 Corinthians 6:15, Paul reminds us that our bodies are "members of Christ." As such, we cannot join ourselves to those who practice sin.

The message is just as strong in 2 Corinthians 6:14–15. "Do not be bound together with unbelievers," Paul says. Why? Believers have nothing "in common" with unbelievers. This is the word *koinonia*. God says we cannot have true fellowship with those who are outside of Christ. Don't try to share a life with people who don't know God.

Christian parents who want their children to come under positive, Christ-centered influences know the importance of the community in which those children live. They don't want their kids lured into drugs, gangs, or crime, so they are concerned about the ones with whom their children practice *koinonia*.

If a child says, "I'm going over to Jack's house," a parent ought to say, "Who are Jack's mama and daddy? What are they like? I need to meet them before you start hanging around Jack too much."

Parents are concerned about their children's fellowship because their children will be sharing their lives with the people in their community. When your children come home from school with words you've never heard before or wish they had not learned, you know what happened. They were in an environment where negative things were said that they picked up. So now you have to correct them.

What you are concerned about for your children, God is concerned about for His children. He wants us in a community that is going to promote righteousness, not drag us down to evil.

The Power of Community

In order to have community, you have to be unselfish. Many people live only for three people: "me, myself, and I." But that's not community.

I'm not condemning taking care of yourself. I'm talking about self-interest that keeps you from serving somebody else, self-interest that says, "I am only concerned with how I benefit." Hebrews 10:24–25 says we need to come together in *koinonia* to "stimulate one another to love and good deeds."

Community also solves the problem of racism. Romans 10:12 says that in Christ, the barriers are broken down. Jesus has built a fence big enough to include everybody in His community.

The story is told of some soldiers who wanted to bury a friend of theirs in the local cemetery. But the priest told them they could not bury their friend in the cemetery because the plots were reserved for members of the community. "You can bury him outside the fence," the priest said, "but you can't bury him inside the fence." So they buried their friend outside the fence.

The friends came back the next day to put some flowers on the grave, but they couldn't find it. They went to the priest and said, "We buried our friend here, but we can't find him. We looked all around outside the fence. What happened?"

The priest said, "I'll tell you what happened. I couldn't sleep last night after I told you you couldn't bury your friend inside the fence. So I got up in the middle of the night and spent the rest of the night moving the fence. Your friend is now inside."

Jesus not only moved the fence; He broke it down (Ephesians 2:14). You and I are now included, and there's room for everybody in Christ. That's why anybody who walks through the door of the church—no matter what color, race, culture, or class—is equal to everybody else inside.

There are no big "I's" and little "you's" in the community of Christ. The cross is the great equalizer, because we are all just sinners in need of a Savior at the cross.

We are a community. Racism and culturalism and classism are answered by our understanding that there is room for everybody at the cross. Jesus broke down the fence for those who accept His death on the cross, so everybody is welcome. Anybody who wants to follow Christ should receive the right hand of fellowship from the community of Christ. Society at large will not find a solution to the problem of racism until it is modeled by the church.

The only unwelcome thing that people can bring into the community of Christ is sin that they don't want to deal with. Sin is not welcome in the community, but people are welcome. So whatever your race or class, don't be so proud about it that you feel it lifts you above someone else. The church is the one place where you ought to be able to be yourself and tell the truth. We lie to each other all the time. Someone says, "How are you doing?" You say, "I'm doing just fine," when actually you are dying inside.

But a true community is a place where you can tell your hurts and struggles and find loving arms of a *koinonia* community, not a cold shoulder.

HOME IMPROVEMENT

I mentioned the television program *Cheers* at the beginning of the chapter. Another top-rated program is *Home Improvement,* a humorous sitcom about two partners who give do-it-yourself tips on television. They show you how to fix what's broken in your home and how to remodel what needs improvement.

We all have room for improvement. If we are going to be a community that models Jesus Christ, that shows Him off, we need to fix what is broken in our lives. We need to do some remodeling.

What needs fixing? We need to fix our selfishness. We need to remodel our schedules so that we have time to follow Christ as His disciples and time for people.

Some homes in the Christian community need some "home improvement."

The church is God's household, the body of Christ, the community of the saved. It is God's context in which authentic fellowship is to be lived out.

Let's get our household in order, let's get the body moving and functioning in every joint and ligament, let's get the homes in our Christian community fixed up and remodeled, so that we will have something believable to export to a watching world.

CHAPTER ELEVEN

THE COMPENSATION OF FELLOWSHIP

A s we wrap up our discussion on the second of four absolute necessities in following Christ, it's time to ask the same question about fellowship that we asked about worship in chapter 7. That is, is there a payoff for practicing authentic *koinonia?* What is the compensation of fellowship for us as Christ's disciples?

There is great compensation—a payoff, if you will— when we practice fellowship as the followers of Jesus Christ. God does something for us that He does not do when *koinonia* does not exist. I find in the New Testament that God rewards us on several levels when we take fellowship seriously. The first compensation of fellowship is that it produces unity.

THE COMPENSATION OF UNITY

We discussed unity at some length in the previous chapter, but I want to look at it again under this heading. When the body of Christ is practicing fellowship, unity is the inevitable result.

Unity in Need

In fact, the church's fellowship was such that when they were devoting themselves to the four essential ministries we are discussing in this book (Acts 2:42), they held all their possessions in common. Everyone and everything was together. They sold these possessions and shared with anyone who had a need (v. 45). And they were "day by day continuing with one mind" (v. 46).

Then in Acts 4, the disciples came together again after the authorities had warned the apostles not to preach anymore in the name of Jesus. The believers got together and prayed, and when they had finished, "the place where they had gathered together was shaken" (v. 31). Then Luke says again that "the congregation of those who believed were of one heart and soul" (v. 32).

The church's fellowship was expressed in their togetherness, both materially and spiritually, and this fellowship contributed to the sense of unity that saturated the church in Jerusalem.

Unity and Diversity

As we said in the previous chapter, the church's unity occurs in the midst of diversity. Unity does not mean trying to make everybody look and sound the same. Praise God for our differences. The challenge is to harness those differences, to team up and reach a common goal.

Many people spend a lot of time trying to change people in the name of unity. What they are seeking is really uniformity. But God intends us to be different. And when genuine fellowship is operative, we can enjoy and even celebrate our differences without allowing discrimination of any kind to divide us.

I have spoken at a lot of Promise Keepers conferences. In Modesto, California, the churches came together cross-racially and cross-culturally to attend the conference, and I saw a great example of unity in the body of Christ in the midst of diversity.

The men from this city all showed up at Promise Keepers wearing the same T-shirt, on which were the words, "The Church of Modesto." These were men from different churches, different races, and different backgrounds, but together they were *the* church from their city.

And I discovered that these brothers had done a lot more than just get T-shirts alike. They have come together across all lines and have shut down many of the topless dance clubs in their city. They decided to get together and unify in the cause of Christ, and things happened.

The Cure of Disunity

The reason we spend so much time being "disunified" in the body of Christ is that we don't have a vision big enough to call all of us together in unity to reach it. We can be different, yet work together, when there is something before us that is bigger than both of us.

See, people fight because they want to win. They fight because they think more highly of themselves than they ought to think (Romans 12:3). But when fellowship is in operation, you understand that you are what you are by the grace of God. There are different functions and job descriptions among Jesus Christ's disciples, but the ground is level at the cross.

It doesn't matter what our titles are at work. It doesn't matter how important we are in the world. In the family of God, we are all sinners saved by grace. And that means you come to serve.

One thing that made the church of Jesus Christ unique in the New Testament was that Jews and Gentiles, who couldn't stand each other, were united in one body. Jesus Christ tore down the wall between them. There was no more separation, just unity.

Of course, the church wasn't perfect. There were squabbles and disagreements. But these believers' hearts were beating as one. They were working from the inside out, not the outside in. They weren't looking at a person's complexion, but at his heart.

That's where you always start. If I have a heart for God and you have a heart for God, we can fix anything. But if we don't have hearts for God, you and I can be the same skin color, or from the same ethnic group, and still have a problem. The issue is first sin, not skin. The issue is what is in our hearts.

THE COMPENSATION OF POWER

A related benefit or payoff we enjoy from unity in our fellowship is the unleashing of the Holy Spirit's power. The book of Acts reveals very clearly that the Spirit's power was unleashed when the people were one in unity and together in fellowship.

Unity and Power

Many of Christ's disciples are not seeing God's power in their lives because they are not operating in unity. When we are disunified, the Holy Spirit backs away. That's why Paul tells us to preserve the unity of the Spirit (Ephesians 4:3). He will only work where there is oneness, not confusion and discord. Going back to Acts 4, I want you to notice that some powerful things began to happen when the Spirit's power fell. In the incident I referred to above, when the disciples had prayed "they were all filled with the Holy Spirit, and began to speak the word of God with boldness" (v. 31). That power was continued as the apostles witnessed with "great power" (v. 33).

Do you want to see some miracles happen? Discover *koinonia*. It's so powerful that God says He will not answer the prayer of a husband who is not in proper fellowship with his wife (1 Peter 3:7). "If a husband is not treating his wife right," God says, "don't call on the Holy Spirit for anything."

Can you see why Satan works so hard to sow the sin of strife and discord among the people of God? The devil knows that as soon as there is confusion, God backs out of the scene. God judges discord; He doesn't bless it with the Spirit's power.

I need to keep stressing this because it is so fundamentally important. Look back at Acts 1:14: "These all [that is, the disciples] with one mind were continually devoting themselves to prayer, along with the women, and Mary the mother of Jesus, and with His brothers."

Then in our basic text for this book, Acts 2:42, I want to point out once more that those early disciples were "continually devoting themselves to . . . fellowship." In other words, both before the Spirit came in great power on the Day of Pentecost, and after His power had been unleashed, the disciples were doing the same thing— coming together in intense prayer and *koinonia*.

I submit to you that the Spirit of God is unleashed when the people of God come together in the presence of God. In Acts 4:31, the building shook when the Holy Ghost showed up. The Spirit was saying, "I'm free to enter in and do My work because they are working with Me."

Power vs. Programs

It's amazing. These people didn't have any programs. God the Holy Spirit just showed up and shook things up. Sometimes we program ourselves to death. We come up with a new program to meet this or that need or to try to get something moving. In most cases, we don't need new programs. We just need new power in the old programs.

Some Christian couples don't just need time away from home to get it together, they need the Holy Spirit's power in their home. The church needs oneness of mind and oneness of heart, because then the Holy Spirit will come in and unleash His power.

When the first disciples came together in intimate, prayerful fellowship, they saw the power of God come down. It's really astounding to sit down and read through the early chapters of Acts. Every time we see the people of God in one accord, the Holy Spirit shows up.

If we are going to have any power in our discipleship, we need to have the Holy Spirit shake us up the way He shook that building in Jerusalem. That happens in the midst of *koinonia*.

THE COMPENSATION OF LOVE

Another payoff for fellowship is that people fall so deeply in love with Jesus that they can't keep Him to themselves.

We preachers are always pounding the pulpit to urge

God's people to witness. "Get out there and witness. Share your faith with someone this week. Tell someone at work about Jesus. It's your responsibility to witness for Christ."

But just telling people to witness will never do the job. The secret to witnessing is not a sermon, but falling in love with the Savior.

Falling in Love

Remember when you first fell in love? You couldn't stop talking about the object of your affections. I have seen quiet folk get loud when they fall in love. I have seen bashful folk whip out pictures you never even asked to see when they're in love.

When you're in love, you are going to talk about it. You get on the phone and say, "Girl, let me tell you, I found him." The guy says, "Let me tell you about this wonderful girl I met." You'll talk about it until people don't want to hear any more—and still you keep talking.

Our problem is that we are not in love with Jesus enough to talk about Him like that. Our faith has become a job, a task, a Sunday ceremony. The believers in Acts didn't have to take a course in evangelism to become powerful witnesses for Christ.

Don't misunderstand. There is nothing wrong with learning to share your faith. But training is not a substitute for love. The disciples' love for Jesus Christ allowed them to overcome any fear about speaking up for Him. Love makes you bold (1 John 4:18).

Just a few weeks before Pentecost, the apostles were running and hiding from the religious authorities. But when the church came together and the Holy Spirit came, they began to speak about Christ with great boldness. All of a sudden, no one could shut them up.

The rulers said to Peter and John, "We are going to beat you if you don't stop talking about Jesus." They answered, "We cannot stop speaking what we have seen and heard" because "we must obey God rather than men" (Acts 4:20; 5:29).

Why can so many of us who claim to be Christ's disciples go day after day, week after week, month after month, without ever bringing up His name? Probably because we don't love Him like we once did (see Revelation 2:4–5).

But when believers come together in a context of *koinonia*, authentic fellowship, one of the benefits is that our love for Christ is intensified. And when our love is intensified, no one will be able to shut us up.

This is exactly what happened at Pentecost. Don't skip over Acts 2:1 too quickly. The disciples were "all together in one place" when they were filled with the Holy Spirit and began to speak in other languages (vv. 1–4). No one could stop them from sharing the message of Christ.

A lot of people are worried about the issue of speaking in tongues. My concern is for all of those disciples who aren't speaking about Jesus in the language they know! Instead of looking for some unusual gift, we need to fall in love with Jesus again and be filled with the Holy Spirit. Then we won't have any problem speaking up for the Lord.

The Fire of Love

What *koinonia* does to believers is what logs stacked in a fireplace do to each other. The fire spreads from one to another. The passion of one believer ignites another believer, and the fire begins to spread. People begin to fall in love with Jesus and start talking about Him.

That's why I like to be around Christians who are excited about Christ. I want some of their fire to warm me. I want their excitement to become my excitement, their joy to be my joy.

You say, "That sounds like what I need, Tony. I don't have any joy in my Christian life." Then find some joyful Christians and begin to fellowship with them.

Do you need peace in your heart? Have fellowship with another Christian who knows what peace is all about. Is your faith not very strong? Find a group of Christians who know what it is to trust God, and let their fire light your faith. This is what discipleship is all about. This is what fellowship does. It pays huge dividends.

Instead of seeking the fire, though, too many believers go the other way. They have trouble trusting God, so they hang around other people who have trouble trusting God. The result is that they become a group of doubters together. They feed each other's problem.

That's not the kind of fellowship the Bible is talking about. True *koinonia* lights a fire of love and devotion to Jesus Christ. A fire soon goes out when there is only one log in the fireplace. Add more logs, and you get a real fire going. That's the payoff of fellowship.

At the 1996 Summer Olympics in Atlanta, we saw Olympic records fall. This happens at every Olympic Games. Why is that? Why haven't we gotten to a place where old records would be "unbreakable"? Well, along with better training, I think one reason is an earthly form of *koinonia*.

When all those athletes and hundreds of thousands of spectators come together, the environment is so "electric," so alive, that it inspires the athletes to put forward a peak performance. They rise above the normal level of their ability. They do great feats because the environment rubs off on them.

This is what I call earthly *koinonia*. The church needs the same dynamic. We will love Jesus greatly and do great things for Him when disciples who are on fire ignite other disciples. When people rub off on each other as they gather in genuine fellowship, the Holy Spirit is free to act.

The Results of Love

Look with me once more at Acts 2:47, the last verse in that great chapter. Notice the very last phrase of that verse. As the disciples were practicing the four necessities, including fellowship, "the Lord was adding to their number day by day those who were being saved."

Their discipleship was producing spectacular results, in other words. The saints were not only igniting each other in their love for Christ, but others were also noticing the fire. When they spread out through the city of Jerusalem to go to work or to socialize, Jesus was so much a part of their lives that sinners came to see what the fire was all about.

Then the saints would say, "Come here and let me explain to you what Jesus did for me. I was lost in sin, but He found me. I was in the pit, but He lifted me out."

As the old people used to say, "I looked at my hands, my hands looked new. I looked at my feet, and they did too. And ever since that wonderful day, my soul's been satisfied."

The beauty of fellowship is that it works not only when we're together, but when we spread out into the world. As we fall in love with Jesus and ignite a fire in each other, the flames will attract unbelievers who want to see what all the fire is about. Then people will hear about Jesus Christ and respond.

A New "Old" Commandment

In John 13:34, Jesus told His disciples, "A new commandment I give to you, that you love one another." Then He added this word: "By this all men will know that you are My disciples, if you have love for one another" (v. 35).

Jesus is saying that the greatest witness you can have as His disciple is your love for other believers. The late Christian philosopher Francis Schaeffer called love the "last apologetic." It's a witness no one can deny.

But it's hard to leave this kind of a witness when there is no fellowship at work among Christ's disciples. Our "connectedness," our sense of belonging, lets people know that Jesus is real. In a culture where people are disconnected, lonely, hurt, and searching for love in all the wrong places, authentic *koinonia* is a powerful apologetic for Christ.

Jesus called the commandment to love one another a "new commandment." But writing about the same thing many years later, the apostle John says, "I am not writing a new commandment to you, but an old commandment which you have had from the beginning" (1 John 2:7).

How can this commandment be new and old at the same time? The same way the sun is both new and old.

The sun has been around since creation. But every day, the sun is new in the sense that the light it brings is new each day. The sun is "from the beginning" of creation, but its effect is new each day.

In the same way the love of Christ, even though it is "from the beginning," ought to rise new every morning in your heart and bring sunshine into other people's lives. When fellowship is working the way it is designed to work, it helps that effect take place. Love is a tremendous compensation of fellowship.

THE COMPENSATION OF SHARING

Now it's time to get gritty, to get down to something that is intensely practical. A final compensation of fellowship I want to consider is what I call the compensation of sharing.

The reality is that when the early church came together in the practice of *koinonia,* the needs of the body of Christ were met. The disciples stepped forward, and dug deep in their pockets when necessary, to share whatever was needed.

Let me give you the implications of this right up front. There were no government programs needed here. No "Great Society" initiatives called for. No "affirmative action" desired. If you know me at all, you know this is a very important principle to me. The church has turned its responsibility and calling over to the government, and we have created a mess that is messing up people's lives.

Material Needs Were Met

Look what was said about the church in Jerusalem:

There was not a needy person among them, for all who were owners of land or houses would sell them and bring the proceeds of the sales, and lay them at the apostles' feet; and they would be distributed to each, as any had need. (Acts 4:34–35)

When the *koinonia* is authentic, the legitimate needs of the body of Christ are covered by the members of the body. When Luke says there was not one needy person in the church at Jerusalem, we need to remember something: They were not just dealing with a few people, but thousands. On the Day of Pentecost, three thousand people were saved (Acts 2:41). Later, five thousand more were saved and added to the church (Acts 4:4). This all happened in a span of just weeks. These were not rich folk either.

What produced this open-hearted, open-handed attitude among the disciples? It was *koinonia.* The disciples were all "of one heart and soul" (Acts 4:32).

We have to realize that fellowship is not some other-worldly, "pie in the sky, by and by" commitment. It gets down to the nitty-gritty issues of life. Notice that this incredible giving was totally voluntary. The disciples did it because they wanted to do it.

That's what got Ananias and Sapphira in trouble in Acts 5. They pretended to make a full commitment when they were actually holding back part of their money. Peter said they didn't even have to give the offering at all (Acts 5:4), but that their pretense of generosity was lying to the Holy Spirit and it brought great damage to the body that was depending on their commitment. Inauthentic *koinonia* cost them their lives. It was not simply that they lied; it was also what they lied about. The well-being of the body was at stake.

Authentic *koinonia,* on the other hand, says, "If my brother or sister has a legitimate need and I have the ability to meet that need, then I will take what God has provided to me and make it available to that brother or sister."

The key word here is *legitimate* need. We know there are people who try to take advantage of the church's generosity for illegitimate needs.

What constitutes a legitimate need? First, it is a need that the person can't meet himself. The church is not obligated to people who simply refuse to work. Paul says if a man won't work, he ought not eat (2 Thessalonians 3:10). The person who says, "I'm not into working," needs to go hungry until he *is* "into working." His hunger is not a legitimate need. If he doesn't do windows, he may need to learn how.

A legitimate need is also a need that a person's family cannot help him meet. Don't bring needs to the church that the family can meet. The family is the first line of responsibility for the needs of its members. We must all bear our "own load" (Galatians 6:5), meaning the normal responsibilities of life.

Another element of a legitimate need is that it truly be a need. The brother who refuses hamburger because he prefers steak is probably not hungry enough yet.

But if a person is unable to meet his own need, and his family is unable to come alongside and help, then you bring the need to the church. This is what the members were doing in Jerusalem, and the disciples gave to meet the needs.

Let me show you what a powerful "payoff" this brings. You may recall the familiar verse, "It is more blessed to give than to receive" (Acts 20:35). Jesus said that, so we know it's important. But we only haul it out and quote it at Christmas when we spend lots of money on people whose happiness is closely tied to our own.

But Jesus is saying that when you give to others who need it, you are "blessed" or happy yourself. How is that? Because when you bless others by giving to them in their time of need, God becomes your "Blesser" by giving to you in your time of need. Think about that for thirty seconds or so and you'll understand why it is more blessed to give than to receive.

Let me show you an example of this principle of giving that will knock your socks off. "Do not neglect to show hospitality to strangers, for by this some have entertained angels without knowing it" (Hebrews 13:2). We need to talk about this.

The writer of Hebrews is saying that when you open your heart and home in hospitality, you may be doing more than you know. The "strangers" here are not just people off the streets who come and say, "I want to stay in your house." These strangers were brothers and sisters in Christ whom the one offering the hospitality did not yet know. We know this because of the context in verse 1, where the writer says, "Let love of the brethren continue."

He's talking about fellowship within the family of God. In that day, traveling evangelists and teachers needed hospitality from local believers as they went from place to place.

When you offer this hospitality, the Bible says you may entertain an "angel." The Greek word for *angel* means "messenger." This could be a literal angel, or it could be a person who is acting on God's behalf as a messenger.

In other words, when God brings a brother or sister in Christ your way, and you have the opportunity to open your home, give freely of what you have. God may have a special message or a blessing for you in their visit.

I saw this happen firsthand on one occasion. Lois and I were asked to host a brother in Christ who was recommended by a reputable person. We took this brother into our home. It so happened that we had a great financial need at that time. I was in school, and there was no money. But we hosted this brother as best we could with what little we had.

After he left, I found in my mailbox at Dallas Seminary a $2,500 check from this messenger of God. If we had turned down an opportunity to host this man, we would have turned down a blessing.

I know what you're thinking. "If that's the case, I'll take in everyone!" But I can't guarantee you a financial return. I *can* say that you will be blessed, "happy," when you help to meet needs in the body of Christ.

A couple of years ago, one of the families in our church lost their house to a fire. The saints who lived in their neighborhood rushed in to help, and *koinonia* was alive in that situation.

Later, this brother came to me and said, "Pastor, I just wanted you to know, Christianity is real." He wasn't talking about my sermons. He was talking about the "sermon" of the people who loved him and his family in a crisis. This is the kind of sermon we need more of; not just a sermon from the pulpit, but a sermon from the pew. That's powerful *koinonia.*

When the church practices true *koinonia,* the church doesn't need welfare. We can save the government a lot of money. The African-American church worked even in the days of slavery, when the people had almost nothing and there was no government assistance, no federal grants, and no social support system.

Yet everybody ate. Kids without a daddy had a daddy. Everybody was extended family. Why did they do that? Because the church understood that when the family of God works, God takes care of His little children.

It's when we don't work that we need welfare. There ought not be one person in the church who is dependent upon a welfare system for the basic needs of life. If a believer has met his personal and family responsibility to the best of his ability and is still in need, the church ought to step in and meet the need.

Emotional Needs Were Met

We think of the apostle Paul as this super-tough saint who could go it alone. But in 2 Corinthians 7:6, he says, "But God, who comforts the depressed, comforted us by the coming of Titus."

Paul was lonely and discouraged at that time in Macedonia. He needed the companionship of his fellow workers in the gospel. He had a legitimate emotional need for comfort and companionship. At the end of his life, Paul was also lonely (2 Timothy 4:9–11).

Paul also helped to meet the emotional needs of his spiritual son, Timothy. After Paul had left Timothy in Ephesus to pastor the church there, he wrote very tenderly to encourage his disciple, who tended to be fearful (2 Timothy 1:3–7).

Without knowing you or your situation, I can say with confidence that there will be lonely believers sitting around you in church next Sunday. How do I know that? Because there are lonely and discouraged people everywhere. It's an epidemic.

This is where we need to practice one of the "one

another" commands of the New Testament we listed in chapter 9: "encourage one another" (1 Thessalonians 5:11).

Of course, encouragement is not the only emotional need that disciples face. Sometimes we need a hand on our shoulder to encourage us, and sometimes we need a push on our shoulder to get us going. Whatever the case, fellowship pays off when we are equipped to meet each other's needs.

Spiritual Needs Were Met

The meeting of spiritual needs is another compensation of fellowship. As we said in chapter 10, this certainly includes rescuing a brother or sister who has been trapped in sin (Galatians 6:1) and one who is more deliberately disobeying God and risking death (James 5:19–20).

It's even better to prevent a fellow believer from slipping off the path. Hebrews 3:13 says, "Encourage one another day after day . . . lest any one of you be hardened by the deceitfulness of sin." This is preventive spiritual maintenance. Since sin is so incredibly deceitful, we do well to warn each other where the traps are.

I also think of the spiritual service that Aquila and Priscilla performed for Apollos (Acts 18:23–27). Apollos was a mighty preacher, but he didn't have all the pieces of his theological puzzle in place yet.

So Aquila and Priscilla took him aside and "explained to him the way of God more accurately" (v. 26).

The lay couple taught the preacher, in other words. And then when Apollos was ready to move on, the disciples in Ephesus wrote a letter of recommendation for him (v. 27).

A CLOSING WORD

As a pastor, I am often asked concerning a need or a problem, "What is the church going to do about this?" The people asking are usually seeking an organizational solution, one that comes from the top down.

But the church isn't designed to work from the top down. Instead, it works from the bottom up. That means believers ought to ask concerning a lot of problems, "What am I doing about it?"

Don't get me wrong. The official structure of the church should do everything it can to embody biblical fellowship. But for this thing to work right, much has to come from the individual disciples as they follow Christ. *Koinonia* requires each member of the body to take a part, to share in the life of Christ.

That's why I am excited about a lot of things that are happening at our church. Believers are carrying sick people to the hospital, visiting the ill, comforting the downhearted, and counseling the broken. Couples who are walking with Christ are helping other couples who want to get out of their marriages learn to strengthen them instead.

Yes, Oak Cliff Bible Fellowship is still a house under construction, just like your church. But allow me to share with you an unusual example of fellowship that we witnessed here in Dallas in the fall of 1995.

We were due to move into our new worship center on October 1 of that year. We had sent out advertisements all over America. People were coming from all over the country to celebrate with us.

But the contractor said, "This is going to be a close call. The only way we're going to make it is if you get the members of your church to help. Once we're done with construction, the cleanup is going to be a massive task. To have this place ready for the first Sunday in October, the church is going to have to get involved."

So two Sundays before the opening date, I told the congregation, "It's now our job. The contractors have done all they can to have the building ready. We need a week where everybody does something, so that everything gets done."

People came by the hundreds on Monday, Tuesday, Wednesday, and every day right on through Friday. It was still a close call, but on October 1 when we opened the doors of the new sanctuary, the floor was clean. There were envelopes in the pew racks. The pews had been wiped and the windows had been cleaned. We celebrated Jesus Christ in our new facility on that date.

How did it happen? We had one mind to accomplish one goal. We could have stood outside and said, "The job is too big to do in one week." Instead, we said, "If everybody does something, everything will get done." We did it because of *koinonia*.

If we as the disciples of Jesus Christ will follow Him with one mind and one heart, with everybody doing his or her part, we will see God send us a "payoff" beyond anything we can imagine.

SCRIPTURE

CHAPTER TWELVE

THE CONCEPT OF SCRIPTURE

We have now come to the third element of what we are calling absolute necessities in following Christ: the Word of God. We need to be men and women of the Word if we're going to develop into mature, growing disciples.

As we refer once again to our foundational passage in Acts 2, I want you to see that when we are told that the believers in the early church "were continually devoting themselves to the apostles' teaching" (v. 42), these people were getting Scripture firsthand because the New Testament had not been written yet. The apostles' teaching was fully authoritative, and the church submitted to that authority.

That's important, because at the core of the whole matter of Scripture and its relationship to our discipleship is the issue of authority. Before we can become growing, maturing disciples of Jesus Christ, we must decide who and what will control the decision-making process in our lives.

SOURCES OF AUTHORITY

The world presents us with a number of options when it comes to answering the question of who and what will be our authority. For example, rationalism or reason is the authority in some people's lives. Their minds are the ultimate foundation for life's choices.

But there are at least two major problems with allowing your mind, your thinking processes, to be your source of authority. The first problem is that your mind is finite. That is, it is subject to limitations. Nobody knows everything. There are lots of things we don't even *suspect*.

A second problem with using reason as your basis of authority is that your mind is sinful. That is, you cannot depend on your mind to give you accurate moral information about life. When you combine finiteness with sinfulness, you've got a messed-up mind that is saddled with great limitations.

Other people don't depend on their minds, but on their feelings. They are moved only by their emotions. I don't want to denigrate the importance of our emotions, but the problem with relying on them as one's source of authority is that emotions are unreliable. They change regularly.

For some of us, in fact, emotions change from moment to moment. We are very emotional people. When things are looking up, we're up. But when things go down, we're down. Emotions were never designed to be our ultimate authority.

Still other people say, "Let your conscience be your guide." They rely on their own moral instincts, their sense of right and wrong.

The problem with making your conscience your source of authority is that your conscience only reflects what it has been fed. If your conscience has been getting the wrong information, you could be feeling right about something wrong, or wrong about something right. You could be operating on a moral instinct that is not altogether accurate. And we know from Scripture that the conscience can be corrupted (Titus 1:15).

If we choose reason, emotion, or conscience as our source of ultimate authority, we're in trouble, because they are all defective. There is only one source of authority on which the decisions of life should rest, and that is the Word of God.

To help you appreciate the absolute necessity of Scripture, in this chapter I want to explore with you three concepts that will enable you to benefit from God's wonderful gift of His Word. These concepts are built upon three important words: revelation, inspiration, and illumination.

THE CONCEPT OF REVELATION

Revelation is divine disclosure, God unveiling information about Himself that He wants His creation to know. Revelation is like pulling back a curtain in order to see what's behind it. It is the displaying of what was covered or hidden.

The reason revelation is critical is that we only get to know about God what He decides to reveal about Himself. God is utterly, totally different from you and me—so different that theologians call Him the "Wholly Other." We were made in His image, but He is distinct from His creation and separate from sin, which puts Him so high above us that to even see Him is to die, apart from Christ.

God is so far outside of and above our realm of functioning that if we are left to our reason, emotions, or conscience to figure Him out, we are going to fall really short. Whatever we come up with is going to be something other than the God of Scripture.

Let's look at why it is important for God to reveal Himself if we are going to know Him. God said through the prophet Isaiah, "'My thoughts are not your thoughts, neither are your ways My ways,' declares the Lord. 'For as the heavens are higher than the earth, so are My ways higher than your ways, and My thoughts than your thoughts'" (Isaiah 55:8–9).

God says two very important things here. First, "I am different from you. My thoughts and ways are different than yours." But instead of recognizing that God is wholly different, people today are trying to create God in their own image. Whenever we try to adjust God to how we think or feel, we are left with something other than the God who reveals Himself.

God also says in Isaiah 55, "I am higher than you." Many of us have had our children come to us and try to advise us as to how to run our homes. They have no experience at being parents, but they think they know how we ought to do our jobs. They don't understand the gap between parents and kids.

What children try to do with their parents, we try to do with God. We try to advise Him on how to be God. We have never been God. We don't even know what it means to be God. We have never created anything, but we want to advise God. However, God must reveal Himself if we are to know Him because He is higher than we are.

Revelation Is Personal

What is the nature of God's self-revelation in Scripture? We have one answer here in Isaiah 55. God's word is that which "goes forth from [His] mouth" (v. 11). That is, God's revelation is intensely personal. It is intimately tied to His Person.

So when you open your Bible, you are not just engaging in academic study. You are really trying to understand a Person. In the Scripture, God unveils Himself. When you look in the Word, you see God.

But you find that God is also looking back at you through His Word. The writer of Hebrews tells us:

> The word of God is living and active and sharper than any two-edged sword, and piercing as far as the division of soul and spirit, of both joints and marrow, and able to judge the thoughts and intentions of the heart. And there is no creature hidden from His sight. (4:12–13a)

The Bible is not just an inanimate object. It is alive because it is the word of the living God who reveals Himself in a personal way. When you read the Bible, you are looking at God and He is looking back at you. That's why the Bible is an absolute necessity for us as Christ's disciples.

Revelation Is Purposeful

God's revelation is also purposeful. He says that when He sends forth His Word, "It shall not return to Me empty, without accomplishing what I desire, and without succeeding in the matter for which I sent it" (Isaiah 55:11).

"All Scripture is inspired by God and profitable" (2 Timothy 3:16). Scripture is beneficial. It acts, it does the things in our lives that God purposes shall be done. God doesn't lay His revelation out for us to look over and vote on. And He doesn't just toss words around with no purpose in mind.

Every word that comes from God's mouth is infused with His purpose. And because God's Word is also infused with His life, it has the power to bring His purpose to pass. God's Word always produces the effect He intends it to produce.

Revelation Is Particular

A third characteristic of revelation is that it is what I want to call particular. That is, the Bible is the complete Word of God for us, but it does not claim to be a total description of what God is like, or a total record of everything God does.

The last verse of John's gospel is important here. The apostle says that if all the things Jesus did were written down in detail, "even the world itself would not contain the books which were written" (John 21:25).

That is an amazing statement. Remember, John is just talking about a brief slice of Jesus' earthly life, His three-year ministry. John says, "I'm not giving you the whole ball of wax, because the Library of Congress couldn't handle the record of what Jesus did."

The Gospels just give us the highlights of Jesus' ministry, the particular details the Holy Spirit wants us to know. Revelation is particular because it is selective.

Deuteronomy 29:29 says, "The secret things belong to the Lord our God, but the things revealed belong to us." What God has told us about Himself is what He wants us to know. But He has not told us everything.

Sometimes we have to say to our children, "That's none of your business," or "When I want you to know, I'll tell you." There are times when you don't feel the need to reveal all that you know. Neither does God.

Why is God particular in what He reveals? One reason is that we could not comprehend it all anyway. And we never will. In fact, after we have been in heaven one hundred million years, we will still not know everything there is to know about God. He is inexhaustible.

Revelation Is Progressive

The opening verse of Hebrews makes clear that the revelation of God is progressive: "God, after He spoke long ago to the fathers in the prophets in many portions and in many ways, in these last days has spoken to us in His Son" (1:1–2a).

The God who spoke through the prophets in the Old Testament spoke through Christ in the New Testament. God gave us His revelation one step at a time, not all at once.

Revelation is progressive. The Bible contains sixty-six books written over a period of about fifteen hundred years by more than forty different authors. Yet it reveals one message. The Bible is God's progressive revelation, not one that was completed in one sitting by one person.

Revelation Is Perfect

The final thing I want you to see about God's revelation is that it is perfect. John 17:17 says, "Thy word is truth." That means there is no utterance of God's that is not truth. Truth is that which corresponds to reality. The Bible is the only place you're guaranteed to find the real deal every time. We are truthful sometimes. But the Scripture is absolute truth.

God's Word is truth because God is truth. His Word corresponds to His character. God is perfect, so His revelation must be perfect (Romans 3:4).

In revelation, God pulls back the curtain so we can

get a glimpse of what He is like. We have enough to know what He expects of us, but not all of Him there is, for the world could not contain it.

I figure that anybody who by opening His mouth and saying, "Let there be," can bring a universe into existence is going to take a while to understand. I'm still trying to understand a personal computer. I'm trying to become "computer literate." But the only way you and I are going to become "God literate" is by His self-revelation. We have that revelation in Scripture.

THE CONCEPT OF INSPIRATION

Here is our second concept regarding Scripture, our second word. Revelation is concerned with the content of Scripture. Inspiration is concerned with the recording of that content.

This word *inspiration* has become watered down in our everyday usage. We say, "I was inspired by the choir." "The preacher inspired me." "That was an inspiring poem." We mean the person or piece made us feel good. It caused our spirit to be elevated.

"God-Breathed"

Well, that's a weak use of the word that does not properly express the biblical concept. We read above in 2 Timothy 3:16 that "all Scripture is inspired by God." The Greek word here, *theopneustos,* is made up of two words, the word for "God" and a word that means "to breathe out" or "exhale." So all Scripture is the "exhaling" of God.

When God gave the Scripture, He exhaled or breathed out the word upon the authors who recorded it. That's what inspiration means. Scripture is the very breath, the very word, of God.

When we talk about inspiration, we are talking about the process by which God oversaw the composition of Scripture so that its message was recorded without error.

All of us have met people who question whether the Bible is inspired at all. Others question whether all of the

Bible is inspired, or just some of it. But 2 Timothy 3:16 says that the inspiration of God applies to everything in Scripture. It's all "God-exhaled." It's all His very breath, His very Word.

Delivered Through Messengers

This helps to explain texts such as Acts 1:16, where Peter is talking about the need to replace Judas among the apostles. He says, "Brethren, the Scripture had to be fulfilled, which the Holy Spirit foretold by the mouth of David concerning Judas, who became a guide to those who arrested Jesus." In verse 20, Peter went on to quote Psalm 69:25 and Psalm 109:8 and apply those texts to Judas.

The question is, who was speaking in the Psalms, the Holy Spirit or David? David wrote the verse, but Peter said the Holy Spirit spoke it. Therefore, the Bible claims that what its human authors wrote is the same as the spoken word of God.

The Scripture is really from God, even though in this case it came out of the mouth of David. God the Holy Spirit spoke through David. Scripture came from the mouth of God, even though it was delivered through a human messenger. That's because of inspiration.

Remember when you were growing up and your parents would give you a message to deliver to your brother or sister? You would go and say, "Momma said to do this," or "Daddy said you have to." That was the voice of authority.

You did not have any authority of your own over your sibling. But once you introduce the formula, "Momma said," you have Momma's authority because now you are delivering her message, not yours.

So if your brother or sister disobeys your word, your parents view it as if that child had disobeyed them directly, because it is really their word delivered through you. But if you try to change the message or add "Momma said" to your own wish, you're in trouble because you are taking unto yourself an authority that doesn't belong to you.

That's what a lot of people are doing today with God's Word. They are either saying that God said things that God never said, or they are denying that God really said what He said, in order to usurp His authority in their lives. They want to take unto themselves authority that God never intended them to have.

This is why for us as disciples of Jesus Christ, Scripture must reign as the supreme authority. The Word of God is not some person's opinion. It is God authoritatively communicating through the pen of another. We must obey Scripture if we claim to follow Christ.

Recorded by Others

So the issue in inspiration is that God breathed the word. How did the process give us a Bible that is free from error even though imperfect human beings were in the picture? The apostle Peter, who was one of those imperfect human beings, tells us how it happened:

> But know this first of all, that no prophecy of Scripture is a matter of one's own interpretation, for no prophecy was ever made by an act of human will, but men moved by the Holy Spirit spoke from God. (2 Peter 1:20–21)

In other words, no biblical writer ever sat down and said, "I'm going to write what I think. I'm going to put my own spin on this doctrine. I'm going to write what I feel like writing." That's not how it worked. The authors of Scripture only wrote as they were "moved" by the Holy Spirit.

This is the key word for understanding inspiration. The Greek word *pheromenoi*, translated "moved," means to be "carried or driven along," like wind driving the sail of a ship.

This word is used in Acts 27:15 to describe what happened when the ship that Paul was on got caught in a terrible storm and was eventually destroyed. "When the ship was caught in [the storm], and could not face the wind, we gave way to it, and let ourselves be driven along." The phrase "driven along" is repeated in verse 17.

Compare this with what we just read in 2 Peter 1:21 and you get the picture of how divine inspiration worked. What the wind was to the sail of that ship, the Holy Spirit was to the writers of Scripture. They were moved by the Spirit where *He* wanted them to go, not where they wanted to go. They wrote what God wanted them to write.

The writers of Scripture were like the sails on a ship that catch the wind and are propelled by it. Just as Paul's ship was overcome by the wind, so the biblical writers were overcome by the "wind" or "breath" of God, the Holy Spirit.

To put it another way, the writers of Scripture were at the mercy of the Spirit, like the ship was at the mercy of the wind. That doesn't mean they simply took dictation from the Spirit. They didn't lose their personalities. Every biblical writer has his own style and vocabulary. But God expressed His perfect revelation through the various personalities of these "men moved by the Holy Spirit."

Guarded by the Spirit

Someone may still say, "As long as people are involved in the process, the result can't be perfect and error-free." That might be true if it were not for the fact that God superintended and controlled the recording of Scripture. Man was involved, but God was in control. That's the difference between the Bible and every other thing in which imperfect humans are involved.

Protecting His Word from error is no harder for God than protecting Jesus Christ from a sin nature even though He was born of a human mother. Jesus was born of a woman who was sinful and imperfect like the rest of us, yet He was without sin (Hebrews 4:15).

How could that be? Because the Holy Spirit was involved. He came upon Mary (Luke 1:35) to protect the sinfulness of man from corrupting the righteousness of God.

In the same way, God inspired imperfect men to record His revelation. That means these men had to let the Spirit rule in their lives.

There's a great spiritual lesson here, by the way. If you let the Holy Ghost take over your life so that He takes you where He wants you to go, rather than your trying to puff your sails to get where you want to go, you'll start getting somewhere.

But as long as you and I try to live by our own will and determination and independence, as long as we blow the winds on our own sails, then we should not be surprised if we don't get anywhere. Following Christ in discipleship means doing what the writers of Scripture did: submitting to the Holy Spirit of God and letting Him direct us wherever He desires.

So just as the Holy Spirit protected Jesus from sin, He protected the Bible from error through His controlling influence in the writing of Scripture. The Spirit guarded the truth of God in a miraculous way so that what was written is what God said. John put it this way:

> If we receive the witness of men, the witness of God is greater; for the witness of God is this, that He has borne witness concerning His Son. . . . And the witness is this, that God has given us eternal life, and this life is in His Son. . . . These things I have written to you. (1 John 5:9, 11, 13a)

Notice that last phrase. The witness from God became a written revelation from God to His people. God the Holy Spirit inspired John to write what He wanted us to know in a language we could understand. Why? So that we would have a permanent record of God's witness.

The Perfect Result

The result of inspiration is this: Because of the overseeing work of the Spirit in the recording of Scripture, what you and I have is the inerrant, authoritative canon of Scripture. The word *canon* refers to the collection of the sixty-six books that make up the Bible.

By the way, the church also believes that the Holy Spirit led in the selection process of these books. There were other epistles and written stories floating around in the early church, but they were not inspired, authoritative Scripture. The Holy Spirit oversaw the process of determining which books were, and which were not, God-breathed.

So let me say it again. The result of inspiration is a canon, a collection of books, that is inerrant (without error). In the Bible, we have the authoritative revelation of God preserved in a written record. We have all that God wants to disclose about Himself.

Why is inerrancy so important? Because if there is a flaw anywhere in Scripture, we don't know whether we can trust it anywhere else. If God calls this His Word, and yet there's a mistake in it, how do I know I can trust God? What other mistakes might He have made (or allowed) that I don't know about?

But let me tell you, if the Bible is a flawless, errorless Book, then you can believe God 100 percent of the time. I have enough people I trust partially. I need a God I can trust completely.

Those who reject the inspiration of Scripture have to do battle with Jesus Christ, because Jesus believed it was the Word of God. He said in Matthew 5:

> Do not think that I came to abolish the Law or the Prophets; I did not come to abolish, but to fulfill. For truly I say to you, until heaven and earth pass away, not the smallest letter or stroke shall pass away from the Law, until all is accomplished. (vv. 17–18)

The "smallest letter or stroke" is the familiar "jot or tittle" (KJV). The smallest letter of the Hebrew alphabet is written like an apostrophe in English ('). A "stroke" is a tiny line that distinguishes one Hebrew letter from another.

Jesus was saying, "God's Word is so true and authoritative that it will be fulfilled down to the most minute portion of a Hebrew letter." In fact, even after this universe is gone God's Word will still be in effect. The result of inspiration is the Word of God that cannot possibly fail.

We can see this kind of detailed accuracy through-out the Scripture. The prophet Micah said the Savior would be born in Bethlehem, a two-bit town in Judea (Micah 5:2). Micah wrote that about seven hundred years before Jesus was born.

How did Micah know that detail so far in advance? Because he was "borne along" by the Spirit of God. Divine revelation came though divine inspiration, result-ing in an accurate record.

Proverbs 30:5–6 says, "Every word of God is tested. . . . Do not add to His words lest He reprove you, and you be proved a liar." God doesn't need your help or mine to get His message recorded. If He had wanted to write more, He would have written more.

Everything we need to know to live holy lives is in the Book. We don't need to be giving God our ideas and our feelings about Scripture. If we try to add to His words, or take away from them for that matter, we are going to be proved the liar, not Him.

In the Upper Room, Jesus prophesied that through the Holy Spirit, He would remind the apostles of every-thing they would need to know (John 14:26; 16:13). So when they sat down to write Scripture, the Spirit saw to it that everything was written just as God willed it to be written. That is inspiration.

Faith and Inspiration

Why is it so important that you believe in the inerrancy and authority of Scripture? Because without faith, it is impossible to please God (Hebrews 11:6). The trouble with a lot of us who call ourselves Jesus' disciples and claim to be following Him is that we don't really trust Him. I'm not talking about our salvation. I'm talk-ing about the outworking of our daily Christian lives.

See, you're not trusting God when you match what God says against your reason, and your reason wins. Or when you match what God says against your feelings, and your feelings win. Or when you match what God says against your conscience, and your conscience wins. That's not living by faith.

And when you're not living by faith, then the power in the living Word doesn't come alive in you. It is impossible to please God without faith. Sometimes, living by faith means you go against what reason tells you. Sometimes it means you go against what others tell you. Sometimes it even means you have to go against everything you were raised to believe.

Authority and Inspiration

Because the Scripture is inspired, it should have authority. When Satan came to tempt Jesus in Matthew 4, Jesus answered him with the authoritative Word of God: "It is written." For Jesus, what was written in Scripture was binding, because "every word" that came from the mouth of God was spiritual sustenance (Matthew 4:4).

Jesus said in John 10:35, "The Scripture cannot be broken." That means it's binding. No single part can be extracted from the whole. It's either all God's Word, or none of it is God's Word.

Some people want to take out the parts of the Bible they don't like. Jesus says no to that approach. In fact, He warned us, "Don't negate the Word of God for the traditions of men. Don't let what men have always done and believed stop you from doing what God says" (see Mark 7:8–9).

THE CONCEPT OF ILLUMINATION

The third concept I want to discuss is illumination. The word *illumination* simply means enlightenment. It is the work of the Holy Spirit that allows us to understand, experience, and apply the truth of God to our lives.

Paul prayed in Ephesians 1:18 that "the eyes of your heart may be enlightened" so that the saints would understand the greatness of God's power and blessings available to them.

The Anointing

First John 2:27 says that every Christian has what John calls "the anointing"—that is, the ability to receive, understand, and apply spiritual truth. There are no "supersaints" when it comes to understanding Scripture. God wants every believer to be illumined concerning His truth. The only difference between us is whether we are committed enough to seek it.

Before cable television came into my neighborhood, I used a television antenna. I had a workman come out one time because I was having problems with my reception. He said, "Your signal is strong, but your antenna is not pointed in the right direction."

The Word of God is strong. There's no problem with the "signal." But our heart's antenna is often not pointed in the right direction. A lot of us are fiddling with our lives trying to fix them when the problem is that our spiritual antenna is not pointed toward God. Therefore, we cannot pick up the Spirit's signal.

But we all have the anointing within us, the illuminating work of the Spirit of God. That's why the psalmist wrote these verses in Psalm 119, "Open my eyes, that I may behold wonderful things from Thy law" (v. 18). "Thy commandments make me wiser than my enemies" (v. 98). "I have more insight than all my teachers" (v. 99). "Thy word is a lamp to my feet, and a light to my path" (v. 105).

The Spirit of God shines His light on the Word of God. Back in Genesis 1:2, we discover that the Spirit was hovering over creation. Then in verse 3 God said, "Let there be light." Light was not present until the Spirit of God hovered.

Why is that important? When the Spirit of God hovers and the Word of God speaks, order comes out of chaos. That's what happened in creation. The earth was "formless and void" before the Spirit and the light came (Genesis 1:2).

Does your life ever feel formless and void? Ever feel empty, chaotic in your life? Guess when you move from chaos to order? You do so when the Word of God is mixed with the hovering Spirit.

That's not just reading your Bible; that's asking God to illumine what you read and submitting your heart to it. Then God brings order out of chaos.

The Mind of Christ

In 1 Corinthians 2, Paul makes some great statements concerning this matter of illumination:

> Just as it is written, "Things which eye has not seen and ear has not heard, and which have not entered the heart of man, all that God has prepared for those who love Him." For to us God revealed them through the Spirit; for the Spirit searches all things, even the depths of God. . . . Now we have received, not the spirit of the world, but the Spirit who is from God, that we might know the things freely given to us by God, which things we also speak, not in words taught by human wisdom, but in those taught by the Spirit, combining spiritual thoughts with spiritual words. (vv. 9–10, 12–13)

When the Spirit takes "spiritual words," the Word of God, and combines them with "spiritual thoughts," a mind and a heart in tune with God, the result is divine illumination. When you combine a spiritually receptive mind with the Word, you have dynamite on your hands.

That's because "he who is spiritual appraises all things" (v. 15) since he has "the mind of Christ" (v. 16). This is the key to illumination. Having the mind of Christ is having your spiritual antenna pointed in the direction of the Holy Spirit's signal. When you are properly attuned, you will understand more things and make more sense out of life than you ever thought possible.

The Process

Luke 24:13–35, the story of the two disciples on the road to Emmaus, gives us a good, real-life look at how the process of illumination works.

You'll remember that as these two walked back to Emmaus from Jerusalem, they were depressed, discouraged, and downcast. Life had fallen in for them because Jesus had been crucified. They saw "no hope, no way, no how."

But then the risen Christ joined them on the road

and asked why they were discouraged (v. 17). They explained the situation and their disappointment, and Jesus said to them, "O foolish men and slow of heart to believe in all that the prophets have spoken!" (v. 25). Then He taught them from the Scriptures.

In other words, they had not been paying attention to the revealed Word of God. Jesus was saying, "You two are discouraged for no reason. If you would have listened to the Word of God, you would know that what has happened is a fulfillment of prophecy."

Because they weren't listening to the Word, they were unnecessarily depressed. But when Jesus began teaching them, they listened. They were all ears. If you want the illumination of the Spirit, the first thing you need is an ear to hear what the Word of God is saying.

Then you need to combine a listening ear with the will to be transformed. Verse 28 says that Jesus "acted as though He would go farther." But they begged Him, "Stay with us" (v. 29). I think Jesus was testing them to see whether they really wanted Him or were just going through the spiritual motions.

God does this with us. He will let us hear the Word, and then He will bring something into our lives to see whether we really heard it, or whether we were just sitting in church or just doing devotions that day. He will bring something into our lives to put to the test that which we have heard. We must have a will that is ready to be transformed.

So we have a listening ear and a willing heart, two key elements in experiencing illumination. The third element is worship. Jesus reclined at the table with these two disciples, and they had a worship service (v. 30).

In fact, we can see many of the same elements in verse 30 that we find later in Acts 2. There was communion in the breaking of bread, prayer, and *koinonia* as Jesus shared it with them.

When all of that was working, what happened next? "Their eyes were opened" (Luke 24:31). Illumination set in. They were enlightened. They recognized Him.

Even though Jesus vanished from their sight in that

instant, everything was changed. They were alive with joy and excitement, and they couldn't wait to share it with others. They got up and ran back to Jerusalem that same night, and excitedly they told the apostles all that had happened to them (vv. 33–35).

You mean the depression was gone? You mean they were happy again? Yes, because they had combined a listening ear with a willing heart and worship of the Lord, and they were illuminated. And when they were illuminated, a transformation took place.

In revelation, God discloses His truth. Through inspiration, He sees that it is recorded for us. And by the illumination of His Spirit, He enables us to understand and apply it. When you get all of this working in your life, you're going to grow as a follower of Christ!

CHAPTER THIRTEEN

THE CONTENT OF SCRIPTURE

I f you looked at the title of this chapter and were afraid we were going to do a review of the Bible's content from Genesis to Revelation, you can relax. That's not the idea I have in mind here.

I believe it *is* an absolute necessity that you know your Bible from Genesis to Revelation. But what I want to talk about here is how we should approach the Scripture, so that its content gets off the page and into our lives.

For this portion of our study, we need to go to a classic passage on how we are to approach Scripture, James 1:18–27. James is an "in-your-face" kind of apostle. He tells the truth without apologizing for it, and he isn't going to worry if someone doesn't like what he says. The Word is there to reform us.

Given his style, it shouldn't surprise us that James wasn't satisfied to have believers read the Word and then walk away from it unchanged. On the contrary, he says that when we look into the Word of God, we must receive it, respond to it, and then reflect it.

WE MUST RECEIVE THE WORD

First of all, if the content of Scripture is going to benefit us, we have to receive it. James writes:

In the exercise of [God's] will He brought us forth by the word of truth. . . . But let everyone be quick to hear, slow to speak and slow to anger; for the anger of man does not achieve the righteousness of God. Therefore putting aside all filthiness and all that remains of wickedness, in humility receive the word implanted, which is able to save your souls. (James 1:18–21)

Please notice that we are commanded to "receive" the Word, which has been "implanted" within us (v. 21). The word *implanted* is in the past tense, meaning that the Scripture is already there inside of us.

What James is referring to here is salvation. When you received Jesus Christ, you were made alive by the Word of truth. We just read that above in verse 18. God used His Word to bring you from spiritual death to spiritual life. There is no new birth without the truth of God.

Believers may have been led to salvation by any number of methods, but we all came via the same Word. God may have used another person to lead you to faith, or you may have come to Him through your own searching of His Word. Whatever person or method God used to get your attention, when you came to Him the Word was planted inside of you.

But James says it is possible to have the Word implanted in your heart, and yet not receive it; that is, not to welcome the truth into your heart and obey what it says. If you don't receive the Word, you don't benefit from it.

Here, James isn't dealing with salvation. He's talking to believers. So we have to ask, how is it possible for us to have the Word and yet need to receive or welcome it?

The Seed Planted

The word *implanted* pictures a seed being placed in soil in order that it might grow. If that seed is going to grow, the conditions must be right. But if the soil is not prepared to nourish that seed, there will be no growth. The seed of God's Word—which is good seed, by the way (see Mark 4:1–20)—cannot flourish in hard soil.

Many Christians go to church every Sunday and

every Wednesday night. They may even read their Bibles every day, yet they are not growing.

What's the problem? It's not the seed. The problem is that the Word does not do its work in our hearts until it is received. The Word is not really heard until it is received.

This is why Jesus would often say, "He who has ears to hear, let him hear" (Mark 4:9). He wasn't talking about a person's auditory canal being open. He was talking about the heart being open and receptive to God's truth. Until the Word is received, it doesn't benefit you.

Jesus said of the people of His day, "While hearing they do not hear, nor do they understand" (Matthew 13:13). Their problem was not physical. It was spiritual. Their ears heard what Jesus said, but they weren't *listening* to what He said.

All of us know what it is like to talk to people who aren't listening. It's very hard to communicate with people who don't really want to hear what you have to say. Hebrews 5:11 warns that even as Christians, we can become dull of hearing. We can hear the Word and not receive it.

How to Receive the Word

Now that we know what it means to receive the Word, I want to back up to James 1:19–21 and look at the conditions James gives for receiving the implanted Word. If these conditions are operative in your life, they will enable the seed of the Word planted in your soul to break open and grow.

We must be quick to hear. The first condition for receiving the Word is to be "quick to hear" (v. 19). If you want to see God's Word flourish and bring forth spiritual fruit in your life, you must make it a priority. That's the idea behind being quick to hear.

This means that you want to know and obey the Word so much that you go to it first. You respond quickly when you hear God speaking to you through His Word.

As Christians, we are to be like the mother who

hears her baby cry and jumps out of bed in the middle of the night. Because she has heard the cry of her own, she's quick to respond. If we are going to see God's Word erupt and grow within us, we must be equally quick to hear.

We saw in James 1:18 that God gave us life through His Word. If God gives you life through the Word, guess what? That same Word is able to develop the life God gave you. But you must be quick to hear it.

Unfortunately, a lot of Christians aren't quick to hear. They are quick to talk, quick to offer their opinion, but not quick to hear. What does this phrase mean in relation to the Scripture?

It means the Word of God ought to be the first thing you appeal to, not the last thing. It ought not be brought into the situation only *after* you have tried everything else. It ought not be your last resort. Your first response ought to be, "Let's see what God has to say about this." That's being quick to hear.

So the question is, where is the first place you turn for guidance, the first place you turn for help when the trials of life hit? James says the first place you should go is to God (1:5). When you are quick to hear, the first thing you want to know in any situation is God's viewpoint on it.

We must be slow to speak. We find this exhortation also in James 1:19. It's significant that all of us have two ears and one mouth. We are to listen more than we talk.

James is saying, "When you do speak, make sure what you say reflects what you heard in the Word." In other words, don't talk before you've heard God's viewpoint, because you just might be wrong.

There are a lot of talkers in the church who haven't checked what they are saying against God's Word, so they don't know what they are talking about. Make sure you have heard God's viewpoint before you offer your thoughts.

If I needed help and I came to you for advice, I would definitely want you to give me something that God gave you, not just something you think. If it's just your opinion, we might both wind up in the ditch.

Being slow to speak also means we don't argue with the Word. When we hear the Word, too many of us Christians are quick to say, "Yes, but . . ." We're quick to respond, quick to speak, rather than quick to listen, understand, and apply what God says.

We must be slow to get angry. Don't get mad, James says, if what the Word says is not what you want to hear. Don't get angry if God is not doing things the way you want Him to do them. Our anger doesn't get us where we want to go. James makes that clear: "The anger of man does not achieve the righteousness of God" (1:20). Our getting mad doesn't make God move any faster.

Have your children ever pouted because you didn't say what they wanted to hear? The message they want you to get is, "Since I am mad, you should change." If you have kids, you know what I'm talking about. Kids throw temper tantrums hoping to change a parent's mind. A good parent isn't impressed by a tantrum.

James wants you to know tantrums don't impress God either. Don't think your getting all bent out of shape is going to shake Him up. God operates according to His will, in His time. Your anger won't help God along or make Him alter His plan. We sure could save ourselves a lot of health problems with this verse.

We often get mad when things don't unfold the way we think they should. Sometimes in our anger we are actually trying to advance God's plan, but it doesn't work.

In the Garden of Gethsemane, Peter cut off the servant's ear in His attempt to protect Jesus and fulfill God's program man's way. But Jesus said, "Put away your sword, Peter; you do not know what you're doing" (see John 18:10–11). Peter's intentions were good, but his actions were dead wrong. His anger caused him to react in a very human way to the unfolding of God's plan for His Son.

We must be pure in life. A fourth condition for receiving the Word of God is a purity of life that includes "putting aside all filthiness and all that remains of wickedness" (James 1:21).

That is, don't bring your old self into this new program. When you got saved, the old you—your old patterns of thinking and acting—came across the border with you. James says, "Don't bring those old habits of wickedness into God's kingdom program." Being Christ's disciples demands that we get rid of the old stuff. Purity of life is an absolute necessity in following Christ.

Being a disciple is not a matter of trying to make our old life fit into God's plan. Neither is it trying to adjust God's plan to fit our program. We can't bring the leftovers of our old ways to God and expect Him to make something out of them. We need to let God's Word sit in judgment on us.

The word *filthiness* is interesting. It means "wax in the ear." James is saying we need to get our spiritual ears cleaned out. We need to get the junk out of our ears so we can hear the Word of God. Many times we don't hear God because our lives are all plugged up. We have "waxy ears." We need to get that junk out of there.

On more than one occasion, I had to say to one of my children who had picked up an attitude at school, "Leave that stuff at school. Don't bring that junk home."

James is saying, "Leave all that stuff from your old life back there. Don't bring that junk into your new life in Christ." If we are going to receive and benefit from the Word, it will be on God's terms, not ours.

A Victorious Life

The word *receive* implies "stop resisting." Why is it important not to resist the work of God's Word in our lives? Because it will "save your souls" (James 1:21). We have already said that James is not talking about justification here. These people were already believers. The Word was planted within them.

But salvation has three tenses. Salvation in the past saves us from the penalty of sin. Salvation in the present saves us from the power of sin. And salvation in the future will save us from the presence of sin.

James is talking about the present tense of salvation here. Receiving the Word will deliver your life to be lived as it ought to be lived. This salvation is not from hell, for that is already settled.

What you will be saved from is the attempt of the world, the flesh, and the devil to rob you of a meaningful, powerful, victorious Christian life. The Word is able to give you life as God would have you live it.

WE MUST RESPOND TO THE WORD

The second requirement when we come to the Scripture is that we must respond to it. First we receive it, we welcome it as God's Word to us. Then we follow up on that reception of the Word by responding to it. James writes:

> But prove yourselves doers of the word, and not merely hearers who delude themselves. For if anyone is a hearer of the word and not a doer, he is like a man who looks at his natural face in a mirror; for once he has looked at himself and gone away, he has immediately forgotten what kind of person he was. But one who looks intently at the perfect law, the law of liberty, and abides by it, not having become a forgetful hearer but an effectual doer, this man shall be blessed in what he does. (1:22–25)

How do you position yourself so that you can be "blessed in what [you] do"? By responding to the Word the way a person is supposed to respond to what he sees in a mirror.

Glancing in the Mirror

We've all seen people who looked like they didn't spend enough time in front of the mirror fixing what was wrong. I find it interesting that the word James uses in verse 23 for the person in the mirror is the Greek word for "male," as opposed to mankind, which would include men and women.

Why does James use a man in this illustration? I think because, all things being equal, men don't spend as much time in front of mirrors as women do. I know I'm on thin ice here, but stay with me.

We men tend to glance in a mirror and go on, whereas women are more apt to study their appearance in a mirror. So James says, "Don't just look into the Word and run on, the way a man might glance in a mirror and not notice what needs to be noticed."

What are mirrors designed to do? They are made to show us exactly what we look like so we can see what is wrong and correct it. The mirror only reflects what is there. We can't get upset at the mirror when it does its job of telling us the truth. If we don't look good, the mirror will tell us so.

I know a guy who got so mad at what the mirror showed him that he smashed the mirror. That's not the idea! A mirror is designed to show you what's really there, things you may not be able to detect on your own.

James calls the Bible a mirror for our souls. It shows us what we really look like inside. We need that, because a lot of us think we look better than we really do.

Have you ever looked into a mirror and been shocked? You thought your hair was in place and your tie was straight. You thought everything was in order, but a glance at the mirror told you that you were a mess.

Once you see that, the issue is what you are going to do about it. If you just take a peek and keep on going, the mirror didn't do you any good. Many Christians mark their Bibles, but never let their Bibles mark them.

James uses another interesting word in verse 23 to describe a person who is only a "hearer" of the Word. This word was used of an audit. If you ever audited a class in college, you were saying, "I want all of the information, but none of the responsibility."

Why is that? When you audit a class, you don't have to do the homework or take the tests, but you get to sit in class and absorb the knowledge.

You cannot "audit" the Christian life, however. You cannot just sit and take in the information, yet accept none of the responsibility for what you hear. A disciple has to do the homework and pass the tests.

Hearing the Word without responding to it is like chewing your food without swallowing: It tastes good, but it has no long-term benefit.

What a lot of us Christians do is chew the Word the way we chew gum. We chew on it until the flavor is gone, then we spit it out until we can get a fresh piece of gum, or Scripture, that's nice and juicy. A lot of Christians like a good sermon, but then they ignore the Word until they hear something else that excites them.

I'm often asked, "What are you going to preach about next?" Sometimes the question sounds like the person chewed on the last sermon, got all the flavor out of it, then wadded it up and threw it away. Now he wants a new piece of spiritual gum to chew on.

As Jesus' disciples, every time we come to His Word we should pray, "Lord, show me myself as You see me." That's very threatening. A lot of us want lying mirrors. We're like the fairy-tale queen who said, "Mirror, mirror on the wall, who's the fairest of them all?" and only accepted one answer.

Most people want mirrors that make them look good. That's why Paul warned Timothy, "Watch out for people who come wanting to have their ears tickled instead of wanting the truth" (see 2 Timothy 4:3). People like that want a false view of themselves.

Did you know that hell will be full of people who looked in the mirror and thought they were OK? They thought they were good enough and righteous enough to stand before a holy God because they refused to believe what they saw in the mirror of the Word.

Staring into the Mirror

We are not just to glance at the mirror of God's Word, but to gaze into it intently (James 1:25). We're to stare at it. Let me go back on that thin ice I was on above. It's amazing to me the way women use mirrors. They want the 360-degree look. They check everything out on the front in one mirror, then they pull another mirror out of their pocketbooks and give the back another look.

In other words, they are looking intently into the mirror. They want to cover all the ground. They don't want to miss anything, because they want to look their impeccable best.

James says, "When you come before the mirror of God's Word, you want that 360-degree look." You want God to show you whatever is there so you can respond to what you see.

Too many Christians approach the Bible like tourists instead of like explorers. Tourists take a quick look at everything and keep on going. "Oh, that's nice. Yes, that's interesting." They're always moving to the next thing.

But explorers look and study and make maps because they want to find out the real deal. They look intently because they want to discover the truth and do something about it.

Let me tell you, when you look into the Word with a heart to respond to what you see, you are not going to like a lot of the things you see. But it's supposed to be that way. When we look into the Word, those of us who think we are pretty are going to find out that, spiritually, we are ugly. Those of us who think we are righteous are going to find out how sinful we really are. But the Bible doesn't show us our true selves so we can just walk away and moan about it. The idea is to see the truth so we can respond to the truth and fix what is wrong.

Some people want the Bible to give them a quick snapshot of themselves, like the pictures you get in those little photo shops in the mall. What we all need, though, is an X-ray machine that penetrates below the surface and gets down to the truth. James says the Bible will do that for the person who is ready to respond to it.

Throughout Scripture, those who came face-to-face with God and saw themselves as they really were had the same reaction. Isaiah said, "Woe is me, for I am ruined!" (Isaiah 6:5). Peter said to Jesus, "Depart from me, for I am a sinful man, O Lord!" (Luke 5:8). Job said, "I abhor myself" (Job 42:6 KJV). And Paul cried out, "Wretched man that I am! Who will set me free from the body of this death?" (Romans 7:24).

When these men looked in the mirror and saw what it reflected back, they saw their true condition as God saw it. And they were motivated to do something about it.

When your heart has an attitude that says, "Lord, make clear what You want, and I'll do it," I have good news for you. You'll hear things in Scripture you never heard before, and you'll see things you never saw before. You'll understand things you never understood before.

Why is that? Because you have given God the freedom to let you see yourself as He sees you. The Holy Spirit can do that because He knows you are going to respond to what you see. You are going to be quick to hear the Word and slow to say, "Oh no, Lord, that's not me."

I get a little worried when I'm preaching and I see people start nudging each other as if to say, "Listen, he's talking to you." I once saw a husband get up and move to another seat because his wife was killing his rib cage! God's Word may be speaking to someone else, for sure. But maybe God is talking to you too.

Understanding the Perfect Law of Liberty

Here's the good part. Look what God is asking us to respond to. James calls it "the perfect law, the law of liberty" (1:25).

The Word of God is flawless. It's without error, as we talked about in the previous chapter. It is the truth, the whole truth, and nothing but the truth. When you look into the Scripture with a heart to respond, you don't have to worry about going astray.

The Word is also liberating. It sets us free from all the things of this world that try to hold us in bondage. What has you in bondage today? Are you being held hostage to sin or fear or defeat? Then come to the Word and let it set you free.

A lot of people have a wrong view of liberty. Liberty to them is being free from all restraint, living without any rules or boundaries.

But that's not biblical liberty, nor is it liberty in any sense of the word. You can't be a liberated baseball player with no foul lines on the field. You can't be a liberated tennis player without base lines. You will simply be a frustrated, out-of-control baseball or tennis player.

Liberty does not mean the absence of rules. True liberty means freedom to play the game as it was meant to be played. Liberty is the freedom to live life as it ought to be lived. The only truly free people are those who are free to be what God created them to be. That's liberty, and that's what God's Word will give us if we will respond to it.

The psalmist said in Psalm 119:45, "I will walk at liberty, for I seek Thy precepts." As long as the psalmist sought God's truth, he knew he would be free. Jesus said, "You shall know the truth, and the truth shall make you free" (John 8:32).

People love to quote that verse, but we have to ask what Pilate asked Jesus, "What is truth?" Jesus answered that for us when He said to His Father, "Thy word is truth" (John 17:17).

In order to know what is true, you have to have a source, a starting point. The starting point and ground of all truth is the revelation of God. When you respond to the Word of God, when you make its truth your own, then you will be set free.

Enjoying God's Blessing

I don't know anyone who doesn't want to be "blessed in what he does" (James 1:25). Even unbelievers want to live blessed lives. But where do you find that kind of blessing? James says it comes in being "an effectual doer" of the Word.

I like the way Paul puts it in 2 Corinthians 3:18: "But we all, with unveiled face beholding as in a mirror the glory of the Lord, are being transformed into the same image from glory to glory, just as from the Lord, the Spirit."

Blessedness comes when the Word of God transforms us into the image of Christ. In the Word, we see the Son of God and are transformed by the Spirit of God so that we are able to live out the will of God.

Responding to the Word is like beginning to work out. You decide you are tired of being out of shape, so you start an exercise program. When you do this, two things become clear very quickly.

First, you are not going to look like Arnold Schwarzenegger in a week. Second, those first workouts are going to hurt. You are using muscles you haven't used in a long time, if ever, so it's going to be painful for a while.

But the only way to work past the pain is to keep exercising. Then those sore muscles will start responding, and you'll find yourself getting in shape. That's the way it works in the spiritual realm too.

WE MUST REFLECT THE WORD

There is a third aspect I want to explore in this matter of approaching Scripture so that we get its content off the page and into our lives. I call this the need to reflect the Word, and I want to talk about it in three areas. James continues:

> If anyone thinks himself to be religious, and yet does not bridle his tongue but deceives his own heart, this man's religion is worthless. This is pure and undefiled religion in the sight of our God and Father, to visit orphans and widows in their distress, and to keep oneself unstained by the world. (1:26–27)

The word *religion* as James uses it here has to do with our external spiritual activity, those things that other people can see and hear us doing.

James isn't saying that religious activity saves us. Remember, he is talking to believers who have already been brought to life by the Word. But James is saying that genuine faith ought to produce genuine works.

In Our Words

It's interesting that James begins with the tongue, a subject he has a whole lot more to say about in chapter 3. No matter what we may be doing, if we cannot control that little appendage in our mouths, our religion is a waste of time.

One proof that you have received the Word and are responding to it is the way you talk. You can't follow Christ for very long and keep talking the way you used to talk.

James says in 3:9 that we sometimes use the same mouth to bless God on Sunday and curse people on Monday. Then he asks a very good question: "Does a fountain send out from the same opening both fresh and bitter water?" (v. 11). The obvious answer is no. So one way you can measure your progress in discipleship is by the way you use your tongue. If you've got the real stuff, it will show up in the way you talk.

In Our Works

Our commitment to the Word of God will also be reflected in our works. James 1:27 talks about helping the helpless, those who can do nothing for us in return. So we're not looking at a business deal here.

When you are "in sync" with the Word, when the truth is getting down into your life, people who may otherwise not get noticed suddenly become very important to you. You no longer look down on them, or consider yourself better than they are. Serving and helping them becomes a real necessity for you.

You probably already know this, but if you follow Jesus Christ you won't usually find yourself in the halls of power and influence and wealth. There are faithful disciples in places of great power and influence, and we can be thankful for that. But for most of us, following Christ will lead us to those who are poor and needy both materially and spiritually. These are the kind of people Jesus sought and hung out with. If indeed the Word is at work in you, it will reflect in what you do.

In Our Walk

Our commitment also reflects itself in our walk. The challenge here is "to keep [our]self unstained by the world."

This is being in the world, but not of the world. We are supposed to mark the world for Christ, not allow the world to leave its mark on us.

What happens when you spill something on your blouse or your tie, and the stain is really obvious? People say things like, "You've got a stain on your blouse." "You must have spilled something on your tie."

They don't say things like, "That's a really nice tie except for that little stain." "You have a spot on your blouse, but the rest of you looks nice." Why don't people say that? Because when you have a stain on your clothes, the stain takes center stage. It attracts all the attention.

It's the same with our spiritual lives. When the world stains you, it shows. Lot allowed the sin of Sodom to spill all over him. He got all stained with the world, and he ended up losing everything. Abraham, on the other hand, kept himself unstained from the world and was blessed in what he did.

How do you keep the stains of sin off you so you can reflect Christ to the world? You pray what David prayed at the end of Psalm 139: "Search me, O God, and know my heart; try me and know my anxious thoughts; and see if there be any hurtful way in me, and lead me in the everlasting way."

In other words, the way you keep from letting the stain of sin spoil God's reflection in you is by opening your heart and life to His intense searching. How does God search us and know us? By the Spirit of God using the Word of God to dissect our hearts (Hebrews 4:12).

We are cracked vessels, no doubt about it. We all have flaws and leaks. The only way to keep a leaky vessel full is to keep the faucet turned on. We have to keep the Word of God flowing through us, keeping us filled and clean. It's an absolute necessity. There's no other way to be a genuine, growing disciple of Jesus Christ.

CHAPTER FOURTEEN

THE CONTEXT OF SCRIPTURE

Someone once said the problem in the modern church is that we have too many "saccharine" Christians.

Saccharine comes in little packages just like sugar packages, but of course saccharine is not the same as sugar. It's an artificial sweetener, designed to look and taste as much like sugar as possible. But it's not the real thing.

I don't want to be a saccharine Christian, do you? I didn't think so! The main reason you are reading this book, I hope, is that you want to be a committed follower of Jesus Christ and you want to learn what that takes. That's what I want too, as a Christian and as a pastor. I don't want to be a "preacherette" preaching saccharine "sermonettes" to "Christianettes."

There are a lot of causes of saccharine Christianity, but I'm convinced that near the top of the list is the fact that Christians fail to take seriously the Word of God. When I say that, I don't mean that people fail to believe the Bible is God's revealed Word. I'm not talking about believing the Word, but *practicing* the Word.

This is a critical issue because your spiritual development and growth as a disciple of Jesus Christ is intimately and intricately tied to what you do with the

Scripture. God's Word is one of the absolute essentials for following Jesus, so let's take the next step and talk about the various contexts in which we need to approach the Scripture.

It's possible to be *under* the Word and yet not be *in* the Word. Many Christians will come to hear a preacher or a Bible teacher they enjoy. But this is the only time they open their Bibles, so they never learn to feed themselves on the Scripture. Therefore, like babies, when they get hungry all they can do is cry for somebody else to feed them.

THREE CONTEXTS OF THE WORD

But that's not the way God meant it to be. He has given us at least three primary contexts to help us receive His Word, feed on it, and grow thereby. I want to review these three contexts with you, and then talk about three areas that give us the tools to learn and apply the Word.

The Personal Context

I have said this before, but it bears repeating here. You and I have a personal responsibility to become men and women of the Word. No one can eat for you, and no one can grow for you.

A mother can mash and mix and soften a baby's food to make it go down easily. In some cultures, mothers even chew their babies' food for them before giving it to them. But a mother can't make the baby swallow that food and grow.

Aren't you glad your mother isn't still feeding you? I am glad my momma doesn't have to sit me down and feed me. And I'm *real* glad she isn't chewing my food for me! How much better it is to be able to sit down to a good meal and feed ourselves.

That's what God wants us to do with His revelation, His Word. It takes time and discipline to feed and nourish ourselves on the Word, but how well we do that has everything to do with how far we progress as Jesus' disciples.

I want to look at a powerful verse of Scripture that we will deal with here and then come back to later in the chapter: "Blessed is he who reads and those who hear the words of the prophecy, and heed the things which are written in it; for the time is near" (Revelation 1:3).

John is speaking specifically, of course, of those reading the book of Revelation, but by way of application there is blessing for us in every part of the Scripture. Notice how John personalizes the promise. It is "he who reads" who is blessed or happy. Knowing the Word is an individual responsibility, a matter of personal effort.

You see the same thing in the risen Lord's messages to the seven churches in Revelation 2–3. "He who has an ear, let him hear what the Spirit says to the churches" (Revelation 2:7). Then Jesus says it is the person "who overcomes" who receives the blessings of His Word.

So even though Jesus was speaking to the church, the benefit was to the individual person who heard the Word and acted on it. The presentation was plural, but the application was personal. We are personally responsible for that which God has revealed. If you are going to grow into a committed follower of Jesus Christ, you must take responsibility for your commitment to Scripture.

The Family Context

We are also told that the Word must be a dynamic, integral part of our family life. The well-known passage in Deuteronomy 6 lays this out clearly:

> Now this is the commandment, the statutes and the judgments which the Lord your God has commanded me to teach you, that you might do them in the land where you are going over to possess it, so that you and your son and your grandson might fear the Lord your God, to keep all His statutes and His commandments. (vv. 1–2a)

Moses said that God's truth was meant to be taught in the home and transferred from generation to generation in the family. He gives the process by which this teaching and transfer are to happen:

> And these words, which I am commanding you today,

shall be on your heart; and you shall teach them diligently to your sons and shall talk of them when you sit
in your house and when you walk by the way and when
you lie down and when you rise up. And you shall bind
them as a sign on your hand and they shall be as
frontals on your forehead. And you shall write them on
the doorposts of your house and on your gates. (vv.
6–9)

This is not exactly being timid about your faith in
your home. If you were to walk in the front door of my
boyhood home in Baltimore, you would see a placard
that my parents put up many years ago when they first
became Christians. It says, "As for me and my house, we
will serve the Lord."

My father is the least private Christian you would
ever want to meet. Everything we did as a family was
based on the Word.

I remember growing up, there were times when I
didn't want to hear any more Bible. I didn't want to hear
my dad say, "We're going to read the Bible before dinner." I didn't want him asking me, "Have you read your
Bible yet?" I didn't want to hear, "We're going to church
to learn more about the Bible."

I can remember many times sucking air through my
teeth in silent disgust. (With my father, I had better be
silent about it!) And then sometimes around the dinner
table, my father would feel sermonic. You know how it
is. Momma had made fried chicken, and Dad wanted to
preach.

He would deliver this long devotion while I sat looking at that fried chicken. If you know me, you know I
was going through great trauma. As a boy, there was
many a day I was exposed to the Word when I didn't
want to be exposed to it.

But here I am today, preaching and teaching the
Word of God. Why? Because Dad fed so much of it to me
I couldn't get away from it.

That's why I say to parents, even though your children may not want the Word now and may not appreciate it now, keep it before them. "Train up a child in the

way he should go, even when he is old he will not depart from it" (Proverbs 22:6). Why is this true? Because he stares it in the face every day of his life.

Don't apologize for that placard on your wall announcing that your home is built on the Word. Deuteronomy 6 says to teach the Word both formally and informally, along the way of life. Drop a little nugget of truth here and there.

Moses laid the primary family responsibility at the feet of the father. I am grateful for the tremendous numbers of men who want to become men of the Word, and for ministries like Promise Keepers that are helping them fulfill this commitment.

But I also want to offer a word of encouragement to the many single parents in the Christian community, the vast majority of whom are mothers. Your home may not have a husband and a father to take responsibility for teaching the Word, but the good news is that the Word of God is not bound by our human limitations. It will still do its work in your family, single parent, if you will adhere to it and teach it faithfully to your children. You can still raise godly kids.

Timothy is a great example. As far as we can tell from Scripture, he never knew a godly father. But Paul could still write to Timothy, "I am mindful of the sincere faith within you, which first dwelt in your grandmother Lois, and your mother Eunice, and I am sure that it is in you as well" (2 Timothy 1:5).

Later in the same book, Paul reminded Timothy, "From childhood you have known the sacred writings" (3:15). Guess where Timothy got his instruction in the Scriptures? From his mother and grandmother.

There are probably a lot of people who are believers today because of what their mothers and grandmothers taught them. Even if your home is missing a parent, you can still raise a Timothy. You can point your children to God as their Father.

The Church Context

As a pastor in Ephesus, Timothy was also charged

with teaching the Word in the third context I want to talk about, the church. Paul told his spiritual son, "Until I come, give attention to the public reading of Scripture, to exhortation and teaching" (1 Timothy 4:13).

That is, Timothy was to explain the Scripture and help God's people put it into practice. And he was to be diligent about it: "Take pains with these things; be absorbed in them, so that your progress may be evident to all" (1 Timothy 4:15).

Why preach the Word in church? Notice verse 16 of this same chapter: "Pay close attention to yourself and to your teaching; persevere in these things; for as you do this you will insure salvation both for yourself and for those who hear you."

The church is the context where the Word of God is to be proclaimed so that we might appreciate it, hear it, understand it, and apply it. The church is the corporate environment for reaffirming the Word of God in the lives of His people.

Let me show you from the Old Testament the power that can invade this corporate context of the Word. In Nehemiah 8, the people of Israel gathered to hear Ezra the priest read from "the book of the law of Moses" (v. 1).

This was after the exiles had returned and rebuilt the walls of Jerusalem under Nehemiah. The people had not had access to the Law for many years. Now the Word was about to be read among them again, and it was a special occasion.

A podium was set up, and Ezra read from the Law for hours (v. 3). The men who stood beside him "explained the law to the people" (v. 7). They read it and translated the Word in a way that the people could understand it. Now look at what happened next:

> Then Nehemiah, who was the governor, and Ezra the priest and scribe, and the Levites who taught the people said to all the people, "This day is holy to the Lord your God; do not mourn or weep." For all the people were weeping when they heard the words of the law. (v. 9)

When was the last time the Word of God made you cry? I'm not saying that crying is the only criterion for taking the Word seriously, but when the Word hits home you feel it. One reason we often lose our sense of awe about the Bible is that we are so used to having it lying around. It becomes common. The Book loses its preciousness. Let's hope we don't have to lose access to the Bible to appreciate it.

Remember how excited you were when you got that first love letter from your first love? Remember how it brought joy to your heart, how you couldn't put it down? That's what the Bible should do for us.

But because we have easy access to the Bible, we can get lazy about it. Or we become convinced that it does no good for us to try to get anything out of our Bible study. For many of us, the Bible is like bran cereal: It's nutritious, but it's dry. It doesn't have much taste to it. Nothing could be further from the truth.

The Word of God is the standard for the church. Pastors are called to "preach the word" (2 Timothy 4:2). Stories come and go, but the Word of God lasts forever. God didn't say He was going to bless my stories. He said He was going to bless His Word. There's nothing wrong with making the Word inviting and encouraging, but it must be the Word.

Even though we are talking about the context of the church, believers also have a personal responsibility here. When you are in church, you ought to have your Bible open to make sure that what the preacher says is true to the Bible.

I tell my congregation not to take the Bible on *my* word. I may eat the wrong thing on Saturday night and have a bad day some Sunday. I may be "off my feed" on another Sunday. People need to check out the Word for themselves.

I always think of the Bereans in Acts 17. They "received the word with great eagerness, examining the Scriptures daily, to see whether these things were so" (v. 11). They didn't take anybody's word for the Word.

What they wanted to know was, "Is it in the book?"

If it's not in the Book, you're off the hook when it comes to someone trying to tell you what God says. We need to test what we hear by the Word.

THREE WAYS TO MAKE
THE WORD COME ALIVE

So these are the three contexts in which we need to receive the Word: personally, in the family, and then in the church. I want to go back to Revelation 1:3 and consider three ways to make the Bible come alive in these three contexts. First let me repeat this verse: "Blessed is he who reads and those who hear the words of the prophecy, and heed the things which are written in it; for the time is near" (Revelation 1:3).

Reading the Word

"Blessed is he who reads," John says. Does this mean reading "a verse a day to keep the devil away"? Hardly. Anyone who picks up the Bible with this idea is using it as a good-luck charm, not as the authoritative Word.

John is not just encouraging us to glance at some words on a page. He has much more in mind. In the Bible, reading has to do with understanding what God has to say to you. The idea is not that you would read and then not know anything about what you just read, or read and say, "There, I read my verse or my chapter for today."

Study the Word. The idea of reading is to grasp God's message to us, to give diligence to our study of the "word of truth" (2 Timothy 2:15). The Greek word translated "Be diligent" in this verse ("study," KJV) means that when you open the Word, you give yourself fully to it. You devour it the way you devoured that first love letter. You take the Bible seriously.

There is a good example of this kind of desire for the Word in 2 Timothy 4:13. Paul was old, he was in prison waiting to die, and he was cold and lonely. Here was a man who had been to the third heaven, who had seen things no one else had seen (2 Corinthians 12:1–4).

But what did Paul want more than anything in that damp prison cell? "When you come," he wrote to Timothy, "bring the cloak which I left at Troas with Carpus, and the books, especially the parchments" (2 Timothy 4:13).

These parchments were Paul's copies of the Old Testament. In other words, Paul was alone, cold, and friendless, but he wanted the Scriptures. He knew that God's Word would supply everything else he needed. Paul wanted to study the Word even in prison.

Memorize the Word. Another way to read the Word is to memorize it. The psalmist said in Psalm 119:11, "Thy word I have treasured in my heart." There's no greater exercise than to memorize Scripture. If you have never done it before, start with a verse a week. At the end of a year, you'll have fifty-two verses in your memory bank.

The purpose of memorizing Scripture is not so you can win a contest or a prize. God's concern is that you have the Word in your heart so that you have it ready to use in any situation.

Why is that important? Because the Word of God is "the sword of the Spirit" (Ephesians 6:17). It's the Word that the Holy Spirit uses to help you when tough times come. But if you don't have the Word in your heart and mind, the Holy Spirit has no sword to pull out and wield.

The best example of the value of knowing Scripture is Jesus in the wilderness being tempted by the devil (Matthew 4:1–11). Jesus answered Satan each time, "It is written." Jesus didn't open a copy of the Old Testament and show Satan the verse. He simply responded out of what was in His heart.

I can't tell you how many times God has brought His Word to my mind to show me which way I should go. That's what the Holy Spirit does. He illumines our minds with the Word so that we can see what we ought to do. But we must first be diligent to put the Word into our minds.

In Proverbs 22:17–18, we read this advice: "Incline your ear and hear the words of the wise, and apply your mind to my knowledge; for it will be pleasant if you keep them within you, that they may be ready on your lips." The Word cannot come to your lips and go out of your mouth until it is first "within you," in your mind.

Then the writer says, "I have taught you today. . . . Have I not written to you excellent things of counsels and knowledge?" (Proverbs 22:19–20).

He is saying, "I wrote what you need, but you have to keep it within you." If you will cooperate with the Spirit by working to memorize Scripture, He can put in your mind what needs to come out of your mouth when you face hard circumstances and difficulties.

You may be saying, "Tony, you don't know me. I'm not good at memorizing things." If you can remember your name, address, telephone number, and the names and phone numbers of a few friends, you can memorize Scripture.

For most of us, the real deal is that we don't feel like doing Bible memory. Suppose you were offered ten thousand dollars for every verse you memorize. You would become the Bible memory champion of the world. That ten thousand dollars would give you brain cells you never knew you had before. Why? The reward would be worth the effort.

The prophet Ezekiel said that when God told him to eat the scroll containing His word to Israel, it was as sweet as honey in Ezekiel's mouth (Ezekiel 3:1–3). It was good to the taste. It was worth the effort. You only know whether something's worth the effort when you put in the effort to find out.

When you see the Word of God become alive in your life, when you see it bubble forth from your heart, and when you see God honor His Word, then the issue of whether you're good at Bible memory will disappear. When you find that you can send the devil packing with the Word the way Jesus did, you'll know it is worth the effort to hide God's Word in your heart.

Many of us have been telling the devil, "Go away, leave me alone." But he doesn't go anywhere, because it's not our word he is afraid of. He's only afraid of God's

Word. Many Christians don't know that Satan can't hang with the Word. Why can't he? Because it is the power of God (see Romans 1:16).

When Satan hears the Word, he hears the voice of God. And he can't handle that voice. Jesus quoted three verses to Satan, and he was gone. Three strikes and he's out.

Try using the Word on the devil when he tries to destroy your life, and you will see the power of the Word when applied in the life of a believer. You need to read the Word; that is, study it diligently and memorize it.

Hearing the Word

The second portion of Revelation 1:3 says that those who hear the Word are blessed.

What does hearing the Word involve? It means more than letting the sounds into your ear canal. To hear in the Bible means to let the Word of God talk to you. Let it sink down into your mind and heart. Remember that Jesus said, "He who has an ear, let him hear" (Revelation 2:7).

Personalize the Word. Some people approach the Bible as a Book that was written two thousand years ago for the people of that day. So they read it as if it were speaking to someone else, not them. They don't really hear God speaking to them in the pages of His Word.

But the Bible was written to us and for us. The Constitution of the United States was written a long time ago. But do we take it as if it were written for us? We sure do.

The reason people can't just break into your house and search it without a warrant is because of that piece of paper written more than two hundred years ago. The reason we have other legitimate civil rights is because of that document written a long time ago.

You get the idea. The Constitution may have been written generations ago, but it is very relevant to the freedoms that we enjoy as citizens of America today.

"All Scripture is inspired by God and profitable for teaching, for reproof, for correction, for training in righteousness," writes Paul (2 Timothy 3:16). To hear the Word is to take its truths and apply them to ourselves. This is God talking to you and me. We have to respond to what He says. Reading the Word without hearing it is like chewing without swallowing.

Meditate on the Word. How do you hear the Word in the way we have been talking about? The key word is meditation. Eight times in Psalm 119, the psalmist's long tribute to the Word, he says he meditates on the Word of God (vv. 15, 23, 27, 48, 78, 97, 99, 148).

Let me give you just a few examples. "I will meditate on Thy precepts," the psalmist writes in verse 15. "Make me understand the way of Thy precepts, so I will meditate on Thy wonders" (v. 27). "O how I love Thy law! It is my meditation all the day" (v. 97). "My eyes anticipate the night watches, that I may meditate on Thy word" (v. 148).

Do you realize what the psalmist is saying in this last verse? He is saying, "I can't wait until it's nighttime so I can think about God's Word. When the kids are quiet, when everything is shut down, when the phone isn't ringing, when I don't have to worry about being distracted, during the night I love to put my head on the pillow and think about God's Word."

Can you and I say that? The power of this is that when you meditate on God and His Word during the night, you go to sleep with God on your mind.

When you do that, you can sing like the old folks used to sing, "Woke up this morning with my mind stayed on Jesus." When you meditate on the Word in the night, the Holy Spirit is able to deal with your pressures and frustrations and wake you up with a calm mind.

How long has it been since you woke up with your mind calm and fixed on Christ? Sounds like a great idea, doesn't it? Try it tonight. If you are facing a trial or a problem tomorrow, make God and His Word the last thing on your mind. You will be amazed at His transforming power when you wake up.

Joshua 1 also shows us how powerful meditation is. Joshua had a big challenge ahead of him. He had to con-

quer the Promised Land with its walled cities and giants.
He was getting ready to face a formidable foe. Did God
give Joshua a surefire military plan? No, He told him:

> This book of the law shall not depart from your mouth,
> but you shall meditate on it day and night, so that you
> may be careful to do according to all that is written in
> it; for then you will make your way prosperous, and
> then you will have success. (Joshua 1:8)

The power of meditation is that it gives you success
in your life. Does that mean a BMW in every believer's
driveway? You and I know better than that. For us as
Christians, success is fulfilling God's purpose for our
lives, whether or not that includes driving a nice car.

God told Joshua, "If you are going to accomplish the
goal for which I am sending you into the Promised Land,
you will need to meditate on My Word until it is part of
your very being, until it guides every step you take and
every decision you make."

If meditation is that important, we'd better find out
what it means to meditate on Scripture day and night.
The word "meditate" makes me think of the activity of a
cow in chewing its cud. I'm a city boy, but I've got this
down.

A cow will eat grass and swallow it. But later, the
cow wants the taste of that grass in its mouth again, so it
regurgitates the grass and chews on it some more. The
cow keeps doing this until the cud is thoroughly chewed
and ready to be swallowed for a final time and taken into
the digestive system to nourish the cow.

That's the picture of what God wants us to do with
His Word. We may chew on it on Sunday and swallow it.
But then on Monday, we bring the Word back to our
minds and think about it some more, turning it over and
over until we absorb more of it.

Or we read and swallow the Word on Tuesday, but
then something happens on Thursday that causes us to
bring the Word back up to meditate on it again. If we do
that often enough, the Word will become so much a part of

us that it infiltrates our entire being. Then we begin to act and react biblically as a way of life.

You say, "Tony, how will I know when to meditate?" You won't have to worry about that. If you are consciously aware of trying to please God through your life, whenever God teaches you something from His Word, He's going to give you a chance to bring it back up again and apply it, meditate on it, and gain insight from it.

The reason many Christians don't experience this process is that they aren't looking for it. They aren't sensitive to the working of the Holy Spirit. They have forgotten most of what they once "ate" from the Word. Meditation is one cure for that problem.

Teach the Word. Here's a third way to help make sure you have heard the Word in the biblical sense of grasping it and letting it do its work. Teach the Word to someone else.

If you are going to be a disciple of Jesus Christ, that means you are going to become a teacher of His Word. You say, "Wait a minute, Tony. I haven't been called to preach. I haven't been called to hold a teaching position in the church."

That may be true, but God has called all of His people to be proclaimers of His Word. A disciple is first of all a learner, but a disciple is also one who teaches what he or she has learned to someone else. All of us are called to "make disciples" (Matthew 28:19).

This is hard, but I need to say it because the Word says it. If you are unable to teach someone else the basics of the Christian faith, it is because you are an immature believer. That's what the author of Hebrews says.

In Hebrews 5:1–10, the writer was going deep with his readers. He was teaching them about the Melchizedek priesthood of Jesus Christ. This is not the stuff you teach new Christians the first week after they are saved. This is part of the deep things of Christ.

So the writer was putting all this down, but then he stopped in verse 11. He had more good things to share about Melchizedek and how he illustrated Christ, but he realized his readers weren't ready to receive them because they had a maturity problem:

> Concerning him we have much to say, and it is hard to explain, since you have become dull of hearing. For though by this time you ought to be teachers, you have need again for someone to teach you the elementary principles of the oracles of God, and you have come to need milk and not solid food. (vv. 11–12)

The problem was that these Jewish Christians had become "mule-headed," the literal meaning of the phrase "dull of hearing." These were everyday believers, ordinary Christians. But the writer says they had been saved long enough to be teaching others. Instead, they were still in spiritual kindergarten playing with the little ABC blocks.

If a new believer came to you and said, "I need help understanding the Bible," could you help? If your child came to you with her Bible and said, "Daddy, Momma, what does this mean?" could you explain it, or at least know where to go to find an answer? People make jokes about it, but there's really nothing funny about Christians who have been saved for years yet still think the epistles are the wives of the apostles or that Phoenicia is the place where people make window blinds. We need a growing, working knowledge of the Scripture so we can help someone else who comes along.

It's like everything else you learn. If you don't use it, you'll lose it. Every time you learn something from the Word, find somebody to share it with. Talk to the dog if you have to, but find a way to teach what you are learning to someone else. That's how you hear the Word.

Heeding the Word

The third key to making the Word come alive in the context of your personal life, the family, and the church is to heed what God has said. John wrote in Revelation 1:3 that those who "heed the things which are written in [the Word]" are blessed.

Obedience is always the goal of knowing Scripture. I want to go back to Psalm 119 once again and look at what the psalmist said about heeding the Word.

Act on it. In verse 57, he says, "The Lord is my portion; I have promised to keep Thy words." Then in verse 106 he makes this pledge: "I have sworn, and I will confirm it, that I will keep Thy righteous ordinances." And finally, "Thy testimonies are wonderful; therefore my soul observes them" (v. 129).

The psalmist knew what to do with the Word—obey it. Jesus said, "If you know these things, you are blessed if you do them" (John 13:17). Not if you heard them only, or can quote them only, but if you practice them.

You may come out of church on Sunday saying, "That was a good sermon." That's great. Now you're ready to go into action. You meditate on the truth you heard. You turn it over in your mind. You discuss it with someone else. Then you put it to work in your own life, and the blessing comes.

The reason the Bible is a dead book to so many Christians is that they are not practicing it. They are not being obedient. So they never see God do anything in their lives that is out of the ordinary, and the Word remains dead letters on a piece of paper as far as they are concerned.

Whenever we talk about obedience, we have to go back to Abraham and God's call to him to offer his son Isaac as a sacrifice (Genesis 22:2).

Abraham must have meditated on that one all night: *God said He was going to make a great nation out of Isaac. Now He's telling me to kill Isaac. This doesn't make sense. It's not logical. But it's not my problem. God told me to do it, and I have to do it. He can give Isaac back to me if He wants to.* Then Abraham got up and obeyed.

This was the key, because it wasn't until Abraham raised the knife to kill Isaac that God stopped him and said, "Now I know that you fear God, since you have not withheld your son, your only son, from Me" (v. 12). In other words, "Abraham, now I know that you don't just talk a good game."

Acquire a taste for it. Someone may ask, "How can I ever get to the point where I can obey God's Word like that? I read the Bible now and nothing sticks. It doesn't change me."

You can become an obedient Christian overnight in the sense that you can start obeying God at any time. But to heed the Word as a way of life, you have to be highly motivated to please God. And where do you acquire the motivation to please God? By acquiring a taste for the Word, the way people acquire a taste for certain foods.

My church people know I don't like squash or its cousin, okra. I've got a thing against that whole vegetable family. I used to feel that way about broccoli too.

But then the doctor told me I needed to get some green stuff in my system, so I set about acquiring a taste for broccoli. I was highly motivated, because I wanted to obey my doctor and prolong my life.

That was a couple of years ago. Guess what? I love broccoli today. And I don't need to smother it in cheese anymore to get it down.

Too many Christians have not acquired their own taste for the Word. They still have to smother it in "preacher" to deal with it. They'll take it from the preacher, but they won't chew the Word and digest it for themselves.

If you want motivation to open the Word and let it change your life, make this your prayer tomorrow morning: "Open my eyes, that I may behold wonderful things from Thy law" (Psalm 119:18). No matter where you are in your discipleship, ask God to open your eyes to His Word.

It may be like castor oil at first. Did your mother or grandmother ever make you drink that stuff? When I was growing up, castor oil was the all-purpose medicine. It didn't matter whether I had a stomachache or a hangnail, Momma would get the castor oil.

That stuff was nasty, but do you know what? After a while, my stomachache would go away. Then the bottlers of castor oil made the stuff taste better, and it was easier to take.

Do you know when the Bible will start tasting good to you? When it makes your spiritual stomach stop hurting. When it makes the spiritual headache go away. When you heed it and see it working. If you will read, hear, and heed the Word, you will see God show His power through it. Then your prayer will be, "Let the words of my mouth and the meditation of my heart be acceptable in Thy sight, O Lord, my rock and my Redeemer" (Psalm 19:14).

CHAPTER FIFTEEN

THE COMPENSATION OF SCRIPTURE

Today people want answers to questions like, "If I do what you're telling me to do, what's the payoff?" and "If I buy this piece of technology, how will it benefit me?"

Most of us Christians wouldn't come right out and ask the benefits of being concerned with the things of God. We're too spiritual for that, or we're afraid of ruining our image of spirituality. But when it comes to knowing and living the Word of God, the spiritual payoff is enormous.

That's what I want to talk about as we wrap up our third absolute necessity in following Christ. I'd like to give you ten benefits you can expect the Scripture to bring into your life, ten good things the Word will accomplish for you if you will commit yourself to know and obey it as a disciple of Jesus Christ. Let's get started.

THE SCRIPTURE IMPARTS LIFE

The first compensation of Scripture is that it imparts spiritual life. The apostle Peter writes:

> Blessed be the God and Father of our Lord Jesus Christ, who according to His great mercy has caused us to be born again to a living hope. . . . For you have

been born again not of seed which is perishable but imperishable, that is, through the living and abiding word of God. (1 Peter 1:3, 23)

If you are saved, it is because the Word of God wrought its work in your soul. You are a Christian today because at some point in the past, God's Word captured you through the ministry of the Holy Spirit and you surrendered in faith to Jesus Christ. There is no substitute for the life-giving "seed" of God's Word.

The apostle James agrees. He says of our salvation, "In the exercise of His will He brought us forth by the word of truth" (James 1:18). No matter what the particulars are in your conversion story, no matter how you came to Christ, nothing can replace the power of God's Word to give life. It is "imperishable" seed that never fails to produce new life.

You can see that even in creation. God spoke, and there was life. No word out of God's mouth will ever return to Him "empty," the prophet Isaiah says (55:11). It will always achieve His will. So when you open the Word, you're dealing with a life-giving reality. The Scripture gives spiritual life.

THE SCRIPTURE CAUSES GROWTH

The Scripture is also indispensable for spiritual growth. For this I want to go back to a familiar passage we have considered before. "Like newborn babes, long for the pure milk of the word, that by it you may grow in respect to salvation" (1 Peter 2:2).

This is one of my favorite biblical analogies. The Bible is your "bottle" for spiritual nourishment. Or to put it another way, what food is to your body, the Word should be to your soul.

Do you like to eat? Me too. Most of us eat when we should eat, and we eat when we *shouldn't* eat. Some people even eat just to eat. Peter says we should approach the Scripture with that kind of hunger.

If you have children, you automatically understand what Peter is saying. You can appreciate this verse because you either are experiencing now or remember what it is like to be asleep at one or two in the morning and hear that little whimper. It's feeding time for your baby.

If you are like me, you never moved on the first whimper. You hoped you were hearing things, you hoped it was a dream, anything but a hungry baby. But that newborn would get louder and louder until you or your spouse got the message: "Get up, I'm hungry."

That baby could not care less that you went to bed late that night. That baby does not want to hear about your hard day at work. Why? Because all that baby cares about is achieving nutritional satisfaction.

In the same way that newborn babies crave milk, we are to crave the nutritional milk of the Word. Why? So that we might grow. The Word that gives you life is the Word that will cause you to grow. The Word that gives you salvation is the Word that will lead you to sanctification.

Jesus prayed in John 17:17, "Sanctify them in the truth; Thy word is truth." You cannot grow without a regular diet of Scripture. If the only biblical "meals" you get are on Sunday and Wednesday, you're not like a newborn baby. Newborns don't take three-day breaks between meals. In fact, most newborns don't even take three-*hour* breaks between meals.

There are a lot of Christians who start off with a real growth spurt because they are so hungry for the Word. They can't get enough of it fast enough.

But then as time goes on, their biblical "feeding schedule" gets off because the Word becomes a convenient extra in their lives. They begin to get spiritually emaciated and weak because they aren't getting enough nourishment for their souls.

What do you do if you've lost your appetite for the Scripture? I like the advice of Dr. David Jeremiah. He says that if you've lost your taste for the Word, you need to force-feed yourself for a while.

That's what the hospital does when, for whatever reason, you can't eat on your own. The doctors put in a tube and feed you directly. In a sense, they force you to eat, because they know you won't get better without nutrition. And God knows you won't grow or get better without the Word.

Spiritually, many of us Christians are losing weight we can't afford to lose. Many believers are spiritually emaciated because they have not been feeding on the Word regularly.

Let me tell you something. Too many believers underestimate the value of simply reading their Bibles. Because the Bible is spiritual nutrition, you can be fed just by reading it, whether you think you're getting anything or not.

The Word is like vitamins. You may not feel an immediate benefit when you take a handful of vitamins. But when you take them consistently, the benefit is staggering as the vitamins do their invisible work in your body.

As I meditated on this, it dawned on me why so many of us neglect the Word of God. We've gotten so filled up on the "junk food" of this world that we have no room in our souls for the Word. Now I know I'm meddling, but stay with me.

If there's something you crave more than God's Word, God will let you fill up on that desire until you're stuffed. It may be television, a hobby, your work—maybe even pornography. But while you're filling up on that desire, God will allow you to become spiritually malnourished until you get sick enough that you turn back to the sustenance of His Word.

Psalm 106 shows you what I mean. In verses 13–14, the psalmist says that the Israelites forgot God's works and did not want to wait for His counsel or Word. Instead, they craved meat for their stomachs. They were tired of eating manna, God's supernatural "corn flakes" from heaven.

"So [God] gave them their request" (v. 15). He showered the camp of Israel with quails. But along with the food, God sent "leanness into their soul" (v. 15b KJV). The people wasted away even while they were feasting on "quail under glass."

Too often we're like the boy who was invited over to his friend's house to eat. His friend's mom had made a banquet-type meal, complete with fried chicken (that's my idea of a banquet!). But the boy didn't know what he was going to have for supper, so he had loaded up on peanut butter and jelly sandwiches. He missed out on a feast because he had settled for a sandwich.

I'm afraid that many of us are "peanut butter and jelly" Christians. We're "donut" saints. We want to pop into a shop and grab a quick fix of spiritual sugar that makes us feel good for the moment, even if it has no lasting nutrition.

But when we do that, we forfeit the benefit of feeding at God's banquet table. Only the Word of God brings spiritual growth.

THE SCRIPTURE LEADS TO MATURITY

The Scripture also leads us to spiritual maturity, which is the goal of our spiritual growth.

No parent is satisfied to see a child continue to look and act like a baby long after infancy should be over. And God is not satisfied to see Christians remain immature.

We looked at Hebrews 5:1–12 in the previous chapter, so I want to pick up here with verses 13–14. The writer had told the Hebrews they weren't ready for solid spiritual food yet because they were not even in kindergarten when it came to God's truth. Then he said:

> For everyone who partakes only of milk is not accustomed to the word of righteousness, for he is a babe. But solid food is for the mature, who because of practice have their senses trained to discern good and evil. (vv. 13–14)

Who can eat solid food? Mature believers. The milk of the Word will cause you to grow. But maturity comes when you can take the Word you are feeding on and use it to meet the various challenges, circumstances, issues, and decisions of life.

That's what the writer of Hebrews says in verse 14.

The mature are those who have practiced the Word so much that their senses are well trained. In the language of James 1:22, they are "doers of the Word, and not merely hearers." God wants you to move from the milk of the Word to the meat of the Word. The way you do that is by practicing the Word.

Let's go back to our illustration of a child growing up. There comes a time when that child is ready to learn to walk. At first, he will try to walk and will fall right back down.

What that child needs is practice. He needs to get up, take maybe half a step, fall down, and get up again. If he practices enough, eventually that marvelous day will come when Mom or Dad backs up four or five steps and says, "Come here. Come to Mommy." The child takes the four or five steps and the video camera starts rolling, because it's a big deal.

How is that child able to walk? The nourishment of the milk he drank and the food he ate strengthened him to the point that now he can do what he couldn't do earlier. His growth is leading to maturity.

The goal of God's Word is that we might become mature adults. Of course, we all know that it's possible to be the chronological age of an adult, yet not be adult in our behavior. Do you know any thirty-year-old kids?

What renders a person mature? One thing is the ability to make responsible decisions on one's own. When you don't have to tell your children every little thing, you know they're maturing. When they decide they're going to do it on their own, you know maturity is setting in.

Maturity comes for us as Christians when we are able to take the meat of God's Word in stronger helpings and apply it to the decisions of life as our natural way of functioning.

That's why you are not mature if you are still living on spiritual milk. You have to digest the meat, the deeper things of God. John 3:16 is wonderful truth. It may be the greatest verse in the Bible. But it's an "ABC" verse (see Hebrews 5:12). There is so much more to learn on the road to spiritual maturity.

THE SCRIPTURE OFFERS GUIDANCE

Here's a fourth benefit of Scripture: It offers you and me spiritual guidance.

In the previous chapter we spent some time in Psalm 119 in relation to meditation and obedience. Let's go back there to learn some more truth from this great portion of Scripture.

One of the most familiar verses in this psalm is verse 105: "Thy word is a lamp to my feet, and a light to my path." What is the job of a lamp or a light? To help you see. The tragedy today is Christians who are spiritually blind.

They can't see evil when it stares them in the face. They can't recognize the devil when he tempts them, because they are looking for a guy with horns, a pitchfork, and a red jumpsuit. They can't even see God clearly. They lack spiritual guidance.

Psalm 119:98 says, "Thy commandments make me wiser than my enemies." Here's the problem a lot of Christians have. They don't know God's commandments, so they are not nearly as wise as their enemies. They are not benefiting from the Word's guidance, which enables us to apply divine truth to life.

Very few of us would enter a room full of people where the lights had just gone out and announce, "I have a flashlight, but I think we will be able to see better to get out of here with our own eyes rather than with this flashlight."

The folk in that room groping to find their way out in the darkness would not be too complimentary in their remarks to the person with the flashlight. The whole point of having the flashlight is that it's too dark for anyone to see with his natural eyesight.

We live in a dark world, headed by the prince of darkness, Satan himself. He has plunged this whole world into pitch darkness. God says, "I have a lamp; I have a light. It's My Word. It will show you the way out." God's Word will give us 20/20 vision.

If we could see everything clearly on our own, we wouldn't need the lamp of the Word. It is because we *cannot* see what we think we can see that we desperately need the truth of God's Word. It is a light that will guide us so we can see and not stumble. Jesus said, "If anyone walks in the day, he does not stumble, because he sees the light of this world" (John 11:9).

THE SCRIPTURE PROVIDES STABILITY

A fifth benefit of learning and living by the Scripture is that you gain spiritual stability.

One of the most familiar stories in the Bible is that of the two houses on two different foundations:

> Everyone who hears these words of Mine, and acts upon them, may be compared to a wise man, who built his house upon the rock. And the rain descended, and the floods came, and the winds blew, and burst against that house; and yet it did not fall, for it had been founded upon the rock. And everyone who hears these words of Mine, and does not act upon them, will be like a foolish man, who built his house upon the sand. And the rain descended, and the floods came, and the winds blew, and burst against that house; and it fell, and great was its fall. (Matthew 7:24–27)

Here we are told of a wise man and a foolish man. Both men built houses, only on different foundations. Let's take a closer look at them.

Why did the foolish man build his house on the sand? Because he miscalculated the weather. He thought every day was going to be sunshine. He thought his life was always going to be smooth. So he figured a sand dune would do as a foundation.

But the wise man didn't trust the weather. He knew the storms would come. So he built his house on something that could defy the weather. He built his house on a rock.

The key thought in this story is repeated twice: "The rain descended, and the floods came, and the winds blew, and burst against that house." I'm here to give you a living witness that it's going to rain.

If it hasn't rained yet in your life, don't sell your spiritual umbrella. It is going to rain, and you can count on it. There is coming into your life a bad-weather day, a bad-weather week, a bad-weather month, or even a bad-weather year. Being Christ's disciple does not exempt you from the rain.

Do you know what a lot of Christians do when it starts raining? They try to change foundations. The rain comes and the house begins to shake and sink, so they pick up the telephone, call the most spiritual people they know, and say, "Help me build a new foundation under my house. It's falling apart."

But you can't change foundations when it's raining. You have to lay your foundation before the rain comes, so that when the rain comes, your house is secure.

Being a Christian doesn't stop the thunderstorms. Being a Christian brings you *through* the thunderstorms. If you want a stable life, one that doesn't cave in when the rain comes, build it on the rock. The Word of God provides spiritual stability.

THE SCRIPTURE PROVIDES INSIGHT

The Word of God provides spiritual insight. This is a sixth benefit of building your life on Scripture as you follow Christ. One of my favorite verses in the Bible is Hebrews 4:12, which says:

> The word of God is living and active and sharper than any two-edged sword, and piercing as far as the division of soul and spirit, of both joints and marrow, and able to judge the thoughts and intentions of the heart.

The Bible says that you and I are wicked of heart, even if we try to cover it up. God's Word is like an X-ray, which looks deep beneath the surface and shows what is there. What an X-ray machine is to medical science, Scripture is to the spiritual life. It penetrates your soul and spirit.

Many of us know what it is to sit under the preaching of the Word and squirm. If the Bible has never made you feel uncomfortable, it's because you are not allowing it to X-ray you. The Word is so powerful that when you really expose yourself to it, it looks right into the heart.

There are a lot of healthy-looking Christians who would find out that something is wrong if they put themselves under the X-ray of the Word. My wife, Lois, recently went through an illness that was detected by X-rays. She didn't feel bad at all. But the X-ray found a problem.

A lot of us think we're spiritually fit because we refuse to let the Scripture X-ray us. Do you know people who won't go to the doctor because they're afraid the doctor might find something? We can approach the Word the same way.

The writer of Hebrews says that Scripture divides "soul and spirit." Why must the soul and spirit be divided? So that you know what's of you and what's of God.

The soul refers to your inner being. The spirit refers to that part of you that communicates with God. God must separate the soul from the spirit so you can detect what is of God and what is of you, because sometimes the two can be very confusing.

When we expose ourselves to the Word, it underlines what is of God, the way a lot of people underline or highlight certain verses in their Bibles. That way, we can sense God moving and directing us to do what He wants. The Word X-rays us and gives us this insight.

THE SCRIPTURE ENABLES PURITY

For the next benefit, purity, I want to go back once more to Psalm 119. In verse 11, the psalmist says, "Thy word I have treasured in my heart, that I may not sin against Thee."

To "treasure" something means to hold it as special, as something precious. When we treasure the Word, it will keep us from sin. Somebody has said, "This Book will keep you from sin, or sin will keep you from this Book."

If you treasure the Word in your heart, it will keep you from displeasing God. Otherwise, the sin that you treasure will keep you from pleasing God. The Word will deal with sin in your life.

The Bible is like a sink full of hot, soapy water into which you place a stack of dirty, food-encrusted dishes that were left on the counter from dinner the night before. That food has dried by now, and it's hard. You can't scrub the stuff off yourself, but soaking those dishes in hot, soapy water will soften and loosen the grime.

The water is able to get in there and work loose that which had become hard and crusty. Many of us have become hardened of soul and crusty of spirit. But taking the Word into our hearts and lives, letting it penetrate and loosen the grime, will clean us up. The Scripture can purify you and keep you pure.

THE SCRIPTURE BRINGS PRODUCTIVITY

How about an eighth benefit of Scripture? You'll find it in another verse we have looked at before: "All Scripture is inspired by God and profitable for teaching, for reproof, for correction, for training in righteousness" (2 Timothy 3:16).

The Word of God is beneficial for teaching, to tell you what God wants; for reproof, to tell you what God does not want; for correction, to tell you how to make right what was wrong; and for training in righteousness, to help you grow from weakness to strength.

Why does God do all of this for us through His Word? "That the man of God may be adequate, equipped for every good work" (v. 17).

Another translation for adequate is *sufficient*. The Word of God is sufficient for "every good work." What is a good work? Simply stated, a good work is whatever God wants you to do. The Scripture is sufficient to equip you for anything God wants you to do. If you will obey the Word, you can come to the end of your life and say the same thing Paul said: "I have fought the good fight, I have finished the course, I have kept the faith" (2 Timothy 4:7). He did all the work God wanted him to do.

We must understand what is meant by the word *sufficient*. It doesn't mean you can study the Word and find out how to be a physician or an attorney or whatever. The Bible doesn't contain those details. But you *can* study the Word and find out how to be a Christian physician or a Christian attorney.

In other words, God's Word sanctifies everything you do, so that what you do is what God wants done. You can't be any more productive than to be doing the will of God. And it's the Word that equips you to be productive; that is, to have a life that achieves God's goals for you so you can say at the end of your life, "I did what God called me to do."

THE SCRIPTURE GIVES VICTORY

The ninth benefit we enjoy through the Scripture is a great one. God's Word enables us to have spiritual victory.

Where else can we go for an example of this but to the temptation of Jesus in Matthew 4? Three times, Satan tempted Jesus to disobey God. And three times, Jesus defeated the devil with "It is written" (vv. 4, 7, 10). By then Satan had had enough. Verse 11 says he left Jesus alone.

If Jesus, the Living Word, believed He needed to use the written Word to defeat the enemy of the Word, how much more do we need to use that same Word against the devil?

One of the main benefits of knowing and living the Bible is that it enables you to handle the devil. When Satan is tempting you to disobey God, quote the Word to him. Use the sword of the Spirit against him.

You can't use a sword you don't feel comfortable wielding. You can't quote the Word if you don't know it. But if you know the Word, you can handle Satan, because he can't handle the Word. Jesus quoted the Word so much to Satan that it weakened him, and he didn't want to hang around anymore.

That's why the demons always got worried when Jesus came. Whenever Jesus showed up, the demons would recognize Him and say, "Our time has not yet come. Don't send us away yet." But Jesus always silenced the demons with a word and sent them away (Mark 1:23–26). We have been fighting Satan with human tools, and we wonder why we are losing.

In 2 Corinthians 10, Paul writes, "For though we walk in the flesh, we do not war according to the flesh, for the weapons of our warfare are not of the flesh, but divinely powerful for the destruction of fortresses" (vv. 3–4).

The King James Version uses the word *strong holds* in verse 4. A stronghold is a place in your life that Satan controls. It's a piece of territory, a patch of ground, on which he has gained a foothold—and he's not about to let go.

In our fancy terminology today we call these strongholds "addictions." They're the place in your life where Satan is in charge, where he calls the shots. It's an area where you are too weak to stand up to him.

Paul says, "You can't fight that kind of battle with tools of the flesh. You've got to have the weapons of the Spirit to tear down those strongholds." But they can be torn down. The Word of God can give us spiritual victory.

THE SCRIPTURE BRINGS BLESSING

The tenth and final benefit of Scripture I want to show you is spiritual blessing. The Word of God is the basis of all spiritual blessing.

Psalm 19 talks about the revelation of God in two ways. The first is the way God is revealed through His works. "The heavens are telling of the glory of God; and their expanse is declaring the work of His hands" (v. 1).

In other words, even a person who doesn't have a Bible doesn't have to be Einstein to see that whoever made this world is strong. Whoever made this universe is good. Even if you don't know His name, you know He's awesome. You can know something about God just by observing nature. That's called general revelation.

But then the psalmist turns to special revelation, the Word of God, in verse 7, and begins enumerating the blessings the Word brings. For example, "The law of the Lord is perfect, restoring the soul" (v. 7).

Has your life ever fallen apart? Have things ever gone downhill? The fastest way back to health in your soul is through the Word of God.

"The testimony of the Lord is sure, making wise the simple" (v. 7b). You don't have to have a string of advanced degrees to have sanctified common sense. Our world is full of people with lots of degrees who have educated themselves into oblivion.

In fact, most people don't even know they're atheists until they go to college. They used to believe in God, but now they want to sound sophisticated, so they say, "I'm an agnostic." Well, fine. The word *agnostic* means "without knowledge," so technically agnostics are know-nothings. They "know nothing" about God, and God can be known. So an honest agnostic will be open to learning about God.

Rejoicing in the Word

"The precepts of the Lord are right, rejoicing the heart" (v. 8). The Word will make you glad you did what God said and not necessarily what other folk said. Somebody always has a story to tell as to why you should do what they did. But if you stay with what the Word says is right, you will wind up rejoicing.

Here is still another blessing in verse 8: "The commandment of the Lord is pure, enlightening the eyes." We've already talked about how the Word will light your path so you can see clearly where you are going.

"The fear of the Lord is clean, enduring forever" (v. 9a). The Word has longevity. "The judgments of the Lord are true; they are righteous altogether" (v. 9b). There is no flaw in the Book. It is perfect from cover to cover. The Word has no errors, no mistakes, no miscalculations.

So how much should we value the Word? Psalm 19:10 says the commandments of the Lord are "more desirable than gold, yes, than much fine gold" (v. 10). And the Word is "sweeter also than honey and the drippings of the honeycomb."

God said David was a man after His own heart, and now you know why. For David, the Word of God was more important than his paycheck. It was more important than his wealth or his throne or anything else. He continues in verses 11–12: "By them Thy servant is warned; in keeping them there is great reward. Who can discern his errors? Acquit me of hidden faults."

The Word of God will show you things wrong you didn't know were wrong. There are times when we think we are on the right track, but we have taken a left turn and don't even know it. The Scripture can reveal these hidden things.

Verse 13 contains an important request: "Also keep back Thy servant from presumptuous sins; let them not rule over me." These are deliberate, high-handed sins—the sins you know you're going to commit, but you do them anyway. If you allow them in your life, they will take over. The only answer for these kinds of sins is to be kept from doing them.

Now notice the second half of verse 13: "Then I shall be blameless, and I shall be acquitted of great transgression." That's a hopeful verse, full of blessing. It means that if you messed up yesterday, if you'll bring your hidden and presumptuous sins to God and deal with them, God will "acquit" you today so you can move on out for Him tomorrow.

A lot of us are controlled by what happened yesterday. But if you let yesterday control you, you'll mess up your today and ruin your tomorrow. Since you can't change yesterday, and since tomorrow hasn't come yet, recommit yourself to God and His Word today.

When you do that, God will overcome the problems of yesterday and fix your tomorrow before you get there because you're on target with Him today. Then you can pray, "Let the words of my mouth and the meditation of my heart be acceptable in Thy sight, O Lord, my rock and my Redeemer" (v. 14).

Enjoying the Benefit

The Word of God will meet whatever need you have, whether it is salvation, wisdom, guidance, maturity, stability, victory, cleansing, or anything else.

Let me suggest how you can start to get a handle on all of this and experience the benefit of Scripture in a way that may be new for you. Psalm 119, an incredible tribute to God's Word and what it can do in our lives, is divided into twenty-two sections of eight verses each. Each of the sections begins with a different letter of the Hebrew alphabet, which accounts for the divisions.

Along with whatever other devotional or Bible reading program you may follow, read one eight-verse section of Psalm 119 every day until you finish the psalm.

But don't just read and go on. Ask the Holy Spirit to enlighten your eyes and open your heart to the Word. As you read, meditate on what you are reading and reflect on what God is saying to you. If a verse jumps off the page at you, mark it so you can come back to it later for further meditation and study.

It will take you twenty-two days to read through Psalm 119 in this way, about five minutes a day. That's not a huge investment of time, but you just may find a huge spiritual payoff in the process.

NECESSITY FOUR
EVANGELISM

CHAPTER SIXTEEN
THE CONCEPT OF EVANGELISM

We're ready to plunge into the fourth and last section of our study—the absolute necessity of evangelism.

The early church was an evangelistic church—to the max, as people would say today! Three thousand people were saved on the Day of Pentecost (Acts 2:41). Just a short time later, five thousand men were saved at one time (4:4). And these were in addition to the people who were being saved "day by day" (Acts 2:47).

We could say the early church grasped the concept of evangelism quite nicely. Those first disciples were paying attention when Jesus commissioned them to "go and tell."

What I want to do in this chapter is review the commissions Jesus gave His disciples in the Gospels and in the book of Acts, because in these we find the concept of evangelism. Each one is a little different and focuses on a different aspect of the task God has given us as His disciples.

SOME BASIC OBSERVATIONS

Before we go to these texts, and then on to the other chapters in this section, I want to make a few foundational observations about evangelism.

The Uniqueness of Evangelism

One of these observations is the uniqueness of evangelism in terms of our ministry here on earth. Did you realize that of the four aspects of discipleship we are studying, only one will cease when we get to heaven?

Think about it. Worship certainly will not cease in heaven. We will continue to worship God throughout eternity. Billions of years from now, we will be worshiping God for who He is and what He has done.

Fellowship will not cease in heaven. We will experience fellowship there as we have never known it before! And our fellowship will be never ending because there is no night in heaven. We will enjoy perfect fellowship with God and with each other as we gather around the throne in heaven.

The Word of God will not disappear in heaven. It is forever settled there (Psalm 119:89). We will spend all of eternity learning facets of God's revelation we didn't know or understand before.

There is only one thing you can do in time that you will never, ever be able to do in eternity: lead unregenerate men and women to Christ. The opportunities we have in history to win people to Christ will be unavailable in eternity, because people's eternal destiny is sealed when they exit this planet.

So if you are going to be serious about following Christ and being His disciple, you must be willing to tell the good news about Him to dying men and women so they can come to faith in Him and know what it is to have eternal life.

The Definition of Evangelism

At its core, evangelism is making known the good news of Jesus Christ to a dying world. A more formal definition might be that evangelism is the verbal and visible declaration of the death and resurrection of Jesus Christ for the sins of mankind, done with the intent of leading people to salvation.

The intent in evangelism is a very important part of

its definition. Paul says he declared the gospel and the Corinthians received it (1 Corinthians 15:1). Simply stating the gospel is not evangelism, because evangelism is more than information. The information is delivered for a purpose.

In evangelism, I'm not only going to tell people the gospel, I'm going to do it with the intent of winning them to the Savior. Some people try to do evangelism by saying, "Look, Jesus died and rose for your sins, and you ought to accept Him as your Savior. If you want to accept Him, you can, but that's up to you."

That isn't evangelism. God is not saying, "Here's the truth. If you want to accept it, fine. If not, that's OK too." The Bible says God is commanding all people everywhere to repent (Acts 17:30). Our task as evangelists is to make God's expectations known.

Jesus said, "I will make you fishers of men." I don't know any fisherman who says, "Oh well, if the fish bite, fine. But if they don't, that's OK. I'm not going to bother baiting my hook or making sure I have a strong line. No big deal either way." Nobody fishes that way. You go fishing to catch something.

Evangelism has to do with presenting the gospel, the good news of the death, burial, and resurrection of Jesus Christ for our sins (1 Corinthians 15:1–4).

The gospel can only be understood as good news when we understand the bad news that all people are lost in sin and condemned apart from Christ. "There is none righteous, not even one," Paul wrote in Romans 3:10.

We need to understand what the gospel is before we can explain it clearly. The reason that's so important is that most people have no clue that the gospel rules out all self-effort to make ourselves acceptable to God.

Most people think they are doing OK, because they are comparing themselves not to Christ, but to their friends and the people around them. Compared to that crowd, they think they look pretty good. They don't see themselves as lost sinners in the sight of a holy God. The bad news is that all of us are separated from God by our sin. But the good news is that Jesus Christ paid for our sins so we can have eternal life.

The Importance of Evangelism

Sometimes Christians are accused of caring about people's souls while ignoring their lives here on earth. So let me say here that I realize there are a lot of other areas of service and ministry the church needs to be involved in. We should do whatever we can to impact the social, political, and economic structures of this world for Christ.

But let me also clarify the issue. If a person is poor, that's bad. But people can recover from poverty.

If a person doesn't have a job, that's bad. But people can recover from unemployment.

If a person doesn't have proper housing, that's bad. If he or she is sleeping under a bridge, that's horrible. But people can recover from homelessness.

If a person doesn't have the best kind of home situation, that's discouraging. We ought to come and help him. But people can recover from bad home situations.

However, men and women who die without knowing Jesus Christ have been hit with a blow they will never recover from for all eternity. Of all the things we need to be involved with, winning people to Christ must be at the core.

The Pragmatics of Evangelism

By this I am referring to a level of involvement that too many Christians never reach. We sing choruses like "This little light of mine, I'm gonna let it shine." We sing about letting it shine in our homes, on the job, and in our neighborhoods.

But I have a pragmatic question to ask. When was the last time you shared Jesus with someone in your family who needs Him? How long has it been since you discussed the gospel with a coworker at your place of employment? Are you taking the gospel to your neighbors?

I don't think I've ever met a true Christian who denied that evangelism was important. But sometimes it's hard to find many Christians who are acting on that belief consistently.

Jesus believed evangelism was important. Anything repeated five times, as the commission to take the gospel to the world is, has to be high on our priority list too. So let's survey the giving of that commission in each of the Gospels and in Acts.

EXERCISING THE AUTHORITY OF CHRIST

The first commission we need to consider is Matthew 28:18–20. Jesus told His disciples:

> All authority has been given to Me in heaven and on earth. Go therefore and make disciples of all the nations, baptizing them in the name of the Father and the Son and the Holy Spirit, teaching them to observe all that I commanded you; and lo, I am with you always, even to the end of the age.

As we go to the nations with His gospel, the risen Christ wants us to know that we go in His authority. This is not just ordinary authority. Jesus has *all* authority in all of creation.

But given the way some Christians approach the work of evangelism, you would never know that they were backed by the authority of Jesus Christ. It is evident that some Christians don't know who they are. They have forgotten the authority that comes with knowing Christ.

If we're not careful, we can become like the circus bear. This bear's owner had it out on the street, rolling over and dancing and doing tricks, entertaining the crowd while its owner played music.

All of a sudden, out of the crowd burst a ferocious dog that began to bark at the bear. The bear cowered in fear, shivering at the thought that this mongrel was going to attack it. Normally that would be highly surprising, because a bear can kill a dog with one slap of his paw.

But this bear had become domesticated. It had become used to being entertained and entertaining others. It had a muzzle over its mouth and it had been declawed. So even though the bear was greater than the dog, it was intimidated by the dog because the bear forgot that it was more than just a circus attraction.

We need to remember that we are not "circus" Christians who have become spiritually domesticated.

God did not save us so that we could be entertained and we could entertain others. We are walking around with muzzles over our mouths, declawed of the gospel, entertaining people with our message but never attacking sin at its core with the good news of Jesus Christ.

Recognize Christ's Total Authority

The word for authority that Jesus uses in Matthew 28:18 is the Greek word *exousia*, which means "legitimate authority." A criminal and a police officer may each have guns, but only the officer has the badge of legitimate authority. Jesus says, "I have the badge."

Jesus' authority is not only legitimate, it is ultimate. There is no higher authority above Jesus. His authority is total.

Satan has authority, but it is neither legitimate nor ultimate. He's just a mongrel dog coming out of the crowd to try to intimidate us with his bark. If we let the devil close our mouths to the witness of the gospel, we are yielding to illegitimate authority.

Satan is the great intimidator. How many times do we think, *You know, I need to share Christ with my co-worker?* But we never get around to doing it because we are afraid of what that person might say. We have the message that will give this person eternal life, and we have Jesus' command to go and tell, yet we clam up because we are afraid of what people might say.

We ought to be more afraid about what Jesus is going to say because we didn't open our mouths and announce the gospel. Being a disciple of Christ means making Him known.

Refuse to Be Intimidated

Jesus tells us in Matthew 28 to go. Actually, the form of the verb here means we should already be going. Jesus assumes we will go, so He tells us what to do when we go.

It's when we go out into the world that we begin to meet with opposition. We are much more comfortable at church in our "holy huddle," talking about how we need to go into all the world and tell others the gospel. It's easy to be a Christian in church. There's no competition. Everyone agrees with you there.

But what Jesus wants us to do is break our huddle and go out to where the people are, demonstrating the reality of who He is by the authority in which we operate.

When it comes to evangelism, the issue is not just what happens in the "huddle" at church on Sunday morning. The issue is whether you will take the "play" Jesus has called, His Great Commission, with you to work on Monday morning and explain the gospel to that coworker or whether you will let Satan intimidate you.

You say, "Well, the Bible says Satan is like a roaring lion seeking to devour us." Yes, Peter does say that (1 Peter 5:8). But Satan is a toothless lion once we realize that he is all roar. Satan roars to intimidate us the way a lion roars to intimidate its foes, particularly jackals, after it has made a kill and has a carcass.

The interesting thing is that if a pack of jackals refuses to be scared off by a lion's roar, the jackals can take the lion's prey away from it. A single lion can't deal with five or ten jackals swarming around its food. So it roars to serve notice, "Don't come over here. This is my dinner. This is my meat. Don't mess with my food." But once a bunch of jackals ignores its roaring, the lion is in trouble.

Satan has a big roar, but he knows that if Christians ever show up and call his bluff, he will have to move out of the way. Our challenge is not to be intimidated by Satan or by people and what they might say. We need to know who we are and whom we serve.

Make Disciples

The central command in Matthew 28 is to "make disciples." Discipleship is what we have been talking about throughout this book. We are trying to discover what it means to follow Jesus. Discipleship is a reproducible concept. We are to help other believers become committed followers of Jesus Christ.

This means that evangelism is not an end in itself. Just getting people "fire insurance" is not God's ultimate goal. His ultimate goal is to conform us to Christ's image (Romans 8:29), and that's biblical discipleship.

We can't send someone else to do the job for us. Jesus promised us that He would be with us as *we* go. But what we often want to do is stay home and send Jesus. That's not what Jesus said. He said, "You go, and I will be with you."

He is saying, "Go to those prisoners who need Me, and I will go into the prison with you. Go to those poor people who need Me, and I will go into that neighborhood with you. Go to those struggling young people who need Me, and I will go with you." We don't send Jesus. He sends us (John 20:21).

Do you know why Islam is the world's fastest growing religion? That religion has evangelists who are not ashamed of their gospel. They will walk the streets and hand out newspapers, and they will go into the neighborhoods and declare their message.

What are Christians doing? Praising God on Sunday morning. Nothing wrong with that, but it's not enough. We need to move out in the authority of Christ, assured of His abiding presence, to share the gospel with the world.

GOING INTO ALL THE WORLD

In Mark 16:15–16, we find this commission from Jesus Christ: "Go into all the world and preach the gospel to all creation. He who has believed and has been baptized shall be saved; but he who has disbelieved shall be condemned."

The emphasis in Mark is on the totality of our evangelistic task. Jesus leaves no corner of the world untouched when He tells us to go to "all the world" and preach the gospel to "all creation." The church comes together not to hide out from the world, but to strategize the play that will best advance the gospel. Then we break from the huddle and put the play into action as we scatter throughout the world.

There should be no place on earth a Christian inhabits where the gospel is not being proclaimed. There should be a witness at your work because God says, "Go and proclaim the gospel." There should be a witness in your neighborhood because God says, "Go and proclaim the gospel." The same is true anywhere on earth. Following Christ means taking the gospel wherever it needs to be heard.

Filled Up to Go

If you're like me, by the time you pull into a gas station your car is on empty. People call it a "filling station" because the idea is to fill your car's gas tank so you can move on. A filling station is not a rest station where you come and hang out for pleasure.

You don't fill up your car and then say, "Car, doesn't it feel good to be full? Let's just stay here and enjoy it." You fill your tank so you can leave the station and start emptying it again by accomplishing the work you have to do.

It's great to get full at church on Sunday morning, but the idea is to leave the station and drive the gospel message into the world. The idea is to go where the ungodly are and let them know about Christ.

The problem with a lot of Christians is that they come to church and gobble up the message, feed on the worship, and stuff themselves with fellowship, but they never use what they know. They just keep getting stuffed. They can barely move because they are stuffed with the things of God.

But they don't realize that the reason God feeds us is so we can be strong to go out and tell somebody else where to find the banquet. A lot of Christians don't evangelize because they are never around any unbelievers. They don't know any ungodly people.

Taking Christ's command seriously will take care of

that problem. You can't go into all the world without rubbing shoulders with non-Christians. Some Christians are afraid of contact with unbelievers because they are afraid the unbelievers' lifestyle will rub off on them.

It won't if you are following Christ the way you should. If you are strong and growing in your faith, the influence will flow from you out to them, not from them in to you. If you find yourself being unduly influenced by the unbelievers around you, you need to step back and try to determine three things: where that influence is coming from, what you might be doing to unnecessarily expose yourself to that influence, and what you need to do to correct the problem. You need to be sure that the influence flows from you to the world, not the other way around. That influence starts with delivering the gospel message.

The Work of the Church

When Jesus' disciples are being obedient to His command to evangelize, the church will become like a maternity ward where every Sunday we hear the cries of newborn babies. You may say, "But I thought that's what we paid our pastor to do."

No, the pastor's primary job is to equip the saints for the work of the ministry. Does that mean the pastor doesn't have to be an evangelist too? Of course not. Every Christian is to be leading other people to Christ.

What I'm saying is that God never intended for us to sit in church every Sunday and wait for unbelievers to show up so they can hear the gospel and get saved. The primary purpose of Sunday worship is not evangelism. Don't get me wrong, there's nothing wrong with an altar call.

But the primary goals of Sunday are worship, the equipping of the saints, and the fellowship of the family of God. Then as we are strengthened and equipped, we go into the world to lead people to Christ.

The Importance of Faith

Mark 16:16 stresses how important it is that people

believe the gospel. This verse has thrown some people for a curve because it seems to emphasize baptism as necessary to salvation. But that's not what the verse says.

The reason Jesus said, "He who has believed and has been baptized shall be saved," is that baptism was so closely associated with the proclamation of the gospel and salvation in the New Testament that an unbaptized believer was inconceivable. The first thing new converts did was publicly identify with Christ in baptism.

Notice the second half of the verse. It's the person "who has disbelieved" who will be condemned. Nothing is said about baptism here. The issue is belief.

Jesus' commission continues in verses 17–18, two more verses that give people a lot of problems because Jesus talks about miraculous signs. But the point simply is that God sovereignly uses miracles at His discretion to validate the truth of the gospel.

The best example of this is in Acts 28:3–5, when Paul was bitten by a deadly snake and shook off the bite. Please note that Paul was not snake-handling! He was not tempting God. Paul was simply carrying out his gospel commission, and God wasn't through with him yet, so He didn't let him die.

What is often missed in these verses is that Jesus says the signs will "accompany" the presentation of the gospel. Drinking poison or allowing deadly snakes to bite you has nothing to do with the gospel. If you aren't presenting the gospel, you don't need to worry about any validating signs. You don't have anything to validate.

BEING WITNESSES OF CHRIST

Christ's commission in the Gospel of Luke empha-sizes that as His disciples, we are to be His witnesses. Jesus said:

> Thus it is written, that the Christ should suffer and rise again from the dead the third day; and that repentance for forgiveness of sins should be proclaimed in His name to all the nations, beginning from Jerusalem. You are witnesses of these things. And behold, I am

sending forth the promise of My Father upon you; but you are to stay in the city until you are clothed with power from on high. (Luke 24:46–49)

A witness is someone who tells what he has seen and heard. You can't be a witness and not be personally involved with people. When you receive a subpoena to come to court and testify, the judge doesn't want you to send someone to relay your message. The judge wants to hear from you.

Sinners are all around us, and they need someone to be a witness to them. How can we stand on the witness stand and not be a witness? How can we not tell them what we have seen and heard about Jesus? We say, "Jesus is the answer." Have you told anyone that lately? We say, "Come to my church next Sunday." That's fine, but it's not enough. They may not make it to church the next Sunday. They need someone who will tell them that forgiveness of their sins is available in Jesus Christ.

Delivering the Message

A witness is someone who delivers the message personally. The story is told of a man who was going into the army. He was deeply in love with a woman, and he didn't want to lose her while he was gone.

He told her, "Darling, I want you to wait for me. And to let you know my heart is committed to you, over the next year you will receive 365 letters from me. I will write you every day for a year to show you how committed I am to you."

So he did it. He wrote her a letter every day for the next year, but at the end of that time he was shocked to learn that she had gotten married—to the mailman! There's no substitute for the personal delivery of the message.

Too many Christians want to do long-distance evangelism. They will help send missionaries overseas, but they won't tell their next-door neighbor about Jesus. We need to send out missionaries, but God needs some witnesses here at home.

If you are not witnessing, you are failing Christ, because one of the reasons He left you on earth after you were saved was so you could tell the world about Him.

Receiving Power to Witness

Luke 24:49 reminds us that we don't just go out and witness in our own power. This verse sounds like the early verses of Acts 1, which we will look at later.

The "promise of My Father" was the coming of the Holy Spirit, who clothes us with power to be His witnesses. God never meant for us to go out under our own head of steam and try to witness for Him.

The fact of the Holy Spirit's power answers the objections people have against witnessing. Someone may say, "But I've only been a Christian for a short while." You are probably the best candidate for a witness, because you have something fresh and exciting to tell. Folk who have been saved for a long time tend to lose their zeal and sit back.

The woman at the well (John 4) had only been saved for a few minutes when she ran into town and started telling people about Jesus. You know the power of God was upon her, because she went to the men who knew her reputation, and they believed her. They saw that something had happened to her.

She invited the men to come, see and hear what she had seen and heard (v. 29). And she led all of her former boyfriends to Jesus Christ because she was willing to be a witness.

You don't have to know the Bible through and through to be a witness. All you need to know is that you were lost in sin, that Jesus died for you, and that He lifted you out of your sin. Of course, you need to learn more of the Bible, but don't wait until you have it all down before you do something.

And, by the way, if you want to be an "on-fire" witness, don't hang out too much with "wet blanket" Christians who have lost their fire. Their lack of zeal will douse your fire if you don't watch out. Find people who have a little fire in them and hang out with them.

Answering the Alarm

A little girl asked her father, "Daddy, what do firemen do in the firehouse all day?"

He said, "Well, they spend a lot of their time waiting for the fire alarm to sound. Then when the alarm sounds, they move out."

I know that firefighters do a lot more than sit around waiting for a fire, but you get the idea. They can't go until the alarm has sounded.

God sounded the fire alarm for His witnesses two thousand years ago. We can't spend our time with other firemen, polishing our "theological fire engines," while people are dying every day without Christ. The call has already been sent out, and God needs people who are ready to go.

DECLARING GOD'S FORGIVENESS

The Gospel of John highlights a different aspect of Christ's command to share the gospel. Beginning in John 20:21, Jesus appeared to the disciples and said:

> "Peace be with you; as the Father has sent Me, I also send you." And when He had said this, He breathed on them, and said to them, "Receive the Holy Spirit. If you forgive the sins of any, their sins have been forgiven them; if you retain the sins of any, they have been retained." (vv. 21–23)

Do you have peace in your Christian life? Jesus makes an important statement about that. In order to have God's peace, you have to be following God's agenda. And since God's agenda includes evangelism, if you are not doing evangelism you are not enjoying what God has for you because you are not doing what He commands for you.

Here Jesus says that He is sending us into the world just as the Father sent Him into the world (John 20:21; see also John 17:18). Jesus went out where the lost people were, and He is calling us to do the same thing. We've already talked about the futility of staying among believers and trying to do evangelism.

A man looked out his window one day and saw his neighbor fishing in his backyard in a tub full of water. The man asked his neighbor, "What do you think you're doing?"

"I'm fishing!" the other guy called back.

"But there are no fish in the tub," the first man said.

"I know, but this sure is convenient."

It sure is convenient for us Christians to go to church. It's necessary, in fact. It's convenient for us to hang out in our own group. But that's not where the fish are.

God did not turn on a loudspeaker in heaven and announce, "You must be born again!" He became a man. He took on flesh and blood in the person of Jesus and walked among us. Jesus mixed it up with sinners. He touched them, He loved them, and He drew them to Himself. And that's the way Jesus sent us into the world.

In John 20:23, Jesus spelled out the authority associated with our evangelism. Being able to forgive or retain the sins of others is a powerful thing. This verse has often been misinterpreted to give human beings too much power in this area. But the Greek language clarifies what Jesus is saying.

The translation before us makes an effort to clarify the verse. Jesus used two Greek tenses, the present tense for "forgive" and "retain," and the perfect tense for "forgiven" and "retained." The perfect tense in Greek specifies past action with a continuing result.

Jesus is saying that we have the authority, not to forgive or retain sins ourselves, but to declare what happens in heaven when a person accepts or rejects Christ. You and I have the privilege of telling someone that if he will accept Christ, his sins are forgiven. We can say that because that person's sins will have already been forgiven by God.

In other words, we have the privilege and authority to announce God's forgiveness for sins. Do you know how many people would love to know they are forgiven?

Someone has said we could empty most of the beds in psychiatric hospitals if people could just know they were forgiven.

We can't repent for other people, and they can only find forgiveness if they will come to Christ. But when a person does that, we have the authority under Christ to announce their forgiveness.

GOING IN THE POWER OF THE SPIRIT

The final commission we will consider is Acts 1:8. Jesus was gathered with the apostles just before His ascension. They were eager to know if He was about to set up His kingdom. Jesus told them:

> It is not for you to know times or epochs which the Father has fixed by His own authority; but you shall receive power when the Holy Spirit has come upon you; and you shall be My witnesses both in Jerusalem, and in all Judea and Samaria, and even to the remotest part of the earth. (vv. 7–8)

Here's a foundational truth we have seen before: Witnessing is not dependent upon you, but upon the power of the Holy Spirit at work in you. Jesus so closely links the coming of the Spirit with being His witnesses that we could make this statement: If talking about your faith to unbelievers is not a regular part of your Christian life, you are, in fact, a nonspiritual Christian.

By that I mean the Holy Spirit's work is not being fully revealed in you. Jesus says, "When the Holy Spirit comes upon you, you will be My witnesses," period.

See, one of the things the Holy Spirit does is talk about Jesus—and He talks about Jesus every chance He gets. If the Spirit is not talking about Jesus through you, and you are never conscious of Him prompting you to talk about Jesus, that's because you and the Spirit are not on the same wavelength.

When the Holy Spirit gives you His power to witness, you won't need prompting or a program. You will just witness because you can't help yourself.

You say, "Well, that's not how I function." Tell me, what do you do on the telephone? You just call your party and start talking because you feel like talking and you have something you want to say. Evangelism should be that natural.

One day, the great evangelist D. L. Moody stopped a stranger on the street and asked him, "Are you a Christian?" The man was put off by the question, so he said, "Mind your own business!"

Moody said, "This is my business!"

The man looked at him and said, "Then you must be Moody."

Wouldn't it be great to be known as "the person whose business is witnessing"? This is your business. You can't be a child of God and not talk about your Father, the one you represent.

So what do we need in order to witness? We need a new injection of Holy Spirit power. We need to get on our faces before God and say, "God, I have failed You in this area of my spiritual life. I have failed to make You known. I now make myself available to the Holy Spirit." Do that, then open your mouth in witness, and you will be surprised at what comes out.

One day, a little boy was in Disneyland having a great time with Mickey Mouse, Donald Duck, and all the rest. But somehow, moving among the masses of people, he got separated from his parents.

He was lost, but he didn't know it because he was having so much fun. His parents were looking for him, but he was too busy having fun to look for them—until about twenty minutes later, when he suddenly looked around for them and realized he was lost. A security officer found him and helped him reunite with his parents.

We live in a sinful world where people are having a good time. They are lost, but they don't know it. It's the Holy Spirit's job to let them know they are lost. Once the Holy Spirit does that, we are God's security officers to unite them with the Father from whom they are separated.

Our problem is that too many of the security officers are also having so much fun with the world's amusements they don't have time to help bring lost people to the Father.

May God help us not to be so busy enjoying the festivities that we fail to bring lost people to the Savior.

CHAPTER SEVENTEEN

THE CONTENT OF EVANGELISM

Did you ever start to deliver a message to someone, only to discover you forgot what you were supposed to say? Or maybe you wrote down some directions, but you got the street number wrong, or you wrote down the turns wrong, and now you can't find the place you're looking for.

We've all done things like that. It's one thing to mess up a message or a set of directions, but it's an entirely different story to muddle up the gospel. If we are going to be telling people the good news (and telling it is an absolute necessity for being a disciple of Jesus Christ), then it is necessary that we get the message straight.

So let's talk about the content of the gospel, lest we be confused about the message Jesus Christ has commissioned us to deliver. I want to do that by turning to the Magna Carta of the Christian faith, the book of Romans. In this great doctrinal statement Paul sets forth the gospel, the good news about Jesus Christ. I want to give you five elements of the gospel from the book of Romans.

OUR PROBLEM

First of all, in order to appreciate the gospel as good

news we must see it against the backdrop of the bad news. The problem the gospel brings to light is stated clearly in Romans 3:23: "All have sinned and fall short of the glory of God."

The Definition of Sin

Since all of us are included in the indictment stated above, we would do well to understand exactly what sin is. The Greek word Paul uses here means literally "to miss the mark." It's an archery term, describing a bowman who draws back his string and releases his arrow, but fails to hit the target.

What is the target we are failing to hit when we sin? What is the bull's-eye we should be aiming at? Paul tells us in the second half of Romans 3:23. The target is "the glory of God." When we sin, we fail to properly reflect God's glory. And we are *all* guilty of missing this mark.

When we are doing evangelism, we need to make sure we are clear on this point with people. One person may be better-looking, wealthier, or smarter than the next person. But each person is still a sinner in God's eyes. It doesn't matter what side of town we live on; all have sinned.

We need to help people see this because when God measures us, He does not measure us against each other. We classify sins into big ones, like murder, and little ones, like telling a small lie. But both are sin, and both are equally offensive to God's character because sin does not reflect what He is like.

Don't misunderstand. I am not saying that killing someone is the same as lying in terms of the damage done, although lies sometimes get people killed. What I'm saying is that when measured against the perfect character of God, all sin is equally offensive.

The Inclusiveness of Sin

Romans 3:23 does not allow for exceptions. All of us have sinned. Back in verse 10 of this same chapter, Paul says, "There is none righteous, not even one."

Every man and every woman is born into this world

alienated from a holy God, because we are born in sin and "brought forth in iniquity" (Psalm 51:5). The Bible makes clear that we are consumed by sin. We try to hide it, cover it, paint over it, and excuse it, but we can't get rid of it.

We call sin by any other name than what it is. What we call accidents, God calls abominations. What we call blunders, God calls blindness. What we call chance, God calls choice. What we call defects, God views as a spiritual disease.

What we call error, God calls enmity. What we call fascination, God calls fatality. What we designate as infirmity, God designates as iniquity. What we view as luxury is leprosy to God. What we see as liberty, God sees as lawlessness. What we call a mistake, God calls madness. And what we call weakness, God says is willingness.

God's view of sin is utterly different than ours. We cannot understand sin, nor can we communicate it to those who need the gospel, unless we clearly understand that there are no degrees of sin with God. When God judges, He does so predicated on a perfect standard, the standard of His holiness.

A Perfect Standard

I've often said that what holiness is to God, cleanliness is to my wife, Lois. She is a cleaning fanatic. She loves the smell of Lysol. To her, every day is just another opportunity to clean something.

I will never forget the time a few years back when Lois was gone for a few days. I thought I would do the good and loving husbandly thing by cleaning the house for her while she was gone. Actually, I planned to oversee the cleaning, not do it myself. So I assembled our four children and gave them their assignments while I supervised. I thought we did a good job, so I was ready for Lois to come home. We had the place looking good, so I expected a big hug and affirming words.

Instead, Lois came in and said, "I thought you were going to clean up for me." She then took me to some forsaken corner of the house and showed me a piece of lint.

I'm talking about something an ant could have missed! She said, "When I say clean, I mean this too."

What was clean to me wasn't clean to Lois because we were operating on two different standards. My standard was get the big stuff in the middle of the house. Her standard included the crevices and the corners.

When God deals with our sin, He measures it against His perfection. Even though we may seem relatively clean compared to the criminal or the drug pusher, we still fall short of the standard of God's perfect holiness.

Two men were exploring a volcanic island when the volcano suddenly erupted. In moments, the two found themselves surrounded by a sea of molten lava. Ahead of them lay a path to safety, but to reach it they would have to jump across a flowing river of molten rock.

The first explorer was an older man. He ran as fast as he could, took the mightiest leap he could, but only traveled a few feet. He met a swift death in the superheated lava.

The second explorer was a much younger man, a virile physical specimen who had once set a record for the broad jump at his college. He put all of his energy into his run, jumped with flawless form, and in fact shattered his old college record. Unfortunately, he landed six inches short of his goal, and he too was swept away.

Although the young man jumped farther than the old man, they both met the same fate, because they both fell short of the standard.

That's the way it is with sin. It doesn't matter how far you can jump. You will still fall short of God's standard. What does it mean to fall short of the glory of God?

The word *glory* means to "show off." Glory is putting something on display in such a way that it is enhanced, made to look good. When we talk about the glory of God, we are talking about putting Him on display.

Anytime we fail to display God as He truly is, we demonstrate that we are sinners. The glory of God is His absolute holiness, His total rulership over all the universe.

How did Adam fall short of the glory of God when he sinned in the Garden of Eden? The issue was not just eating a piece of fruit. The world was plunged into sin when Adam decided he was going to do his own thing with that piece of fruit. He decided he was going to run his own life, be his own god. He was going to live autonomously and leave God out of his life.

Our problem is that we are judged by a perfect standard, and we don't measure up. When I go to the dentist, I brush my teeth really hard beforehand, just like you do. I try to fool him, but he doesn't buy it. He makes me rinse with a red dye that sticks to the plaque on my teeth. I can't fool my dentist because he is using a much more thorough method than I am to determine clean.

Born in Sin

This sin problem is one that all people are born with, as we saw in Psalm 51. Sin entered the human race through Adam, and we were all contaminated (Romans 5:12). Human nature was corrupted by sin, making us sinners by nature as well as by choice.

You don't have to teach a child how to lie. You don't have to give children a course on how to be selfish. Somehow they pick that up all by themselves. That's because what we passed on to our children was not only our looks, but the sinful nature we inherited from Adam.

We are born in sin the way a worm is hatched inside of an apple. When we see an apple with a hole in it, most of us assume that a worm made the hole by boring into the apple. When we cut the apple open, we are looking for the worm.

But we don't usually find a worm, because the wormhole in an apple is made by a worm *exiting* the apple from within, not boring into the apple from without. The egg of the worm is laid on the blossom before the apple is ever formed, and the apple grows up around the worm.

So if you see an apple with a hole in it, it's because a worm has bored its way out of the apple. What you see are the effects of something the apple was created with.

In the same way, the larva of sin is transferred from generation to generation, from parent to child, so that what comes out is what was already there. The result is alienation from a holy God.

The bad news is that "all have sinned." Until we understand and accept the bad news, we are not ready for the good news. When God looks down upon a criminal and a law-abiding citizen, He sees identical twins, because all of us are sinners in His eyes. We have all failed to reach His standard, which is perfection.

THE PREDICAMENT

Our problem has left us with quite a predicament. Paul says in Romans 4:4–5:

> Now to the one who works, his wage is not reckoned as a favor, but as what is due. But to the one who does not work, but believes in Him who justifies the ungodly, his faith is reckoned as righteousness.

Our problem is that we are sinners, and our predicament is that we cannot save ourselves by the works that we do. In verses 1–3 of this chapter, Paul uses the example of Abraham to argue that no one is saved by his own efforts.

Then Paul adds in verse 6 that the only way we can be saved is if God "reckons righteousness" to us "apart from works." To reckon means to put to our account, to credit us with righteousness. Paul is talking about the payment for sin, which we will discuss below.

No Self-Effort

The Bible leaves no doubt that we cannot save ourselves by our own efforts (see Galatians 2:16). This one is tough for a lot of people to accept. They will agree that they are not perfect. They will admit to some degree of sin, but few people are ready to admit that there is nothing they can do about it themselves.

A lot of people are working hard to fix their sin problem because they assume there is some sort of standard they need to meet. The trouble is that they are ignorant of God's true standard, so they set about to establish their own standard of righteousness (Romans 10:3). They are trying to work their way to God.

If there is any one basic misunderstanding of Christianity, it is this idea that we can please God and earn our way to heaven by the good things we do. People attempt to do this in all kinds of ways.

Some practice their religion faithfully. Others try to live a good life and not hurt anyone. Still others figure that being a good citizen is good enough. And there are always those who claim they are trying to keep the Ten Commandments. This last one may be the greatest deception of all.

No one has ever kept the Ten Commandments perfectly. The Israelites were down in the camp breaking them even while Moses was on Mount Sinai receiving them.

The apostle James tells us that if we break even one of God's laws, we are guilty of breaking all of them (James 2:10). And I doubt there are many people alive who have not broken them all.

For example, the sixth commandment says, "You shall not murder" (Exodus 20:13). Someone may say, "I've got you there, Tony. I have never killed anyone."

But Jesus said that if we are angry with our brother, we are guilty enough to go into hell (Matthew 5:22). Why? Being mad enough at another person to commit murder, or wishing someone were dead, is committing murder in your heart.

The seventh commandment says, "You shall not commit adultery" (Exodus 20:14). Someone may say, "I haven't committed that one. Move on to the next one."

But Jesus said that if a man looks at a woman to lust after her, he has committed adultery with her in his heart (Matthew 5:28). The list could go on.

Satisfying God

Do you see why the Bible says that salvation is "not as a result of works" (Ephesians 2:9)? We can't do anything to satisfy God's perfect demands.

Imagine a man convicted of theft standing before the judge for sentencing. He says, "Your honor, before you sentence me I just want you to know that I've never killed anyone." He proceeds to list about twenty-five bad things he hasn't done.

The judge would say, "Well, that's nice, but it's irrelevant. You committed theft, and that's why you are going to prison." You cannot use your righteous deeds to cancel out your unrighteous deeds.

Any and all sin is an infringement of God's standards. The Bible declares that we have a problem, which is sin. And we have a predicament, which is that we can't do anything to solve our problem ourselves. This leaves us liable to God's penalty.

THE PENALTY

Romans 6:23 is crystal clear on the penalty of sin: "The wages of sin is death." Sin carries with it a price tag, a payoff, which is death. The proof that we are all sinners is that we are going to die someday.

In fact, we are going to die by appointment, according to Hebrews 9:27, which says, "It is appointed for men to die once and after this comes judgment." You may be late for a lot of things in your life, but this is one appointment you will keep unless Christ returns first.

Separation from God

In the Bible, death means separation, not the cessation of our existence. We will live forever. The only question is where we will spend eternity.

Physical death is the separation of your soul from your body, and spiritual death is the eternal separation of your soul and body from God in hell. Spiritual and physical death is what Paul is talking about in Romans 6:23. If you want to know how seriously God views sin, look at death.

That's why Solomon said we are better off to go to a funeral than to a party (Ecclesiastes 7:1–4). That sounds strange until you step back and realize what Solomon is saying. He's making the point that the world tries to ignore and deny death by throwing a party. If you go to the world's party, the world will lie to you about man's fate and eternity. At the world's party, you won't get the real deal.

But at a funeral, Solomon says, you get the real deal "because that is the end of every man" (7:2). We are all going to die, but if you are a Christian you will not experience spiritual or eternal death. Paul said that to be "absent from the body" is to be "at home with the Lord" (2 Corinthians 5:8). When a Christian closes his eyes in death, he immediately opens them in the presence of Christ.

The Sting of Death

The Bible says that death has a sting to it. That sting is sin (1 Corinthians 15:56). The person who has not experienced forgiveness of sins through Christ will feel the sting of sin at death. He or she will pay the penalty of sin, which is eternal separation from God and eternal suffering in hell.

This is a traumatic and disturbing concept to most people. I have often had people tell me, "I don't believe a loving God would just send people to hell."

The problem with this is that it is a one-sided statement of the character of God. God is loving, but He is also holy and just. His eyes are too pure even to look at sin (Habakkuk 1:13). It's also important to remember that God did not prepare hell for human beings, but for "the devil and his angels" (Matthew 25:41).

God allows us to make our choice as to whether we will bear the payment for our sin or accept His payment in Christ. If we choose to reject Christ, the only one who can remove our sin, we must bear the repercussion of that choice—eternal separation from God.

When a person rejects God's eternal Son, who died on the cross for the sins of eternal man, he must pay the eternal penalty, eternal separation from God. And so, there is a penalty.

The consequences for our sin are not simply for what we have done, but also because of the One against whom they were done. Since God is an eternal Being, we must pay an eternal price.

I often tell people on Sunday morning, "If you are here today as a non-Christian and you fear death, you have every reason to be afraid. If I can help you to be more afraid, I welcome the opportunity, because you don't want to be caught dead without Jesus Christ."

But if you know Christ, you have nothing to fear from death. Jesus Christ has taken the sting out of death for you by bearing your sin (1 Corinthians 15:55–57).

This reminds me of the two brothers who were playing in their yard. A bee came and stung one of the brothers. He began to cry and hold his arm where he had been stung. He was in great pain. The bee then began circling the other brother, who went into a panic. He was swatting at the bee and yelling to his brother, "Help, he's going to sting me!"

The other boy said, "Quit yelling. It's not going to sting you!"

"How do you know?" his brother asked.

"Because it has already stung me, and a bee only has one stinger. All it can do now is make a lot of noise."

Jesus Christ took our "stinger" upon Himself so that all that death can do now is make a lot of noise. It can't hurt you once you know Jesus Christ. But those who don't accept Him have to pay the penalty for their sins. I know I am reviewing things that may seem really basic to you. But remember our purpose. We are talking about the necessities, the things you need to know and practice to be a disciple of Jesus Christ. We're covering the content of the gospel not just for your own review, but so you can explain it clearly to others as you do evangelism.

THE PROVISION

Aren't you glad the gospel message doesn't stop with the penalty for sin? Romans 5:8 begins with my two favorite words in the Bible: "*But God* demonstrates His own love toward us, in that while we were yet sinners, Christ died for us" (italics added).

Those two words can revolutionize any situation.

Someone may say, "Tony, I realize I am a sinner condemned to face eternal hell." That is true—"but God" has made an eternal provision for your eternal dilemma.

God Gets the Credit

When did Christ die for us? When we got better? When we fixed ourselves up? No, He died for us while we were still sinning against Him.

Why is that? God deserves and demands all the credit for salvation. So He takes sinners just as they are and transforms their lives. He doesn't tell you to straighten out your life and then come to Him. If you could do that, you wouldn't *need* to come to God.

God came to us with the provision for sin because we had nothing to offer Him. We weren't even looking for Him or seeking His forgiveness when Christ died for us. We were going the other way.

A number of things had to happen to secure our salvation. God's holiness and justice had to be satisfied; that's called *propitiation*. God had to be satisfied with the sacrifice for sin. Your good works and mine cannot satisfy God because they are mixed with sin, and God demands a perfect sacrifice.

Then there had to be *redemption*, a payment made to buy us back from the slave market of sin. When we were redeemed, we also experienced *justification*, a legal declaration that we are righteous in God's sight. Salvation also involves *imputation*, the crediting of Jesus' righteousness to our account so that not only is our record of sin cleared, but the goodness of Christ is applied to us.

Paid in Full

Now you understand why Jesus said on the cross, "It is finished!" (John 19:30). That phrase is one word in Greek, a word that means "paid in full." Jesus was saying, "I have picked up the tab for sin."

This is a very picturesque concept. It's drawn from the Old Testament law of the Day of Atonement (Leviticus 16). This was the day each year when the high priest of Israel offered a blood sacrifice for the nation's sins.

The sacrificial goat was killed and its blood drained, and the high priest took the blood into the Holy of Holies and offered it to God. When God accepted the sacrifice as a substitute for the people's sins, He postponed His judgment for another 365 days.

But there were two goats chosen on the Day of Atonement. The other goat was called the "scapegoat" (v. 10). The priest laid his hands on the goat and confessed the sins of the people over it. This signified the transferal of the people's sins to the goat. Then the scapegoat was sent out into the wilderness, signifying that the sins of the people were being taken away for another year (vv. 21–22).

The only problem was that every now and then, a scapegoat wandered back into the Israelites' camp. You can imagine the chaos that ensued when this goat came back, symbolically bearing all the people's sins.

If this happened, someone would take the scapegoat to the edge of a cliff and shove it off. That goat was not coming back anymore.

I want to show you an important distinction here. The Greek word for the payment that was made by the sacrificial goat is *lutrosis*. But when people wanted to talk about a payment that once made would keep sins from ever coming back up again, they strengthened the Greek word to *apolutrosis*.

When Paul talked about "the redemption which is in Christ Jesus" (Romans 3:24), he used the word *apolutrosis*. It means that our sins were shoved off the cliff and they will never come up again.

That's why you can't lose your salvation. Once you are saved, your sins will never be brought up against you again as far as entry into heaven is concerned. The death of Christ guarantees that.

When I stand before God and God says, "Evans, why should I let you into heaven?" my only response will be, "My sins have been washed away by the blood of Your Son, and You told me they will never come up again." I'm going to let the blood of Jesus do my talking for me!

That's why Jesus could tell the thief on the cross,

"Today you shall be with Me in Paradise" (Luke 23:43). How could that man accept Christ and be guaranteed heaven just hours before he died? Because we are not saved by our works of righteousness.

The person who has tried to live a good life for seventy years, but who never accepted Christ, will be lost for eternity, while a thief who makes a dying confession goes to heaven. That's not logical to most people because they are not using God's standard of judgment.

I've often said this before, but it bears repeating here. People like to think God will grade on the curve. But the trouble with the curve is the student in your class who makes one hundred and ruins the curve.

We're not graded on a curve when it comes to holiness, because God is perfectly holy and cannot be around sin. But even if we were, Jesus ruined the "curve" of sin because He lived a perfect life. Before He came, we thought we were OK because we were comparing ourselves to each other. Jesus ruined the curve, but He paid the penalty for our failure to meet God's standard.

THE PARDON

To go to heaven, you must be pardoned. That's what Romans 10:9–10 is all about:

> If you confess with your mouth Jesus as Lord, and believe in your heart that God raised Him from the dead, you shall be saved; for with the heart man believes, resulting in righteousness, and with the mouth he confesses, resulting in salvation.

The death of Christ satisfied the demands of God against the sin of all people for all time. But it is only beneficial to those who accept it. It is *sufficient* for everyone, but it is *efficient* only for those who believe.

Accepting Pardon

Jesus Christ provided the sacrifice, but we must accept God's pardon. Paul says we must "believe in [our] heart." That means your mother can't believe for you.

Your father can't come to Christ for you. Your pastor can't confer salvation on you. You must decide for Christ personally.

Believing in Jesus is a lot different than believing facts about Jesus. Believing in Jesus demands that we personalize our trust in Him. Jesus is Lord, but we must confess that ourselves to be saved. He rose from the dead, but we must believe that for ourselves and accept God's testimony that Jesus' death was sufficient for our sin.

The Proof of Pardon

That's what the Resurrection is all about. The Resurrection is proof that God accepted Jesus' payment. He was raised "because of our justification" (Romans 4:25). If Jesus Christ were still dead today, He could not be our Savior.

The Resurrection separates Jesus Christ from all others who claim to show people the way to God. Buddha, where are you? Mohammed, speak up if you are alive. Confucius, give us another saying if you have anything to say.

The Bible says that Jesus got up out of the grave and showed Himself to the apostles, to five hundred people at another time, and finally to Paul (1 Corinthians 15:5–8). The Resurrection is God's receipt that the payment of Christ for our sins was made and fully accepted.

You must believe that God has raised Jesus from the dead, because a dead Savior can't save you. Don't put your hope in dead people. If they were that good, they wouldn't be dead. You've got to put your hope in a living Savior, Jesus Christ. He alone can offer you a pardon that counts with God. God grants pardon to anyone who comes to Him through Christ, who is the only Mediator between God and man (1 Timothy 2:5).

Our "Umpire"

The Old Testament patriarch Job longed for such a Mediator. He said, "[God] is not a man as I am that I may answer Him, that we may go to court together. There is no umpire between us, who may lay his hand upon us both" (Job 9:32–33).

Job had a problem. He was saying, "I am a sinful man who is trying to reach out to a perfect God. I need an umpire who can come between us. I need someone who is like me and understands how I feel, yet I also need someone who is like God and understands how He feels. This umpire can take my hand and God's hand and bring us together."

That's what Jesus Christ has done for us. He is our "umpire" to settle the sin dispute with God and bring us together. He knows how we feel because He was a man. He knows how God feels because He is God. Jesus is the God-man who can both offer us pardon from God and secure that pardon by His death on the cross and resurrection from the dead.

If you have ever gone to court for a traffic violation, you know what it is to hear the judge pronounce you guilty and announce the fine to be paid. But you have probably never seen a judge leave the bench, reach into his own wallet, pay your fine, then go back to the bench and declare you pardoned because the penalty had been paid!

That's exactly what God did for us in Jesus Christ. We stood before God, the eternal Judge in heaven, and He declared us guilty. Because we had nothing to pay our penalty with, He left the bench of heaven's courtroom and took on humanity in the Person of Christ so He could die to pay the penalty for our sins.

Then He rose from the dead three days later and ascended back to heaven. Now He can say to anyone who throws himself on the mercy of God, "I can't change the law, but I can pay the price." That means there is nothing left for us to do but accept the payment and walk out of heaven's courtroom as pardoned people!

This is the basic message of the gospel. It's too good to keep to ourselves. That's why Jesus told us to go into all the world and announce the good news to anyone who will listen. Evangelism is an absolute necessity if people are to be saved and if we are to be authentic followers of Christ.

CHAPTER EIGHTEEN

THE CONTEXT OF EVANGELISM

Did you know that you were born again to reproduce? You were saved to multiply. God brought the church into existence for the purpose of reproducing the life of Christ in the lives of human beings like you and me. It is His plan that the members of the church, which is His body, reproduce themselves. If there is no reproduction, there is no discipleship.

As we have seen repeatedly, we are called to make disciples. A disciple is a growing, maturing follower of Christ. But before disciples can grow and mature, they have to be born. That's why evangelism is one of the absolute necessities of discipleship.

We've talked about the concept and content of evangelism, which means we are ready to discuss the context of evangelism. I really don't have any surprises here. The God-ordained context in which evangelism is designed to take place is through the ministry of the local church. We have already established that the church is the context in which all of the four necessities are designed to take place.

But what I want to do in this chapter is take that truth a step further and demonstrate that within the church itself, certain things have to be happening for evangelism to be present and effective. The thesis of this chapter is that the church's *inreach* must be in place and working properly before there can be dynamic, effective *outreach.*

SAVED TO REPRODUCE

If a church is not seeing spiritual reproduction taking place on a regular basis, something is wrong. We were born to multiply, saved to reproduce. When a husband and wife are unable to have children, they go to the doctor, because something is wrong.

When a church fails to reproduce new believers, we need to ask why. The church that is healthy and functioning as it should will become, as I suggested in an earlier chapter, a maternity ward where the cries of newborn babes in Christ are heard.

We could change the imagery slightly and say that the church is an incubator for believers, the environment in which we grow and develop. Just as a healthy family prepares its children to be parents themselves someday, so a healthy church enables God's children to become spiritual parents.

But evangelism does not happen in a vacuum. A church that is weak on the other essentials cannot expect to have a healthy ministry of evangelism, because evangelism grows out of a church's commitment to worship, fellowship, and the Scriptures.

Let me show you how all of this comes together by taking you back once more to Acts 2:42–47. I know we have looked at this passage on a number of occasions, but I want us to see it from a slightly different perspective here. These verses demonstrate how the church's inreach gives birth to its outreach. The church Jerusalem definitely knew how to "do church"!

Remember that this church underwent explosive growth the very day it was born (2:41), and that growth continued unabated for days and weeks on end. The church at Jerusalem was reproducing so fast it had new believers hanging out of every door and window.

Compare verses 41 and 47 of Acts 2 and you'll see

something interesting. The church began with three thousand conversions (v. 41), and verse 47 says that "the Lord was adding to their number *day by day* those who were being saved" (italics added). This church was alive with evangelism. Spiritual multiplication was a way of life for these disciples.

SOME OBSERVATIONS

Before we look at what it was about the Jerusalem church that made its outreach so effective, I want to make some observations about evangelism and spiritual multiplication from this text.

Immediate Evangelism

One of the most interesting things to me about the situation in Jerusalem is that people were getting saved so fast there had to be relatively new Christians leading other people to Christ. The church was too young to have any "old-timers" who had been in the faith for years. This tells me that you do not have to be a Christian for ten years before you start reproducing yourself. Yes, there is a lot for new believers to learn. Growth needs to take place. But God's agenda for the church includes evangelism, and a person can start telling others about Christ the day he is saved.

No Need for Programs

It's also worth noting that the Jerusalem church did not have a lot of time to develop elaborate evangelism training programs and strategies. There's nothing wrong with programs and strategies. The church today has it all over the early church when it comes to that.

But those early disciples had something we lack too often today. They were full of the Holy Spirit. You can cut back on programs when you are full of the Spirit. You can get along without a lot of strategies when the Holy Spirit is energizing and empowering your witness.

No Renegade Believers

Here's another observation that is important to note.

Don't miss the phrase "to their number" in verse 47. As people were getting saved in Jerusalem, they were being added to the church. In fact, this phrase or something very similar to it occurs several times throughout the book of Acts.

In other words, there was no such thing as an "unchurched" believer envisioned in the New Testament. This fact is crucial to a central tenet of this book that I have attempted to demonstrate: Discipleship is to be carried on in the context of the local church.

When Christians say they don't need the church, they don't know what they are talking about. They need the church the way a finger needs a body. Should a finger become detached from its hand, it will cease to function.

The reason so many believers don't function properly is that they are detached from the larger body of Christ. They have no nerves or blood vessels, no supply line bringing them the spiritual nutrients they need and dealing with the toxins they produce.

In the human body, there is a name for renegade cells that go off and do their own thing instead of functioning in harmony with all the other cells in the body. We call them cancer cells.

The terrible thing about cancer is that a renegade cell isn't content to rebel all by itself. It starts reproducing itself and gathering other cells around it. As the cells grow, they produce a lump that is often the first sign of cancer.

If the situation is allowed to persist long enough, these renegade cells send cells to other parts of the body, where they also reproduce and spread the cancer. The cancer has now metastasized, making it much harder — in some cases, impossible—to treat successfully.

This is often what happens in the body of Jesus Christ, and it's the wrong kind of spiritual multiplication. But the danger of a spiritual cancer developing does not negate the fact that believers were born to reproduce.

Scattered into the World

In fact, if you look at the opening verses of Acts 8,

you will see that God allowed a "great persecution" to break out against the church in Jerusalem. It seems that the believers were getting comfortable staying in Jerusalem.

Jesus had told them to go into all the world and preach the gospel. God wanted them to metastasize, multiplying themselves in every corner of the Roman empire. So He allowed persecution to arise to get them out of their comfort zone, and the church got the message: "Those who had been scattered went about preaching the word" (Acts 8:4).

Did these people have personal needs? I'm sure they did. Were some of them hurting emotionally? Probably so. Were their needs and hurts important to God? Of course they were. I don't want to diminish one iota the reality of the struggles that many of God's people face.

But when we become too inner focused, when our problems and needs prevent us from reaching out to others and multiplying ourselves through evangelism, Satan has slipped us a "mickey." He can get us so spiritually drowsy from self-analysis that we forget there's a world full of people on their way to hell. God saved us to multiply.

A HEALTHY "INREACH"

With these observations as the background, let's go back to Acts 2 and see what happened between verses 41 and 47 to make the Jerusalem church so successful and dynamic when it came to the ministry of evangelism. How does the church get to be this kind of growing, reproducing body? What kind of inreach did the church at Jerusalem have that produced such an explosive outreach?

A Healthy Devotion

Since we have already worked through these verses in terms of identifying the essential components of discipleship, we don't need to repeat that material here. What I want to focus on is the first half of verse 42, where the writer says that the disciples "were *continually devoting themselves*" (italics added) to the essentials of Scripture, fellowship, and worship.

To devote yourself to something means giving your all to it. The secret to the dynamism of the church at Jerusalem was their total devotion to the things that make for a strong "inreach." The disciples had strong spiritual constitutions because they were fortified by the Word, by biblical fellowship or *koinonia,* and by worship. These formed the context for their work of evangelism.

In other words, they didn't just go through the external motions of "doing church." They were committed to the work of Christ down in the deepest parts of their being. I want to briefly review each of these three essentials to discover what it means to be "continually devoted" to the Scripture, to fellowship, and to worship.

Devoted to the Scripture. These early disciples were devoted to "the apostles' teaching." They wanted to learn. They wanted to know who Jesus was and what the Christian life was all about.

Their situation was dramatically different from ours in two ways. First, they did not have the written New Testament in those days. They were getting the Word firsthand, straight from the apostles' mouths!

That must have been exciting, but these believers could not go home, open their Bibles, and read the finished revelation of God. They hung on every word the apostles spoke, because that was their spiritual food. We have the whole Word of God, conveniently bound into a single volume. How much greater should be our devotion to finding out what God has to say?

A second thing that was very different for these disciples is that everything they were being taught about the church and their new life in Christ was new information to them. They couldn't say, "Oh yeah, I've heard a lot of sermons on that topic."

For some of us, the truths of our faith have become "old hat." We've heard the truth for so long that it no longer strikes us with the force it is supposed to have. We need to be careful that we do not allow our familiarity with Scripture to breed either contempt or complacency toward the truth.

I've said it before, but it bears repeating: You can't grow into a mature follower of Jesus Christ if you are ignorant of the Word. Scriptural knowledge does not come by osmosis. You can't put your Bible under your pillow and hope the truth will seep through into your brain.

Neither can you approach the Scripture the way you approach the assembly manual for your child's bicycle. We all know what those little books are like. If you're like me, you take one look at that thing and you know you will never get through it. So you start skipping around, trying to find the basic instructions, looking for any shortcuts you can take, and wishing all the time you were doing something else. When you finally finish putting that bike together, you toss the manual on the garage shelf, hoping you never have to consult it again.

Some of us are not progressing spiritually because we are not *devoting* ourselves to the Scriptures. It's not that we lack the learning capacity; we lack the inner drive to learn what God has said and what He expects of us. The Jerusalem disciples were devoted to hearing and obeying the Word of God.

Devoted to fellowship. These disciples were also devoted to fellowship (v. 42). We know that the word *koinonia* has to do with what is held in common. We often use the word *sharing.*

Part of their fellowship is described in Acts 2:44–45, where we read that the disciples held all their possessions in common and shared them freely with anyone who had a need. That's being devoted to fellowship!

You can't legislate this kind of sharing, which of course is one of the big mistakes that communism made. The communists tried to force people into a mode where the state held the real title to everything, and no one had any true choice in the matter.

Communism was a dismal failure primarily because

it was a spiritually bankrupt system. But it was also a dismal economic failure because what the communists tried to do is not what God had in mind.

The incident in Acts 5 with Ananias and Sapphira reminds us that the people still held ownership of their property until voluntarily, under the leadership of the Holy Spirit, they gave that property to the church (Acts 5:4).

Even though the disciples had to surrender ownership of their possessions to meet the needs in the church, that was not a problem for them, because they were committed to the greater good of God's family. They were devoted to fellowship.

Isn't this the kind of spirit we try to instill in our families, and especially in our children? We want to create an atmosphere of sharing, a sense that even though this possession or that toy may belong to a particular child, he or she is willing to share it, or even give it up, if the welfare of the family demands it.

We want them to understand that even though they may own the thing in question, they only have it because Mom and Dad bought it for them. Therefore, they need to be willing to share it.

That's *koinonia*. We understand that we have what we have only because our heavenly Father "bought" it for us—whether material possessions or spiritual blessings. Therefore, we need to "be generous and ready to share" (1 Timothy 6:18).

Devoted to worship. The devotion of the church at Jerusalem to worship is evident in Acts 2:46: "Day by day continuing with one mind in the temple, and breaking bread from house to house, they were taking their meals together with gladness and sincerity of heart."

Here is both formal and informal worship. The church gathered in the temple for corporate worship, what we would call the Sunday worship service. Then the members went from house to house for more informal, decentralized worship. This worship included communion, the "breaking of bread," and a meal that was called the "love feast." Remember, the church at Jerusalem had thousands of members even in its earliest days, so they were dealing with large numbers of people.

There was no way everyone in the church could go to one house, so they had house meetings all over the city. In other words, even though the Jerusalem church was very large, they did not allow the size to diminish their worship. They made provision for corporate worship and for worship in smaller, more intimate groups.

From time to time today we hear that a particular church is too large for meaningful worship. We don't hear anyone in the Jerusalem church complaining about that. Even in a big church like the one at Jerusalem, there was a place for people to be involved in a smaller group where they could experience personal involvement. Call them Sunday school classes, shepherding groups, care cells, or whatever you want.

The point is that anyone who is devoted to worship will find a place to worship in the church. The issue is not the size of the congregation. The issue is the depth of your devotion.

A Healthy Testimony

A final context for evangelism is found in Acts 2:47, where Luke reports that the church was "having favor with all the people." The non-church folk in Jerusalem took notice of these Christians. The unbelievers were saying, "Those people are different. There is something odd about them."

We need to ask ourselves whether anybody is saying that about us. The disciples had affected the whole city of Jerusalem by their way of life, and the people could not deny their witness.

The believers were about to fall out of favor with the Jewish leadership, but that's another story. The leaders didn't like the church because the church was threatening their vested interests. But the general populace knew that these Christians were serious.

A DYNAMIC OUTREACH

Once you get through Acts 2:42–47a, you come to

the report that the Lord was adding new believers to the church every day. The Lord added to their number when they took what they were doing in the temple and from house to house into the street. They made it public. The Lord added to their number when they understood that they were saved and brought into the church family in order to be vessels through whom Christ could reproduce Himself.

Daily Growth

You may have already noticed that the phrase "day by day" also occurs in verse 46 in the context of the four elements we are exploring in this book. This answers the question of where the church was getting the power to affect lives and win people to Christ every day.

In other words, believers were worshiping, fellowshiping, learning, and growing day by day, so they were seeing results day by day. There was a direct correlation between their inreach and their outreach.

This doesn't necessarily mean that every Christian was winning somebody else to Christ every day. But it does mean that every day, somebody was winning somebody.

I have often told the people at Oak Cliff Bible Fellowship that, given the size of our church, there ought not to be a day that goes by without someone from the church touching somebody in Dallas with the good news of Jesus Christ. There ought to be a testimony that comes back to us every day of a soul saved or a life changed.

An Evangelistic Challenge

See, God has given the church in America so much that it would be sinful for us to keep what we have to ourselves, to draw our robes around ourselves and say this is all for us only.

We should be dreaming dreams of what God can do through us to affect this world for Christ. I am a dreamer. I dream of things that are not in existence yet as though they were. I probably won't realize all my dreams because of the limitations of time. But I believe it would be wrong to stop dreaming and asking God to do great things through us for His kingdom.

I am not just talking about numerical church growth. I am talking about the Spirit of God changing lives through the dynamic outreach of the church.

My prayer for our church in Dallas and for the church in America is that we not become ingrown and self-satisfied. We can't afford to get complacent when there are still millions of people in America alone who are on their way to hell. We don't have a lot to brag about when there are people in our own neighborhoods we have never introduced to Jesus.

The greatest compliment anyone could pay me as a pastor is not to say, "Good sermon," as much as I appreciate the encouragement. The greatest compliment I could receive would be for someone to say, "What you are doing at Oak Cliff is changing lives for Jesus Christ."

That is a real compliment. That means the message has gone public. It has left the safety of the sanctuary. The people are taking it beyond the security of the pew and out into the marketplace.

THE COMPONENTS OF OUTREACH

The context in which evangelism is to take place is no mystery. Evangelism is the natural outgrowth and overflow of a church that has a vital, dynamic inreach through the experience of the necessities of worship, fellowship, and the Word.

This is so because this type of church is full of the Holy Spirit, and when believers are full of the Spirit, evangelism is natural.

The Holy Spirit and Evangelism

The Spirit's filling also helps to explain the dynamic evangelism that took place in the church at Jerusalem. Jesus had told His disciples to wait on the coming of the Spirit (Acts 1:8). When the Spirit came, these believers did not just go out witnessing; they were *transformed into witnesses*. There's a world of difference between those two realities.

The reason the church has to pull teeth today to get believers to tell of their faith is that evangelism has degenerated into a program we do, rather than being a characteristic of the people we are. When evangelism is just a program, when the program ends so does the evangelism. But when the Spirit gets hold of you, you become a witness.

After His resurrection, Jesus made clear to the disciples that their ministry would be an extension of His when He told them, "As the Father has sent Me, I also send you" (John 20:21).

The question is, How did the Father send the Son? Jesus answered that question for us back in John 17:18 in His prayer to His Father. Jesus said, "As Thou didst send Me *into the world,* I also have sent them into the world" (v. 18, italics added).

The Father sent Jesus "into the world." Jesus did not do long-distance evangelism from heaven. God did not write the gospel message across the sky. Jesus "pitched a tent" among us by taking on human flesh (John 1:14). He became like us so that He could reveal God to us (John 1:18).

In other words, as Jesus' disciples we are to enter into the realm of the unregenerate to proclaim Him. We are not to hide out in the church or to become part of an evangelical ghetto. Jesus' disciples are to go where the unbelievers are and spread the good news of the gospel.

It is unfortunate that so many Christians are depending on the professionals to do the work of evangelism for them. Rather than equipping God's people to go, sometimes the church is encouraging them to stay. Each week Christians all across America sit, soak, and sour as they become spiritual consumers without becoming gospel deliverers.

This reflects a deep spiritual problem, the absence of the Spirit's dynamic. When the Spirit takes over, believers will be like Christ, entering the world of unbelievers with the gospel as a natural overflow of the Spirit's power.

Unity and Evangelism

Not only did Jesus send His disciples into the world of unbelievers with the gospel, He prayed in John 17 "that they may all be one; even as Thou, Father, art in Me, and I in Thee, that they also may be in Us; that the world may believe that Thou didst send Me" (v. 21).

In other words, it would be the unity of Jesus' disciples, and therefore the unity of the church, that would provide a major context for evangelistic success. This is one reason for the strong emphasis on unity in the early church.

On the Day of Pentecost, the believers were "all together in one place" (Acts 2:1). We know they held all their possessions in common. The unity of the church was so important that when a doctrinal question threatened to divide the disciples, they called a church council (Acts 15).

This shows why Satan spends so much time sowing seeds of discord among believers. He knows God won't work in a context of disunity.

Our failure to distinguish between membership and fellowship has added to the problem of disunity. Membership in a certain denomination or group is often based on doctrinal differences, but fellowship is based on our common faith in Christ and His finished work on the cross. We can have fellowship with believers whose particular group we might never join.

When believers are unified, evangelism is a natural result. This, I believe, explains the evangelistic success of a number of organizations that reach far across denominational lines.

God's Spirit has been free to work because people with different views on a number of issues have come together around their common fellowship in the gospel. The church in Acts practiced unprecedented evangelism because they possessed uncommon unity through which the Spirit was free to flow.

Authority and Evangelism

Note also that after Jesus told His disciples He was sending them into the world, He said to them, "Receive the Holy Spirit" (John 20:22). Even before Pentecost, Jesus made clear that His evangelistic commands and instructions are powerless without the presence of the Spirit.

On the other hand, the presence of the Spirit would provide authority in evangelism (v. 23). In chapter 16 we talked about what it means to forgive and retain sins, so I just want to note this verse here.

When the church is obeying Jesus' command, which involves going as a unified body operating in the power of the Spirit to where sinners are, we will experience spiritual authority. If we really believed that the church has this authority by virtue of the Holy Spirit's power, we would be a very different kind of church today.

The bottom line, then, is that if we are going to be authentic disciples of Jesus Christ, we must be involved in evangelism. But this involvement is not just personal, it is part of the local church's mission. The church should provide the fire for evangelism through its dynamic environment of worship, fellowship, and the Word.

Then the world of the unredeemed becomes the place where that spiritual fire is unleashed, so that people might be overwhelmed with the grace of God delivered by a unified body of saints in the power of God's Spirit. When this happens, then, like the believers in Acts, we will see God adding to the church daily those who are being saved.

CHAPTER NINETEEN

THE COMPENSATION OF EVANGELISM

W e've come to the final leg of our journey to discover what matters most. We are at the point where we ask the same question we asked of worship, fellowship, and Scripture: What is the payoff? In what ways are we compensated when we take evangelism seriously and make a commitment to be witnesses of the gospel in obedience to Christ's command?

We are compensated in huge ways! In this chapter, I want to suggest four wonderful benefits that await us when we follow Christ as His disciples by practicing biblical evangelism.

THE GOSPEL RELEASES GOD'S POWER

The apostle Paul wrote in Romans 1:16, "I am not ashamed of the gospel, for it is the power of God for salvation to everyone who believes."

The first benefit you will reap by telling others the gospel is the release and the realization of God's power. That's why Paul says we ought not apologize for the gospel. Why apologize for releasing the power and blessing of God in someone's life? That's nothing to be sorry about.

I don't hear anyone else apologizing for or being

ashamed of their lifestyles. We live in a day when people go public with their evil. The sense of shame that used to characterize sin has been lost. People used to at least try to hide when they sinned. Now they take it out into the streets. What I'm saying is that we need to be just as bold with the gospel, because people need the message of the gospel more than ever today. In fact, no one can experience God's power apart from the gospel.

Why? The gospel, the good news about Jesus Christ, is the message that diffuses God's power in the life of a man or woman. The gospel is the environment in which a person who is bound in sin can come and find freedom and forgiveness.

Mysticism has no power to do this. You can't dial up a psychic and find the power of God for your need. Meditation won't release His power within a person. The New Age "gospel" is simply the enemy's age-old lie. There's no freedom from sin in the New Age. Only the gospel can set people free.

Do you know people who need the power of God in their lives to release them from the curse and bondage of sin? Then you need to tell them of the gospel. Only the death of Jesus Christ in payment for their sins, and His resurrection as the guarantee of God's acceptance of that payment, will provide salvation. It's an absolute necessity that we tell others of this good news.

The "Tenses" of Salvation

In Romans 1:16, Paul tells us clearly the purpose for which the power of God is activated in the gospel. That purpose is salvation to everyone who believes. The power in the gospel is the power for salvation. In the Bible, the word *salvation* means to be delivered from something.

Let me remind you how powerful the gospel is for salvation by reviewing briefly what I call the three tenses of salvation. This may be familiar stuff to you, but it's important to remember what it is that God is offering people when He offers them the gospel through us.

Salvation has three distinct aspects, the first of

which is salvation from the *penalty* of sin. This is called justification, and it takes care of the past.

We defined justification in a previous chapter as God's legal declaration that we are now righteous in His sight. The past tense of salvation cancels the "certificate of debt" that was posted against us in heaven because of our sins (Colossians 2:14). Because of Christ's sacrifice, believers will never face eternal punishment for their sins.

Salvation also has a present tense, our deliverance from the *power* of sin. That's called sanctification, which is really what we have been talking about throughout this book. Sanctification has to do with our growth in Christ, the process by which we become more and more like Christ. You can't be a committed disciple of Christ without growing in your faith.

Then we have the future tense of salvation, which the Bible calls being "glorified" (Romans 8:30). This is the day we still look forward to, when Christ will come for us and deliver us from the very *presence* of sin.

Do you see anything here to be ashamed of? Do you see any reason that we need to stutter or be bashful about telling people what Christ has done and what He offers them? I don't either.

Unsaved people don't stutter when they swear. They come right out with it. They don't shuffle their feet and clear their throats when they tell dirty jokes. They are not ashamed of evil. You and I ought not be ashamed of the gospel. Imagine the benefit of seeing a hell-bound sinner turned around and put on the road to heaven. That's an eternal payoff!

People all around us are missing out on the life-changing power of the gospel because too many of us Christians are ashamed of the gospel. We are embarrassed to be identified with Christ, except on Sunday in church when it's safe.

I'm sure that if I asked you whether you wanted to see everyone saved, you would answer, "Of course." That is God's desire too (2 Peter 3:9). But when does that desire get off the pages of Scripture, out of your heart, and into the lives of lost people? When you and I get serious about our discipleship and begin to make evangelism a part of our daily Christian walk.

The Gospel at Work

The great thing about the power of the gospel is that it doesn't stop when a person accepts Christ. It doesn't just save a sinner from judgment and get him into heaven. The gospel has the power to make us all that God wants us to be today.

Paul makes another great statement about salvation and the gospel in Romans 6:

> What shall we say then? Are we to continue in sin that grace might increase? May it never be! How shall we who died to sin still live in it? Or do you not know that all of us who have been baptized into Christ Jesus have been baptized into His death? Therefore we have been buried with Him through baptism into death, in order that as Christ was raised from the dead through the glory of the Father, so we too might walk in newness of life. (vv. 1–4)

Paul is saying that the gospel can give you power over sin today. It not only solved the sin problem as far as eternity is concerned, but it gives you a power source for your sin problem as far as time is concerned.

I know we're talking about evangelism, but I want you to see a connection here between our own lives and our willingness, or lack of willingness, to do the work of evangelism.

Basically, this connection works two ways. First, if you are not living above the power of sin by the power of God on a day-to-day basis, your witness for Christ is going to be blunted and stymied.

But the connection also goes the other way. If you are ashamed of the gospel in terms of your witness, if you are too embarrassed to be publicly identified with Jesus Christ, then the full power of the gospel is not going to be realized in your life.

You can't tell Christ privately how much you love

Him and how much you want His power in your life, and then refuse to speak up for Him or acknowledge Him publicly. That just doesn't compute. We are called to "walk in newness of life," which means taking that new life with us wherever we go.

In Romans 6, Paul talks about death and resurrection, both ours and Christ's. We know that the Resurrection is central to the gospel (1 Corinthians 15:4) because it validates the death of Christ as the payment for sin. The Resurrection is, as said in an earlier chapter, the "receipt" to show that the payment was made and accepted.

We also experienced a resurrection when we came to Christ. Just as Christ was raised in victory over the power of sin, so we died to our old sin life and were raised to a new life. Our resurrection is "in the likeness" of Christ's resurrection (Romans 6:5).

My point is this. We are resurrected people who don't have to be slaves to sin any longer (Romans 6:6–7). Jesus died to rid us of sin's power as well as to rid us of sin's penalty.

That's why I said the gospel has the power to set us free. But if we are going to go to people and announce the good news that they can be set free from sin's power in Christ, we had better be living in the freedom the gospel purchased for us.

We all know that Christians can get themselves entangled and enslaved to sin. When that happens to us, we aren't going anywhere spiritually—either in our growth in discipleship or in our witness for Christ to others.

Jesus Christ says to us, "I have risen to set you free, that you might walk in a brand-new life." Our challenge is to learn to walk in the newness of life that has been granted to us by Christ's resurrection.

Let me tell you, the resurrection power of Jesus Christ is so potent that any Christian who learns to walk *in* the gospel, as opposed to just accepting the gospel at some point in the past, will experience the full power of the gospel.

An Incredible Deposit

Back in Romans 4:22, Paul said that Abraham's faith was "reckoned to him as righteousness." That word *reckoned* is very interesting. It means to credit something to someone's account. It's like someone going to your bank and making a deposit into your account. That money now belongs to you because it is in your account under your name.

When you got saved, God not only withdrew your sins from your eternal "account," but He also replaced those sins with His righteousness. Talk about compensation! You not only got rid of sin, you gained righteousness, which is both a right standing before God and the power to live a righteous life.

So the question is, why are so many of us Christians not living like the spiritually rich people we are? Why is the power of the gospel not working in us and flowing through us to others? For the same reason that a rich man can have money in the bank and still live in the ghetto: Having something credited to your account does you no good until you draw on it.

The problem with some Christians is that they have never learned how to write spiritual withdrawal slips. They have never learned how to draw on the riches that have been deposited in their heavenly account and apply those riches to their daily lives. The gospel that saved us is the same gospel that gives us the power to live for Christ.

In Ephesians 4:22–24 and Colossians 3:9–10, Paul uses the illustration of getting dressed to explain what it means to live in daily spiritual power. We must get up each morning and "put on" Christ, the way we put on clean clothes every morning to go to work. We have a responsibility to activate the power Christ has given us.

Think of what this means in terms of your evangelism. Your witness will not be effective when people see you every day dressed in the ragged, smelly clothes of the old life. They don't need any more of that. They already have that wardrobe!

But when you go out in public every morning dressed in the righteousness of Christ, you have something to offer people. You're going to look attractive to them.

The gospel is the delivery system for God's righteousness. Our failure to understand what Jesus Christ accomplished on the cross for us keeps us in bondage. So Paul says, "Don't be enslaved any longer. Christ has set you free from the penalty of sin, and He's waiting to set you free from the enslaving power of sin."

Paul is also saying, "Don't short-circuit this whole process by being ashamed of the gospel." It is your power source, and it has a huge benefit waiting for you when you tap into it.

THE GOSPEL TRANSFORMS OUR RELATIONSHIPS

The gospel will not only transform your relationship with God. It will also transform your relationships with people.

For this I want to consider several passages, the first of which is one of my favorites. In Galatians 2, we find a serious problem. It's the famous conflict between Peter and Paul, when Peter sided with the Jews in shunning the Gentile believers, and Paul showed up and called him on it.

Getting the Gospel Straight

Basically, Peter had introduced racism into the church at Galatia. He even got Barnabas to join him (v. 13). I won't review the whole account, but look at the basis of Paul's argument. He opposed Peter "to his face" (v. 11) because Paul saw that ol' Pete was not being "straightforward about the truth of the gospel" (v. 14).

Wait a minute. We're not talking about the death and resurrection of Jesus Christ here—or are we? We're talking about people getting along. But that's part of the gospel, Paul is saying.

In other words, because of the gospel I am to view other people, and they are to view me, in terms of our new relationship to Christ. This means no longer dealing with people on the basis of history, heritage, color, race, or culture. None of those things that divide us has a place in the gospel.

This is crucial to understand because whenever we divide the family of God using secular criteria rather than biblical criteria, we impede the work of the gospel in our own lives. This is a potential problem for homogenous churches; if we are not careful, they can work against the principles the church was designed around. To put it another way, God won't set you free if you are holding a brother or sister in slavery to their history or their race or any other criterion that is a meaningless category in Christ.

That's why the Bible says that when you come to worship, if you have something against a brother or sister, get that thing right before you offer God your worship (Matthew 5:23–24). God won't accept your vertical worship if you refuse to have horizontal fellowship.

The gospel has to do with human relationships. It has to do with how all of us in the body of Christ—blacks, whites, Asians, Hispanics—treat each other. When we are "straightforward about the truth of the gospel," when we tell people what the gospel can do to revolutionize their relationship with God and with others, the payoff is tremendous.

I've said it many times before, but it's still true. The answer to racism is the gospel. The answer to ethnic hostility and the horror of ethnic "cleansing" is the good news that Jesus Christ came to reconcile people to God and to each other. We damage the credibility of the gospel when we put a color or cultural qualification on how we present or live out its message. When we either neglect to present the message to people who are different from us or refuse to fellowship with believers of other backgrounds, we nullify the gospel. Jesus Christ died for all colors, all classes, all backgrounds, all kinds of people.

Time to Get Real

It is far too late for Christians to keep negating the

power of the gospel by our cultural biases. We are taking far too long to get this thing right.

Galatians 2:20 is a great verse, one of my favorites. People memorize this verse and quote it often. People take it as their life's verse. That's great, but we need to remember its context. Verse 20 is part of Paul's answer to Peter's racism.

Paul was telling Peter, "The way you are seeing yourself now is not the right way. Here's how you should look at yourself as a Christian." Paul says first, "I have been crucified with Christ."

This is now our self-identity as Christians. We are walking dead people. Crucifixion results in death. In a crucifixion, someone gets hung on a cross and dies.

Paul says we are to identify completely with Christ in His death on the cross. We saw what that means above in Romans 6. What it also means is that if you and I want to relate to each other properly, we need to relate to each other in terms of who we are in Jesus Christ. Measure me by Christ, not by my race or culture. Relate to me as a fellow believer, a brother in the Lord. And I will do the same for you.

Paul goes on to say in Galatians 2:20, "It is no longer I who live." Do you know why the *I* in you can't be alive? Because the *I* in you is dead. Then what is alive in you? Look at the next phrase: "Christ lives in me."

The reason the *I* in me can't be alive is because the *Christ* in me has taken its place. Therefore, "The life which I now live in the flesh I live by faith in the Son of God, who loved me, and delivered Himself up for me."

A "Christ First" Person

What is Paul talking about? The gospel. What is he saying about the gospel? He is saying the gospel must revolutionize how you think about yourself and about other people.

Peter was peeling off to join the Jews who had come to see him in Galatia when he got caught thinking like a Jew first instead of like a Christian first.

So Paul said to him, "That's not the message of the

gospel, Pete. You can't peel off like that, because you're not a 'Jew first' person anymore, you are a 'Christ first' person." If we had a generation of Christians who knew how to be "Christ first" people, our evangelism would take off in a blaze of glory. The message of Christ would explode into the world.

I don't like to hear people say, "Well, this is just how I was raised." That's a bad opening line with me. We can't say anymore, "But my daddy taught me this." If what your daddy taught you does not conform to the gospel, it was wrong when he taught it to you and it's wrong today.

I'm convinced if we as believers would learn to act on who we are in Christ, we would see unbelievers knocking our doors down to find out how to get what we have. The payoff of evangelism in terms of our relationships is certainly there for us, but much of it is still on deposit waiting for us to withdraw it.

Do you remember those curl activators women used to use? I asked that question in a church service, and a bunch of women winced as if to say, "Don't remind me."

When a woman's hair started hanging down and she wanted a little more bounce in it, she put that curl activator on it and her hair looked curly again. The woman's hair got "activated."

Galatians 2:20 is the "Jesus activator." When Jesus gets activated in our lives and in our evangelism, the issue won't be what we learned back there or how we were raised. We will judge everything by this criterion: Does it agree with our newness in Christ? If it doesn't, it's dead, because we are now alive in Christ.

What the gospel brings is a radical transformation of our thinking. We must judge each other by the content of our spiritual character. That's the measure—not skin color, culture, or any of the things that separate people. The gospel transforms all of our relationships.

THE GOSPEL TRANSFORMS
OUR CIRCUMSTANCES

Here's a third benefit of evangelism I want to show you. In Luke 4:16–30, Jesus went into the synagogue in

His hometown of Nazareth and was asked to speak as a guest rabbi, which was a common custom in those days.

Jesus stood and read from the sixty-first chapter of the book of Isaiah (Luke 4:17). This is what He read:

> The Spirit of the Lord is upon Me, because He anointed Me to preach the gospel to the poor. He has sent Me to proclaim release to the captives, and recovery of sight to the blind, to set free those who are downtrodden, to proclaim the favorable year of the Lord. (vv. 18–19)

Jesus didn't stumble upon this text, of course. He opened to the precise passage He wanted to use for the occasion. In order to understand this passage, we need to remember that in Isaiah 61, Israel was in captivity to Babylon. Those people were looking for and longing for freedom.

The Freedom of Jubilee

In Jesus' day, Israel was captive to Rome. The Jewish people Jesus was speaking to were also looking for and longing for freedom. They were looking for somebody who would set them free, a "freedom fighter."

The Jews wanted somebody who would relieve them of the poverty and debilitation that they suffered because of their oppression by Rome. They wanted a champion who would overthrow their oppressors and release the captives (Luke 4:18b).

Knowing this, Jesus Christ opened the Scriptures and said, "I have come to preach the gospel. I have come to announce the good news of release to people who are caught in slavery."

The last line of Jesus' message is the key to what He was saying. He had come "to proclaim the favorable year of the Lord." The "favorable year of the Lord" in Scripture was the Year of Jubilee, recorded in detail in Leviticus 25:8–55.

Let me summarize the provisions of the jubilee. Jubilee occurred very fiftieth year on Israel's calendar. It was a special year, because it was the year on which people were set free.

For instance, in the Year of Jubilee, Jewish slaves were given their freedom. Debts were forgiven at jubilee. Land that had had to be sold to pay off creditors returned to the family that originally owned it. Even the soil of Israel was given a rest in the Year of Jubilee.

Jubilee was the time when people's difficult circumstances were overturned. It was the year when God took the mess that sinful people had made and made it right.

Jubilee is what Israel wanted in Jesus' day, because their world was topsy-turvy. The people and the land were in bondage to Rome. They were broke and in debt, spiritually and materially.

Jesus came and said, "I have come to announce jubilee, but it won't come by overthrowing Rome. The release I am talking about is the release of sin that comes from the forgiveness of your sins through the gospel." This is the basis for the transformation of our circumstances.

The Prerequisites for Jubilee

The bad news for Israel of Jesus' day is that the nation did not get its jubilee. Let me explain why.

In the Old Testament, God did not bring jubilee until after the Day of Atonement. We discussed the Day of Atonement in some detail in chapter 17. Suffice it to say here that it was the day on which Israel's sins were dealt with before God.

Do you see the connection? God would not give the people jubilee until they had dealt with the sin issue. Salvation sets us free from sin, which always enslaves.

Israel as a nation refused Christ and His salvation, so they failed to enjoy the freedom and release He promised.

Sin blocks God's ability to set people free. If people are not willing to get right with Christ, God is not willing to transform their circumstances.

THE GOSPEL BRINGS CHRIST'S APPROVAL

I want to close this chapter, and the book, by showing you one last benefit of the gospel and giving you a final word of encouragement in your desire to follow Christ.

In Matthew 10:32–33, Jesus said, "Everyone therefore who shall confess Me before men, I will also confess him before My Father who is in heaven. But whoever shall deny Me before men, I will also deny him before My Father who is in heaven."

This is a powerful principle. Jesus says there is a direct connection between your willingness to acknowledge Him publicly, which includes telling the gospel wherever you go, and your current standing before Him.

Let me be very clear. These verses have nothing to do with salvation. The issue in Matthew 10 is not heaven or hell. The issue is your witness, or lack of it, in your day-to-day walk with Christ.

What does Jesus mean when He says that He will confess us before the Father when we confess Him before men? Here's what I believe He is saying. If we are confessing Him openly, He is ready to take our prayers and concerns to the Father when we are in need.

In other words, the only prayers that get answered are the prayers that Jesus signs off on. That's why we end our prayers with, "In Jesus' name." That's not just a nice thought or a convenient way to end a prayer. No, that's asking Jesus to approve a withdrawal from your heavenly account! When you pray in Jesus' name, you are saying, "Jesus, would You please sign off on this request, because the Father won't turn down anything that You ask for."

When my request goes to the Father, delivered by the Spirit, He looks at His Son. "Son, I've just received this request from Evans. Can You sign off on it?"

Jesus says, "Let's see. Has Evans been denying Me before men? Has he been ashamed of Me? Has he been ashamed of My gospel? I can't sign this request until Evans's status before Me has been determined. If he is denying Me and I bless him by signing his request, I will just be confirming to him that his denial of Me is all right."

Oh, but when we are openly confessing Christ in our witness and our walk, when our prayers come before the Father and He asks the Son about us, Jesus will say, "Father, let Me tell You something. This man can't keep his mouth closed about Me. This woman can't say enough about Me. They tell everyone they know about Me at every opportunity. They are not ashamed to be identified with Me. I will gladly sign their requests."

The gospel is the power of God to everyone who believes. It will transform your relationships, your circumstances, and your life. And it can do the same for everyone you share it with.

It's time to go public with the gospel. Let's stop being ashamed. Everybody else is "coming out," so we might as well come out too. The benefits of evangelism are too great to keep to ourselves!

EPILOGUE

My parent's names are Arthur and Evelyn Evans. As I write this book, they are closing in on seventy years of age. Outside of their small life circle of home, church, and neighborhood, very few people know my parents personally. However, many people know their son.

I preach to hundreds of thousands of people each week by radio, by video, and in person. My books, of which this is the twelfth, can be purchased in bookstores throughout America. I have the honor of being the first African-American to graduate from Dallas Theological Seminary with a doctorate in theology. The church I pastor has grown from ten people to four thousand people.

I don't say these things to tout my accomplishments. Rather, they illustrate the thesis of this book: namely, that discipleship is God's means of transforming people into followers of Christ. For, you see, when people respond to my ministry in whatever form, they are really being introduced to my parents. What people see is their impact on my life, which molded and shaped me into what I am today.

My father came to Christ when he was thirty years of age and I was ten. Immediately, he became a passionate follower of Christ. My mother didn't like him as a sinner, and she resented him as a saint. Many times my dad could be found praying and studying the Word in the middle of the night, which was often the safest time for him to pursue God without having to encounter the daily resistance from my mother.

It was about a year after Dad's conversion, as he was studying late one night, that he heard the steps creak as my mother began making her way from their upstairs bedroom to the room where my father was studying. Rather than berating him, however, she approached him with tears in her eyes.

She told Dad how she had been observing his transformed life over the past year, and that whatever it was that was responsible, she wanted it too. That night my father led my mother to Christ. Our home was transformed. After that, Mom and Dad led me, my two brothers, and my sister to Christ.

My conversion put me on the road to discipleship. Biblical values were taught and reinforced on a daily basis in our home, and the church became the center of our family life. Church was where the new life in Christ was lived out in the community, and where I encountered and was molded by the four vital experiences of discipleship.

This inner-city boy began to be transformed into something different from most of the other kids in my neighborhood, and here I am today.

So as you read this book, listen to one of my sermons, or watch one of my videos, say a prayer of thanksgiving to God for my parents, who passed the spiritual baton on to me through the process of biblical discipleship so that I might do the same with my family and those under my charge in the ministry. Because of Arthur and Evelyn Evans, thousands of people will be in heaven praising God for their joyful discovery of *what matters most.*

SUBJECT INDEX

SCRIPTURE INDEX

Moody Press, a ministry of Moody Bible Institute,
is designed for education, evangelization, and edification.
If we may assist you in knowing more about Christ
and the Christian life, please write us without obligation:
Moody Press, c/o MLM, Chicago, Illinois 60610.